# Frommer's®

## The Algarve

### with your family

## The best of Portugal's Southern Coast

by Robin Gauldie

1807
WILEY
2007

John Wiley & Sons, Ltd

Copyright © 2007 John Wiley & Sons Ltd, The Atrium, Southern Gate, Chichester,
West Sussex PO19 8SQ, England
Telephone (+44) 1243 779777

Email (for orders and customer service enquiries): cs-books@wiley.co.uk. Visit our Home Page on
www.wiley.com

UK Publisher: Sally Smith
Executive Project Editor: Daniel Mersey (Frommer's UK)
Commissioning Editor: Mark Henshall (Frommer's UK)
Development Editor: Mark Henshall (Frommer's UK)
Content Editor: Hannah Clement (Frommer's UK)
Cartographer: Tim Lohnes
Photo Research: Jill Emeny (Frommer's UK)

Wiley also publishes its books in a variety of electronic formats. Some content that appears in print may
not be available in electronic books.

Anniversary Logo Design: Richard J. Pacifico

**Library of Congress Cataloging-in-Publication Data**
Gauldie, Robin.
 The Algarve with your family / Robin Gauldie.
    p. cm.
 Includes index.
 ISBN 978-0-470-05526-7
 1. Algarve (Portugal)—Description and travel—Guidebooks. I. Title.
 DP702.A28G38 2007
 914.69'60444—dc22
                              2007034318

**British Library Cataloguing in Publication Data**
A catalogue record for this book is available from the British Library

ISBN: 978-0-470-05526-7

Typeset by Wiley Indianapolis Composition Services
Printed and bound in China by SNP Corporation Ltd.

5  4  3  2  1

# Contents

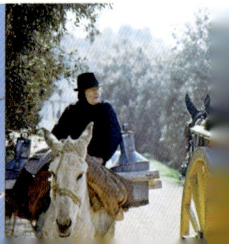

# About the Author

Robin Gauldie began travelling in the early 1970s and has never stopped. He first visited the Algarve and the Alentejo in 1972 and has returned many times since. When not travelling, he divides his time between a home in Edinburgh and a very ramshackle village house in southern France. He has been a full-time travel journalist since 1979.

## Acknowledgements

My thanks are due to Sunvil Portugal and Pousadas of Portugal, Travel PR, and Magellan PR, who all helped to arrange my travels throughout the Algarve and the Alentejo and introduced me to some magnificent pousadas.

## Dedication

For Percy, Fraser and little Zoe.

# An Additional Note

Please be advised that travel information is subject to change at any time and this is especially true of prices. We therefore suggest that you write or call ahead for confirmation when making your travel plans. The authors, editors and publisher cannot be held responsible for experiences of readers while travelling. Your safety is important to us however, so we encourage you to stay alert and be aware of your surroundings.

## Star Ratings, Icons & Abbreviations

Hotels, restaurants and attraction listings in this guide have been ranked for quality, value, service, amenities and special features using a star-rating system. Hotels, restaurants, attractions, shopping and nightlife are rated on a scale of zero stars (recommended) to three (exceptional). In addition to the star rating system, we also use 5 feature icons that point you to the great deals, in-the-know advice and unique experiences. Throughout the book, look for:

**FIND**          Special finds – those places only insiders know about

**MOMENT**          Special moments – those experiences that memories are made of

**VALUE**          Great value – where to get the best deals

**OVERRATED**          Places or experiences not worth your time or money

**GREEN**          Attractions promoting responsible tourism

The following **abbreviations** are used for credit cards:

AE     American Express
MC     Mastercard
V       Visa

## A Note on Prices

Frommer's provides exact prices in each destination's local currency. As this book went to press, the rate of exchange was €1 = £0.68. Rates of exchange are constantly in flux; for up-to-the minute information, consult a currency-conversion website such as www.oanda.com/convert/classic. In the Family-friendly Accommodation sections of this book we have used a price category system.

## An Invitation to the Reader

In researching this book, we discovered many wonderful places – hotels, restaurants, shops and more. We're sure you'll find others. Please tell us about them, so we can share the information with your fellow travellers in upcoming editions. If you were disappointed with a recommendation, we'd love to know that too. Please email: frommers@wiley.co.uk or write to:

*Frommer's The Algarve with Your Family,* 1st Edition
John Wiley & Sons, Ltd
Bicentennial Building
Southern Gate
Chichester
West Sussex, PO19 8SQ

## Additional information

Additional information provided by Anne Dare and Tessa Thorniley.

## Photo Credits

*Cover Credits*
Front cover: Large image: © Michael Howard/Alamy
Small images (from left to right on cover):

© Arco Images/Alamy

© FAN Travelstock

© Cro Magnon

© PCL

Back cover: © John Miller/PCL

*Front Matter*
pi: © Michael Howard/Alamy; piii: © Arco Images/Alamy; © FAN Travelstock; © Cro Magnon; © PCL; piv: © Arco Images/Alamy; © FAN Travelstock; © Cro Magnon; © PCL

# 1 Family Highlights of the Algarve

# THE **ALGARVE**

Montemor-o-Novo
Redondo
Vendas Novas
A12
A13
N5
A6
E90
A6
Évora
N18
N381
SPAIN
A6
N10
E01
N255
N256
IC1
N253
N2
N380
N254
Reguengos
de Monsaraz
Mourao
Sétubal
N253
N253
Vianado Alentejo
N18
Portel
N256
N261
Alcácer do Sala
N384
Barragem
de Alqueva
N120
Alvito
N384
N255
N261
A2
N257
Vidigueira
Alqueva
N385
Grândola
Cuba
Moura
N2
IP2
N258
Santo Madre
IC33
A2
IP8
Serra da Adiça
Santiago do Cacém
IP01
N121
Ferreria do
Alentejo
N260
IC8
N261
N121
N18
Beja
N260
Sines
N120
Serpa
IC4
Aljustrel
N122
E01
N262
IC1
N2
IP2
N264
Parque Natural
do Vale da Guadiana
Vila Nova
de Milfontes
IP2
Castro Verde
N122
N393
N263
Ourique
Mértola
Odemira
N2
N266
Almodôvar
N122
Alcoutim
Zambujeira
do Mar
E01
N124
Rio Guadiana
N120
IC1
N2
IC27
SPAIN
N264
Serra do Aldeirão
Aljezur
Monchique
N267
Castro Marim
A49
Caldas de
Monchique
N124
S. Bras
de Alportel
Vila Real
de Santo
António
Bordeira
N2
Silves
Loulé
E01
Carrapateira
N120
A22
A22
N125
Tavira
Vila do Bispo
Portimão
Lagoa
Albufeira
Quarteira
N2
Olhão
N268
N125
Lagos
Faro
Sagres
ATLANTIC
OCEAN

Lisbon
PORTUGAL
SPAIN
area of
detail

0        10 mi
0        10 km

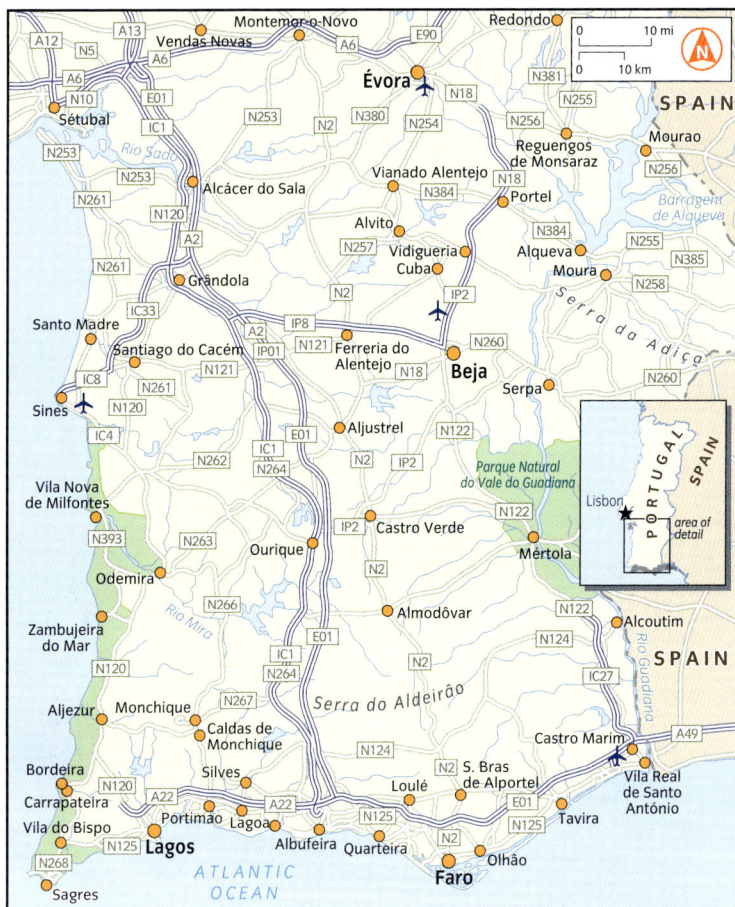

**I** first visited Portugal in 1972 as a long-haired teenager, on the way
home to my first year at university after a summer spent hitchhiking
around France, Spain and Morocco. Crossing the border from Spain
into the quiet hinterland of the Algarve and the Alentejo, I remember
being struck by how peaceful, even backward, the country seemed.
Farmers rode mules or carried their produce to market in donkey
carts, fishermen hauled nets by hand, barefoot children herded fat
sheep and skinny goats in pastures shaded by cork oak groves. That
apparent rural idyll, of course, concealed a great deal of rural poverty.

It's not surprising that, when Portugal's backward-looking dictatorship collapsed three years after my first visit, the people whose lives at
first sight looked so idyllic took to tourism with a will.

Few places in Europe have beaches that can match the Algarve's great sweeps of white and gold sand, stretching from the mouth of the River Guadiana – which forms the border with Spain – all the way to Cape St Vincent and Henry the Navigator's fortress at Sagres, where Portuguese navigators like Vasco da Gama and the wonderfully named Fernando Poo set off into the unknown.

And nowhere has a climate that makes such beaches accessible all year round. While researching part of this book in February 2007 hardy toddlers were splashing in the low-tide shallows of the huge, empty beach at Carrapateira, while wet-suited surfers rode the waves at Sagres's Praia de Beliche and teenage dinghy sailors raced across the waters off Ilha de Tavira. The temperature reached 21°C one afternoon. On most British beaches, that's something we dream about even in mid-summer. Equally family-friendly are summer temperatures that average around 26°C and rarely soar above 30°C – hot, but not too hot, and tempered by cooling Atlantic breezes.

A mixture like that makes a tourism boom inevitable, and the Algarve has boomed indeed since the first time I went there. Thousands of British families visit every year, and enterprising locals have built an array of purpose-made, family-friendly visitor attractions to complement the Algarve's natural advantages – from tennis academies and riding schools to karting tracks, zoos, and a plethora of water parks, boat rides and other intriguing choices for families.

Let's not forget the region's history. There's a limit to how many Manueline churches you can drag the children round before the whingeing starts (about one, in my experience) but even boring old cathedrals can throw up surprise treats – like a spooky chapel full of skulls and bones, or a bell-tower occupied by a family of fledgling storks. And almost every hilltop, harbour and headland has a castle or fortress with a story to tell of knights and princesses, from the wars against the Moors and the Spaniards to the battles of Wellington's redcoats and their Portuguese allies against the French.

Getting back to basics, the Algarve's tourism has been driven mainly by British families, so resorts are user friendly – it's rare to find a restaurant without an English version of the menu, there are zillions of child-friendly ice-cream parlours (enough for a different flavour for every day of the week), and if you can't persuade the family to sample easy-to-like Portuguese dishes such as grilled sardines it's easy enough to find comfort-food standbys such as fish fingers, burgers and beans on toast.

Most town centres have a pedestrian zone covering the main shopping and strolling areas, and many hotels are right on the beach. That said, the less you pay for your accommodation, the less family friendly it is likely to be and the more likely you are to have roads to cross to get to the sand. On top of this, many of the resorts in the west – such as Portimão – are perched on cliffs above the beach, making for fantastic views but meaning that the beach is less accessible to families with toddlers, who may have to be carried up long flights of steps when tired. When planning your day remember many shops and businesses, along with museums and heritage attractions, close down for a couple of hours in the middle of the day.

For any family – whether with tots and toddlers, pre-teens or active teenagers – the Algarve is a great holiday destination, offering almost year-round sunshine, superb beaches, and just enough purpose-built visitor attractions and heritage sites to keep the family entertained and engaged. So, what are you waiting for?

# ALGARVE FAMILY HIGHLIGHTS

**Best Family Events** The Algarve has a full calendar of events, ranging from deeply tra-ditional religious festivals that have been held for more than 1,000 years to an array of world-class cultural and sporting fix-tures including major tennis, golf and motor sports events. The less important religious events – such as local saints' days – are beyond the comprehension of most non-Portuguese families, and the big-ticket sporting dates are aimed more at an adult audience, but there are a handful of events

that are perfect for families with children of all ages.

Carnival is celebrated all over Portugal in mid-February, and the **Loulé Carnival** is far and away

Loulé Carnival

## Onward to Spain

**It's very easy to travel on from the Algarve into western Andalusia –** and if you have a taste for sightseeing, a trip across the border is highly recommended. No formalities are required. If the Algarve has one small drawback, it is the lack of city sights with a high 'wow factor' and a real sense of history. If this is the kind of thing you want from a holiday, you'll find it in Seville, Huelva, Jerez de la Frontera and Cádiz, just across the now transparent Spanish frontier, and along with piles of heritage you will also discover some of Spain's finest beaches along the Costa de la Luz – the last relatively undeveloped stretch of coastline in Spain. Two fantastic regions in two countries for the price of one!

the most colourful and accessible in the Algarve. From deep religious roots, it has evolved into a three-day event with flower-covered floats and parades, street dancing and music. Anyone can join in – OK, it's not Carnival in Rio or Mardi Gras in New Orleans, but the smaller scale means it's a lot less overwhelming for smaller children and most children will be enthralled and enjoy the spectacularly costumed dancers (see p. 54).

From 7th June to 7th October, the **International Sand Art Festival (FIESA)** at Areias de Pêra has to be the Algarve's top family fixture. Every year, 'sand artists' from all over the world descend on this stretch of beach near Albufeira to create a 'city' of gobsmacking, colossal wonders of the world, from gigantic Buddha images to Lord of the Rings style castles, cathedrals and monsters. Prepare for the children to be inspired – but prepare too to spend the rest of your holiday as a hod carrier while they construct a scale copy of Hogwarts Academy or Snow White's Castle (see p. 83).

The unspoilt seaside village of Cacela Velha, east of Faro, goes all Arabian Nights for four evenings in July in a kitschy but fun recreation of the Algarve's 10th–13th century Moorish past, the **Moorish Nights**. There's a Moroccan-style open-air market in the square outside Cacela Velha's miniature medieval castle, giving children the chance to blow their holiday pocket money on souvenirs

brought over from Tangier (not so very far away) and you can sit cross-legged on cushions eating Moroccan dishes and sipping mint tea, while watching belly dancers and listening to Berber musicians create a reverberating wall of sound (see p. 156).

**Best Towns & Cities** On the map, the Algarve appears to have a good share of fair-sized cities. In fact, it hasn't got a single big city in the true sense of the word. The suburban sprawls that have mushroomed around Faro, Lagos and Portimão are products of the tourism boom of the last 30 years – all geared to comprehensive resort holidays. However, if you're looking for a slice of easily accessible heritage that even younger children can relate to – and that will provide young people aged 10 and up with plenty of fodder for the next school history project – head for the historic core of Faro or the lovely old riverside towns of Tavira and Vila Real de Santo António.

Faro's old quarter, within the remnants of its medieval walls, is a medley of cobbled streets overlooked by the bell-tower of the cathedral (which is often occupied by a family of storks), and outside the walls is a traffic-free zone of shops, cafés and ice-cream parlours. Tavira has a pretty riverside esplanade, the remains of a medieval castle, islands to visit just offshore and – best of all – a quirky and unique attraction, the camera obscura, sited in a former water tower and offering a seemingly magical 360-degree panorama of the city. It also hosts a lively array of summer markets and street entertainment that will keep children entranced for hours (see p. 157). Vila Real de Santo António has a special feel as it looks across the river to Spain – just a short drive away across a highly scenic new suspension bridge – and on its doorstep are some of the Algarve's hugest and least crowded beaches at Monte Gordo. Inland, only a 10–15 minute drive away, is the atmospheric stronghold of Castro Marim, surrounded by the wild wetlands of a natural park (see p. 153).

But, if you must build an outstanding historic city into your trip, the thing to do is head east, across the Spanish border, to Seville – it's doable as a day trip (by car or train) from the central and eastern Algarve, but well worth an overnight stay (see p. 180).

**Best Resorts** In a sense, the Algarve from Faro west as far as Lagos is one big resort, with miles of hotels, apartments and villa developments spreading either side of former fishing villages such as Quarteira, Albufeira, Portimão and Lagos, and golf courses and tennis course resorts stretching inland as far as the A22 motorway – all served by Faro's international airport. Each has its stretch of sandy beach, often merging imperceptibly with other strands to east and west offering Brits a great choice. Families looking for resorts with all the trimmings will probably want to

stick to this central stretch of coast. Those with cash to flash will like the more upscale enclaves – notably Vilamoura and its surroundings and the Algarve's ultimate big-spender's oasis, Vale do Lobo. Quarteira and Albufeira are bucket-and-spade brigade havens.

To the west, Portimão's beaches are among the Algarve's postcard icons and are about as well supplied with family-friendly facilities as it is possible to imagine (though getting to them from a clifftop hotel can be a challenge for the pushchair-encumbered). Still further west, Lagos is less a resort than a fishing port on steroids – its beaches, and its satellite resort at Luz, are well out of town. Heading out into the Atlantic, the small resorts between Luz and Sagres are less than ideal for families – great beaches, but the surf can be intimidating and facilities are limited. East of Faro, the beaches are more sheltered and the resorts are smaller and much more low key – perfect for families with smaller children looking for no more than soft sand, warm sun and gentle waves, and mainly geared for those looking for a holiday in a self-catering villa or apartment complex. The only full-service resort at this end of the Algarve is the much-maligned Monte Gordo, which deserves a much better write up than it usually gets – the beach goes on for miles and miles, there are still touches of fishing village colour in the shadow of its high-rises, and it has family-friendly facilities without the urban sprawl of the big resorts to the west.

**Best Water Parks** You might think the Algarve is already blessed with enough natural sandy beaches to satisfy the most demanding family, but get to a good water park and the temptation will always be there to return. Some parents end up going back two or three times to the same site once children are hooked on a certain attraction or show. There's a spaghetti junction of flumes, pools and rubber-raft rides (as well as sun-loungers, bars and restaurants) across the Algarve waiting to be delved into.

The longest established of these great days out is **Aqualand**, at Alcantarilha; the best pick for families with toddlers as there is a special pool and play area for younger children. It has plenty for gung-ho older children too – the literally breathtaking 92-metre Kamikaze is the Algarve's longest speed chute, and the 23-metre Banzai is Portugal's highest water slide. The downside is that in high season – which is, inevitably, when British families are most likely to be there – there can be long queues for the most popular rides. This is unfortunately true, also, of the Algarve's other top water park, **Slide and Splash**, near Estombar – which has an even bigger choice of thrills and spills. If standing in line for 20 minutes for a 30-second plunge is likely to shred your nerves avoid weekends, when local families as well as holidaymakers flock here for rides such as the terrifying Black Hole. Aqualand and Slide and Splash add new rides most summers so visit their websites (see p. 97 and p. 96) for the latest developments.

**Best Animal Parks & Aquariums** It takes a bit of finding, because it's not in fact in Lagos but tucked away in the countryside about 20 minutes from the city centre, but **Lagos Zoo** is bound to please children, with its friendly macaws and cockatoos, hooting gibbon

Fisherman's Beach, Albufeira

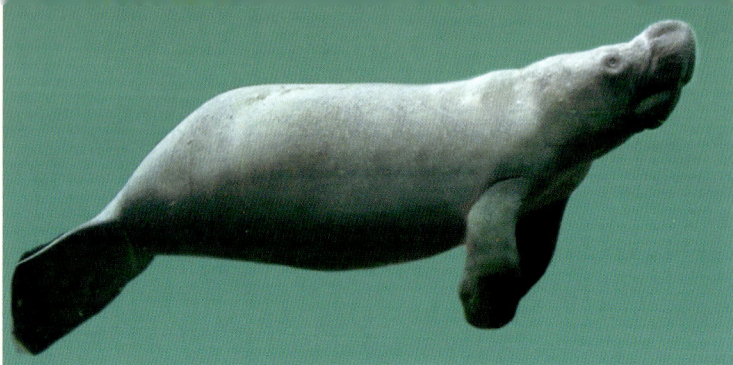

Zoomarine

family, and island-dwelling troops of lemurs and marmosets (see p. 132). **Zoomarine**, just outside Guia off the A22 motor-way, claims green credentials, but with its dolphin show, trained seals and sea-lions, sharks, sea turtles and coral reef fish, it has more than a touch of the circus. Some eco-conscious parents may have qualms about this (I know I do), but there is no doubt that it delights children (see p. 97).

**Best Islands** Separated from the quintessentially pretty town of Tavira by a narrow channel, **Ilha de Tavira** is the perfect castaway island for families. It's easy to get to, has a choice of places to eat, is completely traffic free, and best of all has a beach of white sand peppered with seashells where young beach-combers can paddle, swim and explore for hours. If you're pre-pared to camp, you can even stay here (see p. 154).

**Ilha da Armona,** a 15-minute ferry ride from Olhão, has shel-tered lagoon beaches and even more bars and restaurants, but because it's so close to Faro it

does get crowded, especially on summer weekends (see p. 67).

For a bit more peace and quiet, try neighbouring **Ilha da Culatra**, a 45-minute boat ride from Olhão, or **Ilha da Barreta**, a 30-minute ferry ride from Faro.

**Best Natural Attractions** Your first view of the **Parque Natural da Ria Formosa** will be from the air, as your holiday jet banks in to land at Faro airport – from a window seat, you should have a good view of the Natural Park's tidal labyrinth of sandbanks, islands and narrow channels, and the white, v-shaped wakes of fishing boats. The gliding storks, flamingos and wading spoonbills make this a special place for any-one with an interest in the natu-ral world, and the web-footed Portuguese water dogs make it even more special (see p. 158).

**Best Boat Trips** With more energetic older children, you can explore the Ria Formosa (see above) on foot or by bike, but it's a huge area and with smaller chil-dren the way to see it is from a boat (especially if dad is, like the author, a fan of Francis Ford Coppola's quintessential going-up-a-muddy-river-in-a-boat movie, *Apocalypse Now.* Key quote: 'Never get off the boat'). (See p. 159.)

Other great boat trips include the **schooner sunset cruise** from Vilamoura Marina, which has mass appeal; while from Sagres you can take a deep-sea fishing trip that's probably better as a father-and-son bonding **experience** than as fun for all the family (see p. 126).

**Best Outdoor Activities** The Algarve opens a cornucopia of outdoor activities for older children, ranging from **surfing** on the beaches of **Sagres** and **Carrapateira on** the west coast (see p. 126 and p. 129), where there are several surf schools that welcome young teenagers, to tutored **dinghy sailing** in the more sheltered waters around **Ilha de Tavira** or on the estuary of the **Rio Arade**, near Portimão (see p. 151 and p. 100). Across the border into Spain, east of Cádiz, some of Europe's best surf, kite-boarding and windsurfing beaches can be found.

On land, upscale sports resorts such as **Vale do Lobo** and **Quinta do Lago** offer tennis academies and golf coaching for youngsters – though at a price that is well beyond the reach of most parents (see p. 67). Several companies also offer four-wheel-drive trips into the wilder hinterland of the Algarve, which can be a good laugh for older children but not for anyone under 10.

Luckily the Algarve is set up for less structured activities from running down the beach, the simple family pleasures of beach-combing on the mile-long sands between Faro and Tavira or burying dad's car keys!

**Best Markets** Local tourist boards and many tour operators and hotels make much of the region's so-called 'gypsy markets', but their claims need to be taken with a pinch of salt. Some Portuguese attitudes to its 'gypsy' community are deeply tainted by what can sometimes be interpreted as racism, so that promoting markets that were once picturesque is cynical at best. Political correctness aside, 'gypsy markets' in Faro and else-where now have little claim to colourful authenticity, and their stock in trade tends to be the cheapest of cheap tat. Most children will find them disappointing and even a little scary.

Mértola Market

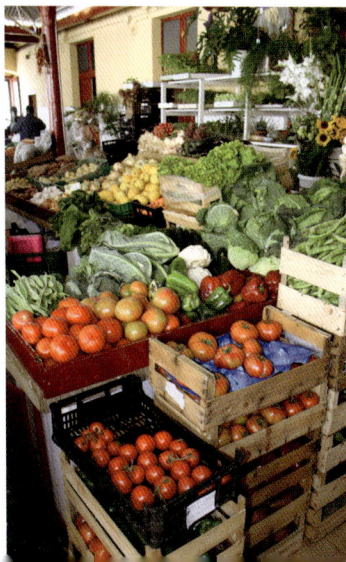

A lot more authentic, and much more interesting, are the region's fish and produce markets. For an education in edible marine life, take them to the morning fish markets at Quarteira or Olhão, and for an eye-opening change from your local supermarket, seek out the main municipal market in any of the region's major towns – especially Faro, Tavira, Portimão and Lagos – where the sight of local housewives sorting through heaps of fresh fruit and vegetables and butcher's stalls where recently slaughtered calves, chickens and piglets hang is guaranteed to give the entire family a Hugh Fearnley-Whittingstall style reality check.

Tavira's indoor market, which is housed in a vast new building at the east end of town (at the end of Rua João Anas, opposite the Hotel Vila Galé) is one of the most user friendly and good for a visit in all weathers.

**Best Castles** Dotted at strategic points around the Algarve are castles built by crusading Portuguese kings (and their Moorish, Roman and even Carthaginian predecessors). One or two, like the little fortress overlooking the sea at **Cacela Velha**, are still in use by the Portuguese armed forces. On the waterfront at **Lagos**, the fairy-tale miniature fortress now houses a museum and art gallery.

Much more imposing (and free) is **Castro Marim**, with its battlements commanding a hilltop with a view across the river to Portugal's old enemy, Spain. All that remains of **Tavira's** castle is a pretty walled garden and a square tower with great views across the old town, but like Castro Marim, entrance is free. The daddy of them all, however, has to be Henry the Navigator's **Fortaleza** at Sagres, where a line of ramparts defends the neck of one of the world's great natural defensive sites, a peninsula ringed by unscaleable cliffs hundreds of feet high.

## THE BEST ACCOMMODATION

The Algarve has a well-deserved reputation for luxury villas and golf resorts at one end of the budget scale – and for cheap and cheerful apartment complexes at the other. But look beyond these to find a much wider and imaginative choice of places to stay.

For those with deep pockets, there are lavish five-star hotels and villa complexes that are self-contained resorts in their own right.

Windmill

These are perfect for a stay-put holiday, with everything you could want right on your doorstep, and enough facilities and activities to keep the whole family busy for a week or even a fortnight without ever leaving the resort. Less gleamingly new, but perhaps with more genuine Portuguese character, are the (surprisingly affordable) *pousadas*. Most of these are historic buildings – convents, monasteries and even palaces – that have been converted into comfortable and individual hotels, with pools, courtyards and gardens that are safe places for children to play in, some excellent restaurants, and secure off-street parking, and most are located slap in the historic centre of some of the region's most attractive towns. That said, they're perhaps better for a shorter stay, or as part of a multi-stop touring holiday, than for a long holiday.

At the other end of the price scale, well-managed campsites are strategically located along the coast, and for those who can't be bothered lugging a tent all the way to Portugal they offer tent rentals and even simple beach chalets with en-suite shower and WC. Away from the beach, the Algarve and the Alentejo also have a growing number of guest-house-style places to stay in former farms or country estates – some of which still have chickens, pigs, sheep and horses, children will be happy to know.

### Best Self-Contained Resorts

Covering 400 hectares of groomed grounds and set on a 2-km stretch of beach, **Vale do Lobo** is the swankiest address in the Algarve, with gorgeous villas and apartments, facilities including baby-sitters and nannies on request, a large children's village with animators, child-minders and its own pool and mini-golf course, and a tennis academy where your budding Wimbledon stars can be coached by world-class tennis aces. It also has its own supermarket and designer boutiques, 15 very good restaurants, tennis courts, golf courses, and other activities ranging from lawn bowls to volleyball, yoga, aerobics and wooden-top spinning (see p. 56).

**Le Méridien Penina** scores equally highly – and a smidge more affordably – with its Penguin Village for children, offering everything from an adventure playground to a children's pool and slide, crèche, paints and craft materials, bikes, movies and a bouncy castle, along with five-star rooms and suites, cots (in both Penguin Village and in parents' rooms), and babysitting (see p. 112).

### Best Inland Accommodation

Almost all the Algarve's accommodation is on the beaches, but if you prefer to seek out something away from the resorts, **Quinta dos Amigos** is a former farm (it has pools for grown-ups and children) on three acres of gardens and farmland, with accommodation in two-person studios and one-, two- and three-bedroom apartments (the largest sleep up to seven people) in converted farm buildings. It has its own riding stables (for riding lessons, beach rides and guided trail riding) and babysitting is available on request. Breakfast and dinner are not included in the price, but can also be arranged. It's an excellent compromise between self-catering and hotel-style accommodation (see p. 71).

**Best Grand Hotels** Set among gardens and palm trees, just a minute's walk from Tavira's ruined castle, the **Hotel Convento da Graca** is outstandingly dignified and grand without being intimidating. There's a large inner courtyard, and behind the hotel are grassy lawns in which you'll find a toddlers' pool as well as a full-sized pool with umbrellas and sun-loungers. With fewer than 40 rooms and suites, it's not too crowded even when full. If your budget will stretch to it, go for the best of the five suites, which has its own terrace and garden. Breakfast is buffet-style, which is handy for picky and impatient children, and parents in need of a discreet hair of the dog can start the day by helping themselves to a complimentary glass of sparkling wine. It also has off-street parking (see p. 167).

**Best Stay Near an Unspoilt Beach** On a verdant hilltop within sight of the rolling surf of the west coast at Carrapateira, where there's not a sign of a high-rise hotel or apartment block, the **Monte Velho Nature Resort** is run by the friendly

Balsemão family, who have young children themselves and so understand family needs. Accommodation is in single-storey, ranch-house style abodes opening onto a pretty garden (with a toddlers' pool); this is definitely for people looking for a self-sufficient, quiet holiday as there is very little to Carrapateira apart from sand, surf and scenery. Peace at last! See p. 141.

**Best Pousadas** In the rolling hinterlands of the Alentejo, luxury pousadas are surprisingly suitable for families with younger children. Housed in a former convent, the **Pousada de São Francisco** in the historic centre of sleepy Beja has big, safely enclosed gardens full of palm trees, goldfish ponds, nesting swallows and swimming pools for adults and children, plus a small play area with a tree house, swings and slide. It also has off-street car parking. See p. 221.

In Alvito, a very pretty small town that is a great base for exploring the Alentejo countryside, the **Pousada Castelo de**

Pousada Castelo de Alvito

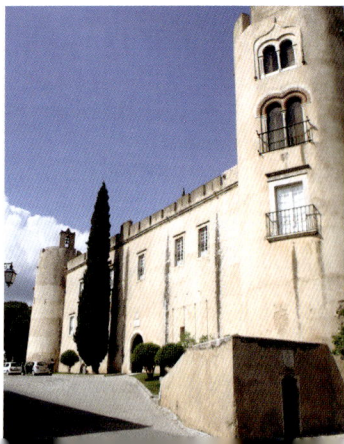

**Alvito** is in a medieval castle complete with turrets and battlements with views for miles around, and safe, pretty lawned gardens with a pool suitable for tots under supervision as well as parents, and a resident mob of rare and magical white peacocks that occasionally hop over the wall to roam the village streets. Wannabe princesses should book the Queen's Room, with its four-poster bed. See p. 223.

**Best Campsite** Camping Tavira, under pine trees on Ilha de Tavira, is the perfect castaway campsite. You can only get there by boat (a five-minute hop from the jetty at Quatro Águas) and it's just one minute's toddle to the island's huge sandy beach (with lifeguards, a first-aid station and half a dozen cafés and restaurants, so even if you're in tents you needn't live out of tins). It's Robinson Crusoe Algarve style with all the nice extras (and company) Daniel Defoe didn't provide. Bring your own tent or rent one for up to six people complete with mattresses, sheets and sleeping bags. Older children may enjoy sleeping in their own pup-tent next door to mum and dad. The site has security guards, and there's a store room where you can lock up valuables (see p. 168).

## THE BEST EATING OPTIONS

The Algarve is purpose-built for family tourism – 40 years ago, it hardly existed as a holiday destination, and most of the restaurants, bars and cafés that now exist have been built quite recently with holidaymakers in mind. The positive aspect of this is that virtually all are very well accustomed to the needs of British families, but the downside is a certain uniformity. In addition, the lifespan of an Algarve restaurant is often short – last year's favourite fish restaurant may close down and reopen under new management next year as a Tex-Mex burger bar.

Families looking for familiarity will be reassured by a tourism infrastructure built on British requirements, but more independent families should look to areas offering both convenience and a range of cuisine. There are very few restaurants with special options for children, such as highchairs, outside major resort hotels or ex-pat establishments, however, the Portuguese are very welcoming of children, flexible and used to having them gambolling around. Parents won't be fussed about child-specific amenities when the welcome is so friendly.

Even more positively in Portugal – if your children can be wheedled into sampling unfamiliar dishes – the typical Portuguese menu features an array of small snack dishes. With a range from sausages and olives to shrimps, sardines and other seafood, as well as salads, there is rarely any objection to ordering a tapas-style selection of small dishes for children to sample, rather than full-sized adult main dishes.

Sardines

## Restaurants on Beaches

Restaurants right on the beach are the best of all worlds for families, allowing parents to linger over coffee while children hopping up and down to do something else can head straight back to the sand after lunch. Fortunately, the Algarve has plenty, clustered along the beach boardwalks at the main holiday centres. There's a particularly good choice of purpose-built eating places on Portimão's spectacular **Praia da Rocha**, overlooked by steep cliffs, where restaurants such as Castelos and O Âncora stand on a wooden boardwalk that stretches all the way along the beach. Just outside Faro, **Praia de Faro** has the biggest choice of beach restaurants (often very busy on summer weekends). In the east, traffic-free **Ilha de Tavira** has a cluster of restaurants and cafés on a huge beach, including the value-for-money Restaurante Ilha Formosa, and the cheap-as-chips Dinoself self-service café. There are more in the very shadow of the giant apartment pyramids of Monte Gordo, and at Praia Verde, where Pézinhos n'Areia is popular with locals for its wide seafood menu and where children can play on the beach within sight while parents eat. It's worth noting that not many of these places stay open all through the winter, though you will usually find at least one restaurant serving lunch on any of the beaches on winter weekends, if not through the week (see p. 151).

## Restaurants in Resort Hotels

For the full works such as crayons and high chairs, most of the Algarve's resort hotels have a range of eating places that cater especially for families and even just for children. The luxury **Le Méridien Penina**, near Alvor, has a special children's restaurant, **Penguin Mac**, as part of its Penguin Village for children, as well as children's menus at its other restaurants (see p. 112).

**Fish Restaurants Portimão** wins hands-down when it comes to fish and seafood restaurants, with a string of half-a-dozen modern establishments serving fresh-caught sardines at sunny outdoor tables on the quayside north of Largo Francisco A. Maurício, where you can watch the fishing boats and yachts on the river while you wait for your meal. More authentic fish restaurants can be found hidden beneath the arches of the road bridge, just inland from the former fish market at Largo da Barca, where at **Forte y Fejo** (see p. 115) you can select your sea bass, bream or huge grouper from trays of crushed ice, or choose your lobster from those living beneath the aquarium-style dining-room floor.

### British-style Pubs & Restaurants

Around half of those who visit the Algarve each year come from the UK, and there's also a large expatriate population. British-style (and often British-run) pubs and restaurants have appeared to service this captive market, so families who get homesick for familiar home cooking (from roast beef and fish and chips through to chicken masala, pizza and chilli burgers) are spoilt for choice. The biggest hot-spots for this kind of culinary experience are Quarteira and Albufeira's famous (some would say notorious) strip, a continuous avenue of pubs, bars and restaurants – including, at last visit, the Kilt and Celt pub, the Rover's Return and the Dog and Duck,

which gives you some idea of the ambience of the area. A great compromise in Quarteira is **Fernando's Hideaway** – a local institution that serves massive steaks, Sunday roasts and fish and chips as well as Portuguese standards, and has a children's menu and some vegetarian specials.

**Vegetarian Restaurants** Like the rest of Portugal, the Algarve could do more for vegetarians. Portuguese cooking leans heavily towards meat and fish, sometimes in unusual combinations such as pork with clams, and in most places veggies will be fobbed off with omelettes and uninspired salads. **Restaurant Ribatejano**, in Faro (see p. 74) promotes itself as a purely vegetarian eating place but strict vegetarians will be surprised to see bacalhau (dried salt cod) dishes on the menu along with vegetable rissoles, tofu omelette and soya burgers. More upscale restaurants within the upmarket hotels and pousadas generally make a bigger effort, with at least one gourmet veggie offering on their costly menus, but at street level vegetarians are better off choosing self-catering accommodation and relying on the plentiful supply of lovely fresh fruit and vegetables, local cheeses, olives and other non-meat treats in local markets and shops.

**Luxury Restaurants** The Algarve has more than its fair share of very posh restaurants for special occasions, including some with Michelin stars. At the **Hotel Vila Joya** in Albufeira, Austrian chef Dieter Koschina's cooking stands head and shoulders above the rest – he's the only chef in Portugal to hold two Michelin stars. Koschina sources the finest ingredients – such as lobster, crayfish and turbot – from local markets and imports truffles, goose liver and caviar for superb combinations.

**Henrique Leis**, whose restaurant is located between the Vale do Lobo and Quinta do Lago resorts, ensuring a steady flow of well-heeled customers, has one Michelin star.

**Restaurant Willies**, at Vilamoura, has not yet earned a Michelin star but as owner-chef Willie Weger has won stars elsewhere this may only be a matter of time.

**Places for Picnics** You really need to take a picnic along to make the most of some of the Algarve's more extensive beaches, such as the huge stretches of **Ilha de Tavira** and the vast sands of **Carrapateira**. You can buy the essential kit – an insulated chillybin for cold drinks, plastic cups and plates, something to sit on,

Hotel Vila Joya

and a sharp knife for cutting things up – at any local supermarket (there's a good choice of picnic equipment in branches of the Intermarché supermarket chain) and stocking up on picnic snacks is dead easy in local markets and supermarkets. Beaches can be blisteringly hot in summer and a sun umbrella is a must. There are cooler picnic spots inland, such as those on the shores of the fjord-like **Barragem de Bravura**, an artificial freshwater reservoir of jade-green water about 15 minutes' drive inland from Lagos, or the **Barragem do Arade**, a five-minute drive northeast of Silves.

# 2 Planning a Trip to the Algarve

**P**lanning any holiday takes a certain amount of time and organisation, but when travelling with children it's imperative to do your homework about your destination and any possible hazards, be that health precautions or simply the risk of boredom, before you go. Certain aspects, such as transport and accommodation, should not be left to chance – hanging around at airports or train stations, or not having a room for the night are a recipe for disaster with little ones in tow. Other aspects, however, should always retain an element of spontaneity – spotting a theme park or interesting museum en route and allowing a stop to look at the animals for example. It's usually these surprise encounters that stay in children's memories long after they return home. What's important is building a schedule that allows for this flexibility.

Children will also get much more out of any holiday if you involve them in some of the planning stages – sit them down with a map of the region and explain where you're going and what you're likely to see and do. You can be sure that will start a debate! Building up excitement prior to the trip is not only all part of the experience, but will also keep them going should you encounter any hitches such as flight delays. Take their interests into account too – if one child loves the outdoors while the other has more fun exploring castles and playing king over ramparts, make sure you've built in both options for the trip. Ultimately, whether your child wants to be a pirate or a princess, some fun preparation will help you get more out of your adventure.

## THE REGION IN BRIEF

If you haven't yet visited the Algarve – and even if you have – you may think that this southernmost stretch of sandy shore is no more than a gaggle of golf courses, villa complexes and cheap and cheerful beach resorts.

Up to a point, you'd be right, but Faro airport is the gateway to so much more than just the manicured greens and spotless sands of resorts such as Vilamoura, Albufeira, Quarteira and Portimão.

Head all the way west, and in a surprisingly short space of time (less than a 90-minute drive from Faro) you're on the wild west coast, a region of endless sands, spectacular coastlines and Atlantic surf.

Take off in the opposite direction, and in only half an hour you're in Tavira or Vila Real de Santo António, gorgeous historic towns that haven't turned into booming tourism resorts because they're not right on the coast – but both of which have splendid sandy beaches just minutes away.

Push on a little further east and you can be across the border into Spain's 'sherry triangle' and the stunning historic cities of Seville, Jerez and Cádiz, and a whole different culture of gypsy violinists, flamenco dancers and prancing stallions – and of cutting-edge adrenaline water sports.

Or go inland, across the rolling plains and winding river valleys of the Baixa Alentejo. Spattered with scarlet, purple and yellow wildflowers in spring and early summer, the Alentejo's prairies bake under endless sun in summer, but the region is dotted with dozens of freshwater reservoirs, including Europe's newest and largest artificial lake, that are super, uncrowded family picnic spots.

This is a region that seems a world away from the busy coast, but that is very easy to get to. And all of the holiday honeypots of the Algarve, the Alentejo and Andalusia's western corner are packed into a remarkably compact space: none of the attractions and destinations that we have highlighted in this book is more than two hours from Faro airport, at maximum. With buses and trains linking everywhere along the coast and inland, you don't even need a car to explore.

Further south, Monchique, around an hour's drive from Sagres and about half an hour from Lagos or Portimão, is a pleasant enough little town for a break to let the family stretch their legs and grab a cold drink if you're tempted to take a drive through the hills inland from the coast – but from the point of view of parents with children it isn't really a destination worth making a special trip to.

Yes, go to the Algarve for some of the most spectacular beaches in Europe, for lovely villas and excellent family resorts – but go too to explore wild Atlantic beaches, flamingo-haunted wetlands, traffic-free historic town centres, cool river valleys and the big skies of the back country. There is much more to the Algarve than the world of the holiday brochures.

## VISITOR INFORMATION

Most families these days have access to the Internet, either within their own home or at local libraries or Internet cafés. This is the fastest and easiest way to do some preparatory groundwork for your holiday, both in terms of planning where to go and what to see as well as opportunities to book accommodation and transport. The website of Portugal's national tourist office, *www.visitportugal.com*, provides detailed information about the whole country including, of course, the Algarve, and links to hotels and restaurants. There are also a number of themed itineraries that are recommended, many of which are family-specific. If you are looking for any information that is not included on the site they can be e-mailed at E: info@visitportugal.com.

If you prefer a more personal approach, the tourist office, under the name **ICEP (Investimentos, Comércio e Turismo de Portugal)**, has an

## Beach Guide

**Pick up the Algarve Tourist Board's** *Guide to the Beaches of Algarve* (*Guia de Praias do Algarve*) – it lists 116 different beaches, with lots of pictures and all the information you could need, including tips on where to park. Launched in 2006 in Portuguese, an English edition was due for publication in 2007 and should be available through the Portuguese National Tourist Office in London as well as from *www.rtalgarve.pt*.

office at the Portuguese Embassy in London at 11 Belgrave Square, SW1X 8PP (📞 *0845 355 1212*).

The tourist office's other main website, *www.portugaloffice.org.uk*, provides very useful links to all the UK tour operators that organise holidays in Portugal, including more than 50 that specialise in the Algarve. The advantages of a good tour operator for families are the overall package, organisation, advice, peace of mind and support if anything goes wrong. Other websites that are devoted solely to information about the Algarve include *www.algarve.org* and *www.algarve-gids.com*, offering up-to-the-minute information about villas, golf courses, weather and more.

In addition to the official tourist office sites, there are several privately run information sites that offer a wide range of information on activities, attractions and where to eat and drink. Most of these are run by British expats who live in the Algarve, so they are well informed and up to date – but also opinionated and occasionally eccentric. Some of the most useful for families are the sites: *www.algarve.org*; *www.algarve-beach-life.com*; *www.*

*visitalgarve.pt*; *www.algarve-gids.com*; *www.thealgarve.net*.

### Family-friendly Websites

There are numerous websites offering information particularly geared towards families and the best child-friendly options in the region, from activities to practicalities. On *www.takethefamily.com*, for instance, there are recommendations for child-friendly hotels, suggestions of what to do during your trip and how much you can expect to spend for an average family of four. Equally *www.babygoes2.com* offers pros and cons for your trip with a special emphasis on toddlers. Non-destination specific but nevertheless useful and reassuring is *www.deabirkett.com*, run by the former *Guardian* children's travel specialist, where a forum between parents and families allows you to share tips and questions about travelling abroad with children.

If you're planning to drive to the Algarve from the UK, or simply want to do a bit of travelling around when you're there, you can take a lot of stress out of the journey by using the Internet to plan routes well in advance. Among the many sites are *www.viamichelin.com*, *www.map orama.com* and *www.mapquest. com*, all of which offer point-to-point directions as well as map information for specific addresses. The added advantage of viamichelin is that it also offers invaluable information on current roadworks, speed camera locations and tollbooth locations and charges if applicable.

## Entry Requirements & Customs

### Passports & Visas

British and Irish citizens require only a valid passport to enter Portugal and stay for a period of 180 days or less. For longer stays a residency permit is required, which can be applied for locally at the **Portuguese Immigration Authority (Serviço de Estrangeiros e Fronteiras)** or in advance at the Portuguese Embassy (see above).

### Travelling as a Single Parent

Any child under the age of 18 travelling with only one parent is required to carry a letter of authority from the absent parent remaining at home. Although these are rarely requested to be seen, they are a legal requirement designed to prevent child abduction.

### Taking Your Pet

Under the **Pet Travel Scheme (PETS)**, UK-resident dogs and cats can now travel to many other EU countries and return to the UK without being quarantined. Dogs and cats are issued with a passport (by a vet) after being fitted with a microchip and vaccinated against rabies at least 21 days prior to travel. On re-entry to the UK, you need to get your pet treated against ticks and tapeworm (by any EU vet 24–48 hours before being checked in with a transport company approved by the scheme). For full details, see *www.defra.gov.uk/ animalh/quarantine/index.htm*.

Many hotels and self-catering accommodation are also happy to have pets on their premises but it is vital to check in advance. Some may also charge a small extra fee to cover any damage the animal might incur.

### Customs

In theory EU citizens can import and export an unlimited amount of duty-paid goods provided it can be proved that they are for personal use and not for resale. Reasonable limits that fulfil these criteria are 800 cigarettes, 10 litres of spirits, 90 litres of wine and 110 litres of beer. If entering the country, however, particularly from the UK, all of the above goods are considerably cheaper in Portugal so it makes little sense to import anything other than what you might require for your journey.

## Money

### The Euro

Portugal's currency is the **euro** €. There are 100 **cents** in a euro

| What Things Cost in the Algarve | € | £ |
| --- | --- | --- |
| 1 litre unleaded petrol | 1.35 | 0.92 |
| Hire of medium-sized car (per week) | 160–200 | 107.20–134 |
| Taxi ride | 8.00 (approx. 5 km) | 5.45 |
| City/town bus fare, adult | 1.50 | 1.02 |
| City/town bus fare, child 5 or over | 0.50 | 0.35 |
| Single train fare, adult | 6.70 | 4.55 |
| Single train fare, child | 3.35 | 2.28 |
| Single air fare, adult | 74–222 | 50–150 |
| Single air fare, child | 74–222 | 50–150 |
| Family room in luxury hotel | 150–250 | 102–170 |
| Family room in mid-range hotel | 100–150 | 68–102 |
| Family room in budget hotel | 50–100 | 34–68 |
| Admission to zoo, adult | 3.00 | 2.05 |
| Admission to zoo, child | 1.50 | 1.02 |
| Admission to public museum | 2.50 | 1.70 |
| Cinema ticket, adult | 5.00 | 3.40 |
| Cinema ticket, child | 2.50 | 1.70 |
| British newspaper | 3– 5 | 2.05–3.40 |
| Local telephone call (per minute) | 0.14 | 0.10 |
| European telephone call (per minute) | 0.21 | 0.14 |
| Fixed-price menu at mid-priced restaurant | 10 | 6.80 |
| Fixed-price menu at budget restaurant | 8.00 | 5.45 |
| Under 12s menu at budget restaurant | 1.50 | 1.02 |
| 1 litre milk in supermarket | 1.00 | 0.68 |
| 1 litre apple juice in supermarket | 1.00 | 0.68 |
| 1.5 litre bottle still water in supermarket | 1.25 | 0.85 |
| 1kg bananas in supermarket | 1.50 | 1.02 |
| Sandwich from takeaway counter | 1.00–2.50 | 0.68–1.70 |
| Packet of 20 small Pampers in supermarket | 5.00 | 3.40 |
| 330ml infant milk in supermarket | 3.50 | 2.38 |

*Assuming a conversion rate of £1 = €1.48*

and coins range in denominations from 1 cent to €2. Notes come in denominations of €5–500.

As of writing the **euro–sterling exchange rate** was €1.46 to £1 (68p to €1), so to convert prices to a quick rounded-up sum simply drop a third off the euro price for the average cost in pounds). For current rates and a currency converter see **www.xe.com**.

### Credit & Debit Cards

Most shops, restaurants and hotels in the Algarve accept the international credit cards **Visa** and **Mastercard**. **American Express** and **Diner's Club** are usually the preserve of the most expensive establishments because they apply charges for use. Most places, however, will be reluctant to receive payment by any credit card for any transaction under €5. If you're in more rural areas or in smaller campsites and B&Bs, check in advance whether they accept cards – many remain cash-only operations.

ATMs (cashpoint machines) can be found in towns all over the Algarve, at both banks and in hole-in-the-wall outlets, and will accept international debit cards if they display corresponding symbols such as Cirrus. Most of them are accessible 24 hours a day. You simply need to use the same PIN number that you use at home to withdraw cash. Most will also give you the option to change the usage instructions from Portuguese to English. Cash can also be withdrawn from ATMs using a credit card but there is a higher rate of interest charged on these transactions.

It's worth informing your credit card company that you're going abroad before you leave home. Many companies put a block on cards if they see unusual or foreign activity on the account and are unable to reach you to discuss it, in order to prevent credit card fraud.

For **lost or stolen cards** see p. 43.

### Budget Tips

Obviously prices for accommodation can be considerably lower in the winter months while the climate is still pleasantly balmy. School holidays as well as high season boost up prices because of popularity. As most families are tied to the school calendar, camping, youth hostelling or staying in private homes (*quartos*) are a good way to keep costs down.

**Discount cards** that cover many attractions and transport are also available for anyone in your party under 26 or over 65, available from tourist offices.

## When to Go

Spring and autumn are the ideal times to visit the Algarve, although the winter months still have a pleasant climate and prices for both accommodation and airfares are greatly reduced. The high summer months of July and August are not only very crowded but the weather can be sticky at best and highly uncomfortable at worst, particularly for young children.

For the latest real-time weather reports from the region, visit the websites: *www.vale-do-lobo-guide.com*, *www.wunderground.com*, *www.Easyjet.com* or *www.ryanair.com*.

| Average Daytime Temperature & Rainfall in the Algarve | | | | | | | | | | | | |
|---|---|---|---|---|---|---|---|---|---|---|---|---|
| | Jan | Feb | Mar | Apr | May | June | July | Aug | Sept | Oct | Nov | Dec |
| Temp. (°C) | 15 | 16 | 17 | 20 | 22 | 25 | 28 | 28 | 26 | 22 | 19 | 16 |
| Rainfall (mm) | 70 | 70 | 35 | 31 | 25 | 5 | 1 | 1 | 5 | 51 | 55 | 65 |

## Public & School Holidays

The following days are public (bank) holidays in Portugal, when museums, banks and most shops will be closed:
1 Jan: New Year's Day
Feb: Shrove Tuesday*
Mar/Apr: Good Friday*
25 Apr: Freedom Day
1 May: Labour Day
May/June: Corpus Christi*
10 June: Portugal Day
15 Aug: Feast of the
    Assumption
5 Oct: Republic Day
1 Nov: All Saints' Day
1 Dec: National Independence
    Day
8 Dec: Immaculate Conception
25 Dec: Christmas Day

*Dates vary year to year

The Portuguese love a good party so many of these events are marked by parades and carnivals, which can be spectacular affairs and well worth a look.
Portuguese **school holidays** coincide almost exactly with UK equivalents, so expect beaches and attractions to be full of many local children too during these periods. It does also mean, however, that far more events are staged to appeal to children.

## Special Events

### Family Events

#### Loulé

**Loulé's Carnival**, held each year over three days in the run up to Easter (March or April, contact tourist office for annual dates) is the most colourful in the

Algarve and one of the liveliest in Portugal, with a parade of fancy-dressed floats, folk music, fireworks and dancing from dusk until dawn (see p. 53). *www.visitalgarve.pt*.

### Albufeira

**Albufeira Carnival** takes its mid-February carnival less seriously than most other Portuguese towns, with a special children's carnival parade on the Friday closest to 14th February – floats, children in costume, and baby, toddler, pre-teen and teenage carnival princesses and princes. To take part, contact the tourist office in Albufeira (see p. 79).
The **International Sand Art Festival (FIESA)** has to be the Algarve's top family fixture. Every year, from June to October, 'sand artists' from all over the world descend on this stretch of beach at Areias de Pêra near Albufeira to create a 'city' of gobsmacking, colossal wonders of the world, from gigantic idols and copies of famous statues to castles, dragons, temples and monsters. There is a different theme each year. Everybody loves this one, and children are inspired to even greater sand-castle-building efforts of their own (see p. 83).
( 00 351 969 459 261; *www.pro sandart.com*). *Open* daily 7th Jun–7th Oct, 10am–midnight. *Admission*: adults €7, children (6–12) €4, under 5s free.

**Festa da Ourada** held on 14th August, the religious procession which begins Albufeira's biggest summer festival is as solemn as it gets around here, with local fisher folk heading for church to beseech the help of the Virgin Mary in her role as *Stella Maris* – the 'Star of the Sea' and protector of fishermen. Things loosen up and become more tourist-accessible after mass at Albufeira's main church, with a procession of fishing boats, and reach a crescendo with a phenomenal fireworks display on the beach. Small children will find the crowds, the noise and the flash-bangs a bit much, and dads should be willing to carry children shoulder high so they can get a decent view of the pyrotechnics (see p. 83). *www. visitalgarve.pt*.

### Portimão

Children who think sardines grow in tins (and come without heads) will be either fascinated or appalled by **Portimão's Sardine Festival**, an actual celebration of the sardine, which has grown into a week-long party in mid-August (dates vary) where the sardine is honoured, praised and finally grilled (with the head on) and eaten. The old-town streets and waterfront are a family-friendly and mainly car-free setting for this happy street party every evening, with fireworks, live music, market stalls and many other attractions (see p. 81). *www.visitalgarve.pt*.

### Silves

**Silves Medieval Fair** is one for the Dr Who fans in the family, when the Castle of the Moors and the old town of Silves are transported back to the Moorish Middle Ages. Held in August,

everybody dresses in Moorish costume, and musicians, dancers, knights and veiled damsels, snake-charmers, jugglers and jesters roam the streets and everyone can join in (see p. 83). *www.visitalgarve.pt*.

### Fatacil

A celebration of traditional Portuguese music, handicrafts and food at this nine-day festival in the middle of August in Lagoa (see p. 87).

📞 *00 351 282 353 453; www. carvoiero.com/guide/fatacil/ index.html)*

### Castro Marim

Step back in time to the Middle Ages where lively jesters add to the atmosphere of horseback jousting through the streets of Castro Marim. Music, food and traditional crafts add to the spectacle. Last four days of August (see p. 154).

📞 *00 351 281 510 740; www.cm-castromarim.pt)*

## What to Pack

In summer lightweight cotton clothes and swimwear are all that you'll need, but make sure you also include a sunhat for every family member, as the heat can be oppressive. In spring and autumn nights are cooler so some kind of jacket or fleece to cover up with is recommended, as is a waterproof light jacket in winter. The Portuguese are casual by nature, particularly in the Algarve, so you're unlikely to need very smart clothing unless you're dining or staying at a high-class establishment.

In summer **insect-repellent** and **sun cream** with the appropriate factor number are essentials.

Portugal is a family-orientated country and you should have no problem at all in finding goods to fulfil children's needs, whether it be day-to-day items such as nappies and formula milk, to cheap buckets and spades, rubber rings, beach balls and any number of toys that are affordable enough to be disposed of when it's time to go home.

## Health, Insurance & Safety

### Health

There are no real health risks travelling in the Algarve and no vaccinations are required. **Mosquitoes**, however, although harmless, can be a nuisance and **sunburn** is particularly unpleasant for children so make sure you have relevant creams and repellents. **Tap water** is safe to drink, although you may find bottled water more palatable.

### Travel Insurance

Unlike many European countries, UK residents do not need to apply for an EHIC (European Health Insurance Card) before visiting Portugal. There is an organised agreement between the two countries that UK visitors receive free or reduced medical treatment in the case of emergency.

However, if you require medical treatment that is not considered of an emergency nature – a nagging toothache, for example, or a sprained wrist that is certain to ruin your holiday if left untreated – costs of health care in Portugal are very high.

It's therefore essential to take out **comprehensive travel insurance** for all the family before leaving home. This should not only cover any medical treatment necessary either in state or private facilities, but also repatriation costs if you need to fly any family member home. A good policy will also cover baggage loss and travel cancellation. If you're planning on pursuing adventure sports on your trip you should also build in cover for that within your policy.

Travel insurance is a drop in the ocean when compared with the other costs of your holiday – around £10 for a family of four per week – but the costs that can incur without it can often seem infinite should disaster strike. Don't skimp on this area – it's not worth it. If you're buying travel insurance through a travel agent or tour operator, make sure the company is a member of the Association of British Travel Agents (ABTA), which regulates insurance sales by holiday companies. If you buy your insurance independently, make sure the broker and the insurance company are registered with the Financial Services Authority (FSA), which regulates all other insurance sales in the UK.

## If You Fall Ill

For **emergency treatment, doctors** and **chemists** see p. 43 and p. 42.

If you have an ongoing medical condition that requires **prescription medicine** bring enough with you to cover your stay as well as copies of the prescriptions. You should also know the generic name of the medicine as different countries often identify the same medicines under different brand names. Keep the medicines in your hand luggage while travelling in case of baggage loss or disruption, but make sure that they are clearly labelled for airport officials to see.

If you or your child has an illness that may make explanation of what's happening impossible, and that needs swift and accurate treatment (such as epilepsy, diabetes, asthma or a food allergy), the charity **MedicAlert** (*www.medicalert.org.uk*) provides bracelets or necklets engraved with the wearer's medical condition. It also includes details such as an ID number and a 24-hour telephone number that accepts reverse charge calls so the medical details can be accessed from anywhere in more than 100 languages.

## Travelling Safely with Children

Portugal and the Algarve are, in general, safe places where crime is rare but, as with everywhere else, where tourists go **petty crime** thrives. Lock your car doors even when you're inside and don't carry any more cash on you than you need for that day. Be especially alert for pickpockets during carnivals or parades. It's also frighteningly easy during such events to lose sight of a child within moments. If your children are old enough, agree **a meeting place** with them in advance in the event that you get separated and make sure that they have your mobile phone number, accommodation address and the skills to ask for a policeman. Don't, however, make their name visible – children can be very trusting to anyone who reassures them by name. With younger children, as you would anywhere, keep hold of their hands at all times.

**Beaches** should, quite rightly, be areas of fun and freedom, but it's also all too easy to doze off in the sun and wake up to a missing child, and with the sea on your doorstep this doesn't bear thinking about. Make sure one adult is always alert and awake. For peace of mind, especially if you're with a group of children who are finding it hard to curb their excitement, invest in **Boardbug** wrist-worn monitors. They can monitor up to three children at a time from distances of 2 m to 150 m. They're available from *www.travellingwithchildren.co.uk* at approximately £55 each, but it's a small price to pay for the knowledge that you can locate them easily and quickly, with minimum panic.

ABTA has launched a new free web-based service for families providing added reassurance for parents travelling abroad with their children (*www.family safeholidays.co.uk*).

The website has essential pre-travel information, printable emergency contact details and a registration service, where the most important holiday details can be stored; it can be accessed online or via a 24-hour call centre anywhere in the world if something goes wrong.

The registration service can store travel itineraries, copies of passports and insurance policy details. It can also store details of the family with photos, medical conditions, medication and allergies. If the worst happens, families can utilise the service to immediately produce a missing poster of a lost child or adult, which can be viewed in six languages and made available on the Internet or via e-mail.

## Specialised Resources

### For Single Parents

For helpful 'Holidays' pages with contact details of useful associations and operators in the UK, see *www.singleparents.org.uk*. **One Parent Families** (☎ *0800 018 5026*; *www.oneparentfamilies.org.uk*) is a British charity offering information and advice for lone parents; **Gingerbread** (☎ *0800 018 4318*; *www.gingerbread.org.uk*) is similar, with members getting regular e-mails with discounts and holiday ideas. Members of both get discounts with tour operator **Eurocamp** (p. 33), which has an Arrival Survival service to help lone parents unpack and settle in

and has two sites in the Algarve. Most youth hostels offer single-parent discounts too.

### For Grandparents

The Algarve is a very popular destination for grandparents, many of whom spend all or part of the year in the region in their retirement because of the year-round sun. This is particularly true, of course, of golf fanatics. Many children, therefore, will have the advantage of holidaying with their grandparents in privately owned homes. Otherwise, the most convenient way to include grandparents in the holiday is to rent out villa accommodation, which allows more flexibility to cater to different age groups. Travellers over the age of 65 are also entitled to discounts on many attractions as well as transport (see p. 23).

### For Families with Special Needs

Like much of southern Europe, the Algarve is somewhat behind in providing disabled facilities and the beauty of old towns lined with cobbled streets can lose much of their charm if you're struggling with a wheelchair. However, the newer modern villas are beginning to take these issues into account, as are larger hotels. One of the best places to find out about accessible accommodation, transport and other issues is **Wheeling Around the Algarve** (*www.player.pt*). **Holiday Care** (☎ *0845 124 9971*; *www. holidaycare.org.uk*) also publishes information guides to foreign destinations for disabled travellers.

## The 21st-Century Traveller

### Mobile Phones

The advent of mobile phone technology has vastly improved many of the situations that can occur when travelling with children. It's simple and easy to use British mobile phones in Europe: when you arrive in the Algarve it will simply switch over to a **Portuguese network** and you can call any number, whether at home or abroad, directly, although you do need to add the international dialling code even for Portuguese numbers.

However, it's still wise to check with your service provider that your phone is set up for international roaming, particularly for receiving voice mails, which can sometimes be a bit more complicated.

**Call charges** to both UK and Portuguese numbers will be higher than they would be at home and you also pay for incoming calls from the UK. Anyone you phone on his or her mobile at home will also be charged. Therefore if you're going to be making and receiving a lot of calls or you travel a lot it's more economical to buy an **international SIM card** to temporarily replace your UK one, which will give you a local number and lower rates. The website *www.0044.co.uk* offers more information on this. Equally, if you're in the Algarve often or for a long period you can buy a standard **pay-as-you-go** mobile from any telecommunications shop. Making and receiving foreign calls will also use up more battery time so you will find you'll need to recharge your phone more regularly than you would at home.

### Other Phones

For information about **area and international dialling codes** and **public phones**, see p. 44.

### The Internet

Cities such as Faro and the large resorts have an array of Internet options, from cyber cafés to Internet ports in bars and restaurants.

To retrieve your e-mails, ask your Internet Service Provider (ISP) if it has a **web-based interface** tied to your existing account, such as *www.btyahoo.co.uk* for British Telecom. If it does, you can simply go to their site, type in your e-mail address and password, and access and send mail from your own address. If it doesn't provide this you can set up a **free web-based e-mail account** with companies such as *www.yahoo.com* or *www.hotmail.com*. It's not a bad idea to have one of these anyway, in case there are any problems with your regular ISP.

Most hotels of any size will also have an Internet point, which can be used for a small fee, usually based on a 15-minute time span. Larger hotels may also have a **modem connection or dataport** in each room or a **Wi-Fi** ('wireless fidelity') area, which means you can work directly from your own laptop providing that it is Wi-Fi enabled. This is a more expensive option (you'll be charged a telephone rate) but more flexible and private.

Do be aware that **Portuguese keyboards** are different from the UK qwerty keyboard, with additional characters, and the @ key can sometimes be frustratingly hard to locate.

# ESSENTIALS

## Getting There

**By Plane** Portugal has long been the preserve of charter airlines largely carrying package holiday tourists, but the **low-cost or no-frills airlines** have opened up the Algarve for independent travel as they have done all over Europe. The low-cost airlines that run regular flights to **Faro International Airport** are **Ryanair** from Shannon and Dublin, Ireland (📞 *0818 303 030*; *www.ryanair.com*), **Easyjet** from Luton, Stansted, Gatwick, Belfast, Bristol, East Midlands, Liverpool and Newcastle (📞 *0905 821 0905*; *www.easyjet.com*), **bmibaby** from Birmingham, Cardiff and East Midlands (UK: 📞 *0871 224 0224*; *www.bmibaby.com*), and **Flybe** from Exeter and Southampton (UK: 📞 *0871 700 0535*; *www.flybe.com*). The charter airline **Monarch** also operates regular flights from Birmingham, Gatwick, Luton and Manchester (UK: 📞 *08700 405 040*, Portugal:

📞 *0800 860 270*; *www.flymonarch.com*). Globespan flies from Aberdeen, Durham, Edinburgh and Glasgow (UK: 📞 *08712 710 415*; *www.flyglobespan.com*).

Other scheduled airlines that operate between the UK and the Algarve are **British Airways** from London Gatwick (UK: 📞 *0870 850 9850*; *www.britishairways.com*) and **Aer Lingus** from Dublin (UK: 📞 *0870 876 5000*, Ireland: 📞 *08181 365 000*; *www.flyaerlingus.com*).

As a general rule, **under-twos travel free** and need to sit on one parent's lap. From the age of three they need to have their own seat so pay the same fare as adults. For low-cost airlines **fares** can genuinely start as low as £0.01, depending on when you book and whether there are any special offers operating to your destination, but **airport taxes** can add as much as £20 to each fare. The low-cost airlines also have far more restrictions on size and weight of baggage than do scheduled airlines.

**Luggage on flights:** Passengers between the UK and Portugal are allowed a laptop-sized bag as their hand luggage. You are only allowed to take small quantities of liquids in your cabin luggage or on your person. These liquids must be in individual containers with a maximum capacity of 100 millilitres each. You must pack these containers in one transparent, resealable plastic bag of not more than one-litre capacity. Drinks and toiletries can, however, be purchased in airport shops once you've passed through security. Remember that the situation may change at short notice for security reasons. Check with your airline prior to packing about current regulations so you don't waste time repacking at the airport. Also, look at the British Airports Authority website, which posts new security regulations regularly (*www.baa.com*).

**By Car** Most visitors to the Algarve arrive by plane and pick up their hire car from the airport. However, if you want to bring your own vehicle and drive from the UK the easiest option is to take an **overnight car ferry** from southern England (Portsmouth or Plymouth) to the northern Spanish cities of **Bilbao** or **Santander**. Journey times range between 24 hours to 35 hours, but the ships are packed with activities for children, including swimming pools and games rooms and children's entertainments shows are usually also staged. However, be warned that this is a considerable undertaking with children; holiday time may well be better spent at the destination. Long sailings are obviously more costly than shorter cross-Channel services, averaging around £500 for a standard vehicle and four-berth cabin on a return trip, but long car journeys with children are considerably more stressful so it's worth the extra expense if possible. And with petrol costs, a long drive doesn't save a significant amount anyway. Prices are obviously higher in high season.

The main operator on this route is **Brittany Ferries** (UK: ☎ *08709 076 103*, Spain: ☎ *00 34 942 360 611*; *www.brittany-ferries. co.uk*). From here, drivers should follow the N620 to northern Portugal and then the E1 tolled motorway south to the Algarve. The journey is approximately 1,000 km so an overnight stop in Portugal is recommended.

**By Train** A rail journey from the UK to the Algarve would be non-sensical for adults to undertake, let alone the prospect of doing it with increasingly bored children. The journey would involve taking the Eurostar from London or Kent to the Gare du Nord in Paris, crossing the city to the Gare d'Austerlitz to link up with the routes to Spain and then down through Portugal – an entire trip of around 40 hours. What's more, you'll pay through the nose for the privilege.

**By Bus** If the 40-hour rail journey were not enough to put you off, only the most sadistic or unthinking parent would inflict a bus journey on their children. Forget about it.

## Package Deals & Activity Holidays

**Package holidays** are among the most popular options for visiting the Algarve. Booking a package holiday means that a designated tour operator handles all aspects for your trip, from plane or ferry, to accommodation and, if required, car hire as well. They also offer different options such

## Flying with Children

**If you plan carefully, you can make it fun to fly with your children.**

- You'll save yourself a good bit of aggravation by reserving a seat in the bulkhead row. You'll have more legroom, your children will be able to spread out and play on the floor underfoot, and the airline might provide bassinets (ask in advance). You're also more likely to find sympathetic company in the bulkhead area, as families with children tend to be seated there.
- Have a long talk with your children before you depart for your trip. If they've never flown before, explain to them what to expect. If they're old enough, you may even want to describe how flight works and how air travel is even safer than riding in a car. Explain to your children the importance of good behaviour in the air – how their own safety can depend upon their being quiet and staying in their seats during the trip.
- Pay extra careful attention to the safety instructions before takeoff. Consult the safety chart behind the seat in front of you and show it to your children. Be sure you know how to operate the oxygen masks, as you will be expected to secure your own first and then help your children. Be especially mindful of the location of emergency exits.
- Make a member of the crew aware of any medical problems your children have that could manifest during flight.
- Be sure you've slept sufficiently for your trip. If you fall asleep in the air and your child manages to break away, there are all sorts of sharp objects that could cause injury.

as full- or half-board accommodation. Booking all the elements separately and independently can, these days, often save you money, but it won't save you time, which is after all the quality most at a premium for families. **Activity holidays** include all of the above elements but with the addition of other themed options, be it sporty, creative or cultural.

Although **escorted tours**, where you have a guide taking you to various sights, usually by coach, do operate in the region they are an ill-advised option for children. Children rarely enjoy

schlepping around sights as part of a regimented group, with no freedom to explore on their own and parents will be tied to a fixed schedule. If you want your children to get to know the area do it with them alone, which also gives them the option to contribute and suggest ideas of where to go.

The following are just some of the tour operators who handle packages to the Algarve (see *www.abta.com* and *www.aito.co.uk* for more) although there are many more on the **Internet** and advertised in weekend travel

- Be sure your child's seatbelt remains fastened properly, and try to reserve the seat closest to the aisle for yourself. This will make it harder for your children to wander off – in case, for instance, you're tired and you do happen to nod off. You will also protect your child from jostling passersby and falling objects – in the rare but entirely possible instance that an overhead bin pops open.

  For the same reason, sudden turbulence is also a danger to children who are not buckled into their own seat belt or seat restraint.

- On crowded flights, the flight crew may need as much as an hour to serve dinner. It's wise to encourage your children to use the toilet as you see the attendants preparing to serve.

- Be sure to bring self-containing compact toys. Magnetic checkers sets are a perfect distraction, and small colouring books and crayons also work well, as do card games like Go Fish.

- Make sure you have your child's comforter and dummy; having two or three favourite identical comforters can be a life saver in the hustle and bustle of holiday travel when things tend to get dropped, lost or forgotten.

- Some airlines serve children's meals first. When you board, ask a flight attendant if this is possible, especially if your children are very young or seated toward the back of the plane.

sections of **newspapers**. If you're booking with a small company make sure that your travel insurance (see p. 26) covers you if the company goes bust.

**Destination Portugal** This travel agency has specialised in holidays to Portugal for more than 30 years and has a wide range of hotels, villas and resorts on offer to suit most budgets, as well as a range of pousadas. They can arrange all manner of your trip from flights, to car hire to insurance and also offer a range of supervised children's activities to keep the little ones amused

(📞 *01993 773 269*; *www.destination-portugal.co.uk*).

**Eurocamp** One of the most successful of Europe's holiday park companies has two parks in the Algarve that offer fun for all the family. Not only is everything on site that you could wish for, from shops, restaurants, beach and pool, but there are also tennis courts, bicycles for hire, football pitches and basketball courts. Accommodation ranges from tents to mobile homes to chalets, all of differing facilities depending on price (📞 *0870 901 9410*; *www.eurocamp.co.uk*).

**First Choice** Another well-known company that has a large number of resorts in the Algarve, with a strong focus on children's activities and children's clubs. Accommodation ranges from self-catering to full board, depending on resort and your preference, and family rooms with four or five beds are also regularly available. Prices are extremely reasonable too – a family of four could expect to pay around £500 in spring, all-inclusive, for a week's break depending on how early you have booked ahead ( ☎ *0870 850 3999*; *www.firstchoice.co.uk*).

**Sunvil** This long-standing travel company offers a range of tailor-made holidays in the Algarve, which offer something a little different than a standard holiday resort. Accommodation can be arranged in more interesting and characterful buildings as well as pousadas (see p. 38). There are also a number of activity holidays on offer. Full details can be downloaded from its website or you can request a brochure to be posted to you ( ☎ *0208 758 4722*; *www.sunvil.co.uk*).

## Getting Around

**By Car** If you're planning to travel around the Algarve at all, driving is undoubtedly the best way to go. Not only does having your own wheels ensure greater flexibility, which is usually essential for children, but it allows you to get off the beaten track and explore more rural areas.

You will need to bring your **driving licence** and, if bringing your own car (see p. 36), your **vehicle registration document** and current **insurance certificate**. It's also recommended to apply for a green card from your insurer, which gives you fully comprehensive cover in Europe. If you are a member of the AA or RAC check with them whether they have an agreement with a Portuguese breakdown service, which will reduce costs should you need to call out their services. If you're in your own car you must also display an international **sign plate** (i.e. 'GB') on the rear of your car and you should carry a **red warning triangle** in case of breakdown.

The roads in the Algarve are of a high standard although they can become frustratingly log-jammed in summer. There is only one **motorway** in the region, the Ayamonte-Huelva that links the Algarve with southern Spain. The other main roads (Estrada Nacional) are classified as either IP roads (Itinerário Principal) or IC (Itinerário Complementar). The latter charge **toll fees** but tend to be faster routes as a result. **Petrol stations** can be found en route but are not as frequent as in some other European countries so it's always advisable to fill the tank in major towns, particularly if you're planning a long trip.

**Driving rules and advice:** Whatever you do, keep in mind at all times that traffic in Portugal *drives on the right*. Traffic from the right also has priority at junctions

**Driving times**

Faro–Albufeira: 40 minutes
Faro–Portimão: 60 minutes
Faro–Sagres: 90 minutes
Faro–Tavira: 35 minutes
Faro–Vila Real de Santo António:
  50 minutes
Faro–Seville: 3 hours
Faro–Beja: 90 minutes

and crossroads. Road signs follow the international standard.

**Speed limits** are 120 km/h (80 mph) on the motorway, 90 km/h (60 mph) on the national roads and 50 km/h (35 mph) in towns. Although there is an alcohol limit of 5 ml per litre for drivers, if you're travelling with children on board it should go without saying that no alcohol should be consumed at all by the driver. Seatbelts, front and back, must be worn at all times during movement.

The best **driving maps** of the Algarve are published by Michelin, Collins and the AA and are available at most motorway stops and at the airport.

For ease of mind, particularly in high season, it's advisable to hire cars in advance of your holiday from one of the reputable car hire firms on the Internet. This provides **proof of booking** and alleviates any misunderstandings on arrival.

When picking up your car you will need to present the **driving licences** of all people intending to get behind the wheel, your passport and a credit card in one of the drivers' names. The **minimum age** for

car hire in Portugal is 23, and the driver must have had a full international driving licence for one year prior to this.

Car hire in Portugal is relatively cheap in comparison to other EU countries (there are deals available as low as £50 for a week's rental), but prices do vary depending on the size of the car and whether you want additional features such as convertibles. When getting a quotation, make sure it includes unlimited mileage, full insurance, tax and 24-hour breakdown assistance.

Major car hire firms in the Algarve include the usual international firms as well as local outfits, with more details of prices and vehicles on their websites. They all have offices at Faro airport:

**Avis:** *www.avis.co.uk*

**easyCar:** *www.easycar.com*

**Europcar:** *www.europcar.com*

**Hertz:** *www.hertz.co.uk*

**Sixt:** *www.e-sixt.com*

**Motorhomes** Motorhomes must abide by all the same road rules as cars.

While you are not allowed to stop overnight by the roadside, the Algarve has a vast collection of **campsites** where you can hook up. Prices are obviously higher than car rental, with high season costs for a four-person vehicle coming in at around €800 per week, but this is offset by no or low accommodation costs. Numerous companies hire out motorhomes in the region:

# Travelling by Car

**If you're driving your own vehicle to the Algarve, an** **in-car satellite navigation system** might be worth investing in – long journeys bore children and trying to keep them entertained while map-reading too can be extremely stressful for all concerned.

In case of emergency make sure at least one **mobile phone** on board is fully charged.

**Europ Assistance** (📞 *01444 442 211*; *www.europ-assistance.co.uk*) is a highly recommended company that can provide breakdown cover abroad with your own vehicle. It will also prioritise families with children.

It's illegal in Portugal for children under 12 years to sit in the front passenger seat. **Child seats** are also required for all children up to the age of five. These can be hired along with your car rental but you'll need to specify the age of the children, as the seats vary in size according to the height and age of the children.

Other miscellaneous items that can prove invaluable on both long and short car journeys with children include: a **first-aid kit; window shades**; a **cooler box** to house cool drinks and snacks; **wipes** and **plastic bags**; **nappies**, if necessary; a lightweight **sweater** or **blanket** for each child; activities such as **books** and **crayons**, or the increasing range of **magnetic games** such as Hangman that are now on the market and **travel pillows**.

try *www.algarvecampers.com* or *www.camperrent.pt/ingles*.

**By Plane** Both TAP (*www.flytap.com*) and Portugália operate services between Lisbon and Faro.

**By Train** The **Portuguese State Railway** (Caminhos de Ferro Portugueses, or **CP** for short) offers good services around the Algarve, with major stations at Faro, Lagos, Silves, Albufeira and Tavira. The high-speed and comfortable Alfa route covers the distance between Braga and Faro, via Lisbon.

Prices are also incredibly good value, especially if you're used to British rail fares. The journey from Lagos to Faro, for instance, with a travelling time of just under two hours, costs €6.40 for a single adult fare, with children under 12 travelling at half price. Children under four travel for free if they sit on an adult's lap. Most of the discount offers are not applicable for regional routes, but if you're covering more of Portugal than just the Algarve, the *cartão de família* can save money, although with prices so low it's hardly worth the effort unless you're planning on spending the whole holiday on the train.

**Tickets** for regional trains can be bought at the station on the day of travel, although you can book the national routes up to 30 days in advance. **Timetables** of the entire system are displayed in all major stations. For more information visit *www.cp.pt*.

**By Bus** The main bus and coach company to cover the Algarve is **EVA**, which operates a route right across the region from Lagos and over the Spanish border to Seville (note that the service does not run at weekends between October and May). The buses are comfortable and offer a good chance to see the landscape. The main bus station in Faro is at Avenida da República (📞 *00 351 289 899 700*). Or visit the website (*www.eva-bus.net*) for more information.

**By Bike** The relatively flat landscape of the Algarve can make getting around by bike a fun and pleasant family activity. Tourist offices (see p. 19) will provide information about where you can hire bikes. Given the Portuguese reputation for bad driving, staying off the main roads is advisable (imperative for smaller children) and helmets should be worn by all cyclists. Bikes have a habit of disappearing, too, if you leave them out of sight, so make sure you lock them when unattended.

# ACCOMMODATION & EATING OUT

## Accommodation

As one might expect from such a popular tourist region, the Algarve has a vast variety of accommodation options, from high-end hotels and large-scale resorts to charming rural family-run ventures. In high season it's essential to book all accommodation in advance – this would apply to any visitor, but is even more vital for families so that children are not left stranded with no bed in sight.

Hotels must display their **rack rates** (published price per room) clearly for all their customers, although unless you've found yourself with nowhere to go, these rates should rarely be paid. Travel agents and tour operators all receive **discounts** on these rates that they then pass on to their customers. And, if you're outside of the busy season, you can usually negotiate with the hotels themselves – after all they'd rather have a room full at a lower rate than empty at no charge at all.

There are also innumerable discount hotel sites on the Internet that offer substantial savings – just search Algarve Hotels and you'll see how many come up. This is certainly a good price comparison tool so long as you have the time and patience to wade through them. If not, a tour operator may be a better option.

Most hotels offer a half-price discount for children under eight.

Hotels are **graded in stars** from one (lowest) to five (highest), although on many occasions this can be misleading. The stars are based on facilities provided (restaurant, pool, lift etc.) but this doesn't take into account the quality or maintenance of such facilities. On many occasions a three-star B&B may well be far more comfortable than a four-star hotel.

The following **price guidelines** that are used throughout this book are based on one night's accommodation for two adults and two children, excluding breakfast (other than B&Bs and unless otherwise mentioned):

**Very expensive:** Over €300

**Expensive:** €200–299

**Moderate:** €100–199

**Inexpensive:** Less than €100

The very expensive hotels in the Algarve tend to be recognised international luxury chains such as Sheraton, or large golf resorts where no stone has been left unturned in terms of pampering and facilities. Resorts range from moderate to expensive, depending on what's on offer, but there will always be at least one swimming pool. Some resorts insist on half-board accommodation, meaning you're paying for breakfast and dinner every day, but this is often a welcome stability for children and the regular hours help to retain sleep patterns. For a far more local and intimate feel as well as lower costs, B&Bs offer good options, although not all

will have pools and smaller children may become bored – traditional architecture fades very quickly against water slides and children's clubs.

**Pousadas**

Pousadas are heritage hotels that are often set within renovated historic buildings, and are usually in the historic centres of towns such as Faro, Tavira, Beja and Évora, as opposed to seaside settings. Service is usually intimate and friendly, they lack all the brashness of large-scale resorts, and they can be a surprisingly good option for families with younger children as they all have large walled gardens – usually with a pool for children as well as grown-ups, and sometimes with slides and swings for toddlers – and secure off-street parking, and are very welcoming to (well-behaved) little ones. Older children and teenagers may find the tranquillity and the old-town surroundings of most pousadas claustrophobic and a bit dull, but the chain also has hotels in rural and lakeside locations with lots of outdoor activities.

**Resorts**

The Algarve is one of the major resort regions of Europe and all along the coast the sight of high-rise complexes is in evidence. They may add little to the beauty of the landscape and some travellers can be snobbish about them but for a family holiday they can supply everything you need for a week or two in the sun. All have pools and most have a shallow children's pool area as well. In addition, the larger resorts will provide a range of activities from supervised children's clubs, to water games, to evening entertainment. The majority of resort hotels are booked as part of a package holiday deal via travel agents and tour operators.

## Guesthouses

Known as *pensães* in Portugal, these offer clean and comfortable basic accommodation usually sharing bathroom facilities with a couple of other rooms. If you're on a tight budget and want to go the independent route rather than package, these are a great option.

## Campsites

The Algarve is littered with campsites, from the large-scale affairs that include all the facilities such as pools, bars and restaurants, that one would expect from resort hotels, but with added freedom, to smaller more rural areas. Some are tent-only sites, while others provide hook ups for caravans and motor homes. The smaller sites will usually charge an extra fee for use of washing facilities. The main chain of Portuguese camping is Orbitur (*www.orbitur.com*).

Unlike the rest of Portugal, it is strictly forbidden in the Algarve to camp anywhere except in designated sites.

## Hotels

Small-scale, personal hotels in the Algarve are rather thin on the ground in comparison to other regions of the country. Most hotel accommodation comes in the guise of resorts, as mentioned above, or large-scale golfing complexes, many of them run by luxury chains such as Sheraton, Sofitel and Le Méridien. Unless you have a budding Tiger Woods among your young clan, these are rarely going to be an affordable or wise option for families. Other individual hotels in the region that we would recommend can be found within the sightseeing sections of this book.

## Self-catering

There are two unique and recommended self-catering options available in the Algarve and these can be a wonderful choice for families, combining flexibility with facilities.

The *Aldeamento Turísticos* are 'tourist villages' that provide apartment-style accommodation as part of a resort complex, so you have all the advantages of resort accommodation without being confined to a single room and on-site restaurant. Away from the resort complexes themselves but still in popular tourist areas are *Apartamento Turísticos*, which vary in size and comfort, but also offer self-catering advantages. Perfect for picky eaters or children who find sitting still in the formality of a restaurant tiresome.

## Eating Out

The abundance of **fish and seafood** in the Algarve can be one of the highlights of the holiday for adults, although parents are well aware that many children turn their noses up at the sight of fruits from the sea. That said, the local speciality of grilled **sardines** could be a good introduction for children to fish because of their small size. Most menus will also offer plenty of meat options, however. The dish of the day (*prato do día*) is usually a good option for adults – it's generally the catch of the day and very good value. Beachfront restaurants will usually have the staple pizzas and pasta on their menu and these filling options can often be the best bet for children who appreciate the familiarity. Most restaurants within resort hotels are well versed on catering for children, from portion sizes to favoured dishes. The menus may seem a little too home from home for mum and dad, but little ones rarely push spaghetti bolognaise or burgers round a plate. Equally many resorts offer **buffet** dining allowing for individual choice all round.

**Vegetarians** will, unfortunately, be a little short of options – salads and omelettes are usually the most on offer.

Do be aware that it's very common for bread, olives and pâté to be brought to the table as soon as you sit down. These are *not* complimentary, so if you eat them you will be charged for them. **Tipping** is the same as the rest of Europe – usually around 10% of the total bill.

For a Portuguese **food vocabulary** see p. 235.

Most restaurants will, on asking, offer a **half-portion** (*mini-prato*) for children and a few will sometimes have one or two **high chairs** on offer.

Portugal has yet to join the growing trend of banning **smoking** in public places, so it is still legal to smoke in restaurants. If you or your children are sensitive to this try and find a table outside – the weather is generally accommodating.

**Eating hours** are generally noon to 2pm for lunch and between 7pm and 10pm for dinner although these, particularly dinner, are rarely set in stone.

The **price guidelines** below, which correspond to all the restaurants mentioned in the guide, are based on two adults and two children for a two-course meal including drinks:

**Expensive:** More than €75

**Moderate:** €45–69

**Inexpensive:** Less than €45.

## GETTING CHILDREN INTERESTED IN THE ALGARVE

For a smooth holiday with the family, getting everyone involved from the start in the planning and preparation is essential. It will help you gauge what may or may not be enjoyable abroad and what is realistic in terms of an itinerary, as well as building interest and expectations before the trip:

● Involve the children in the planning, and give them some control over where you're going.

● Ask then to research the Algarve: the main areas and beaches, language, best buys and so on. Have family quizzes based on this information.

● Let them help with drawing up lists for packing, and let each child have his/her own small suitcase or backpack.

● Encourage children to put together a scrapbook of pictures and text about the places you'll be visiting – there's lots of material available in brochures and on the Internet, and from tourism boards.

● Download Frommer's Holiday Fun Pack from *www.frommers.co. uk* for an enjoyable bunch of games and ideas for before, during and after your trip.

● Get the children to send to national and regional tourist boards for information and maps – they'll love getting post.

● Suggest that they research the airline with which you're travelling, how long it takes and how big it is.

● Let them practise currency conversion and language pronunciation for Portugal.

● On holiday let each child have a digital camera – they love taking pictures. If that's not possible, buy some cheap fun cameras or let them try the family camera.

● Take addresses with you, so that children can play their part in writing postcards home.

## Making Movies

Look out for cameras, stars and film crews around the Algarve's beaches, streets and castles – they are often used as movie locations, and the Algarve Film Commission (AFC), which was set up in 2007, wants to bring more cameras and action to the region. The AFC's president is Portugal's biggest film star, Joaquim de Almeida – he was the baddie in *Desperado* (1995) opposite Antonio Banderas and starred in 2007's *The Heart of the Earth*, which was partly shot in the Algarve.

## Famous Footy Players

Manchester United star player Cristiano Ronaldo is Portuguese, born in Madeira, Portugal in 1985. By age 10 his reputation was growing in Portugal with Madeira's top two teams, CS Maritimo and CD Nacional, both interested in signing him. In 2003 he was signed to Manchester United for £12.24 million. During the 2006–7 season, Ronaldo won the PFA Players' Player of the Year and PFA Young Player of the Year awards. Ronaldo was named the national team captain for the first time in a friendly match against Brazil on 6th February, 2007.

**Monster Dollies**

**Algarve artist Claudia Brito makes weird and wonderful dollies out of** brightly coloured felt and fabric. Dolls made this way are an Algarve tradition but Claudia's 'Sushi Dolls' look more like Japanese manga comic characters and monsters than old-style costumed dolls. Find a list of where to buy them, or order online at **www.dollsinsushi.blogspot.com**.

## Tigers & Dogs

Vista Iberica is a publisher offering English language books, maps and magazines. For children these include, *The Algarve Tiger*, written to enhance awareness of the Iberian Lynx and *Bica, the Portuguese Water Dog*, for three to six year olds, a fun yarn about a nature-loving canine (**www.vistaiberica.com**).

## FAST FACTS: THE ALGARVE

**Babysitters** Many larger hotels and resort hotels can arrange babysitting services on request, either from their own staff or from a list of known locals. You will normally need to provide 24 hours' notice.

**Business Hours** Shops are generally open 9am to 1pm and 3pm to 7pm Monday to Friday, with a two-hour siesta period in the afternoon. On Saturdays they open for the morning period only. Supermarkets in larger towns, however, often stay open later, until around 9pm.

Banks are open 8.30am to 3pm Monday to Friday but 24-hour ATM machines can be found in all tourist areas.

Restaurants open on average from noon to 2pm for lunch and from 7pm to 10pm for dinner, although international fast food chains and more casual venues such as beachfront bars will remain open throughout the day. Museum hours are 10am to 12.30pm and 2pm to 5pm.

**Car Hire** See p. 35.

**Chemists** Most staff at chemists (*farmácias*) are qualified to diagnose minor ailments and recommend treatments. Chemists, identified by a green cross outside their premises, are open from 9am to 1pm and 3pm to 7pm. If you need medical assistance after these hours, there will be a card in the window informing you of the nearest all-night chemist.

**Climate** See 'When to Go', p. 23.

**Currency** See 'Money', p. 21.

**Driving Rules** See p. 34.

**Electricity** Portugal runs its electricity on 220 volts AC. Visitors from the UK and Ireland will require a two-pin adaptor in order to plug in any electrical items brought from home. Many larger hotels can loan out adaptors if necessary although it's always more convenient to have your own.

**Embassies & Consulates UK:**
Rua São Bernardo 33, Lisbon
(📞 *00 351 21 392 40 00*).
Ireland: Rua de Imprensa à
Estrêla 1, Lisbon (📞 *00 351 21 392
94 40*).

**Emergencies** Police, fire and
ambulance (📞 *112*).
There are three hospitals in the
Algarve that are equipped to deal
with emergencies:

Faro: Rua Leão Penedo (📞 *00 351
289 891 100*).

Portimão: Sitio do Poço Seco
(📞 *00 351 282 450 300*).

Lagos: Rua Castelo dos
Governadores (📞 *00 351 282
763 034*).

**Internet Access** All the main
towns and even some smaller villages now have Internet cafés
and facilities, while large hotels
will also usually have a business
area where you can use their
computers. For details of specific
locations, see individual sightseeing chapters.

**Language** For useful words and
phrases see the Appendix.

**Lost Property** The lost property office at Faro Airport can be
contacted on 📞 *00 351 289 818
302*. For any other missing items
during your holiday, your best
bet is to report it to a local
police station, taking your passport with you for identification.

**Mail** Opening hours for post
offices are 9am to 6pm Monday

to Friday although in large
towns such as Faro they may also
be open on Saturday mornings.
The cost for sending a postcard
from Portugal to the UK is currently €0.74.

**Maps** See p. 35.

**Mobile Phones** If you have
roaming capabilities set up on
your own mobile you will be
able to use it in the Algarve,
although if you are planning on
making a lot of calls it's cheaper
to hire a local phone. Mobiles
(*telemóvel*) can be rented at Faro
Airport and at other Telecel
offices in the region. There is
quite a hefty deposit – around
€350 – but this is refundable
when you return the phone and
you then only pay for any calls
you have made.

**Newspapers & Magazines**
The main daily newspapers in the
Algarve are the *Diário de Notícias*,
*Público*, and *Correio da Manhã*.
The major British broadsheets
and tabloids are also available a
day old in the major tourist
centres. There are three English-
language local papers too: the
*Algarve Gazette*, the *Algarve News*
and *Anglo-Portuguese News*
(*www.the-news.net*).

**Pets** Portugal is a member of
the EU Pet Passport Scheme,
which allows families to travel
with up to five domestic pets
more than three months old
around Europe as long as the
following criteria are followed.
   Prior to travel pets must be
fitted with a microchip and

vaccinated against rabies by a qualified vet. They will then be issued with a passport that contains proof of vaccine and their own identification number, which must accompany them during travel. If it is the animal's first rabies injection, a period of 21 days must elapse before travel.

**Pharmacies** See 'Chemists', p. 42.

**Police** In an emergency: ☏ *112*. If you are a victim of theft or any other crime, report it immediately to the local police station where you will be required to file a report.

**Taxes** A value-added tax (IVA) of 17.5% is added to all hotel and restaurant bills and car rental. More expensive goods, such as jewellery, can be taxed as high as 30%, however. Non-EU residents can claim back this money if they have spent more than €175 at any store that advertises tax-free shopping. You will need to fill out a form at the time of purchase and then present this at the airport to claim your refund.

**Telephones** Public payphones, found on the street and in bars, cafés and post offices, can be used either with coins or with prepaid telephone cards (*cartão telefónico*) available in post offices and newsagents. You will need to dial the area code to call other regions in Portugal but you can drop this code for local calls. To telephone abroad, dial *00*, followed by the area code.

Be warned that making calls from hotel rooms is prohibitively expensive.

For directory enquiries within Portugal: ☏ *118*.

**Time Zone** Portugal is on the same time zone (GMT) as Great Britain and moves the clocks forward by one hour every March and back one hour every October. Crossing the border into Spain takes you into a different time zone, one hour ahead of Portugal and the UK.

**Tipping** Tips are not obligatory in any establishment, but they are generally expected to boost the low earnings of the staff. In restaurants you should add approximately 10% on top of your bill. Doormen and porters should be tipped around €1 in hotels. Taxis expect a tip of around 15–20% on top of the fare.

**Water** Tap water is safe to drink in Portugal but is usually very heavily chlorinated and tastes unpleasant. Bottled table water is available everywhere and is much more palatable. In most restaurants, you will be asked whether you prefer it chilled, or at room temperature – which is how the Portuguese drink it.

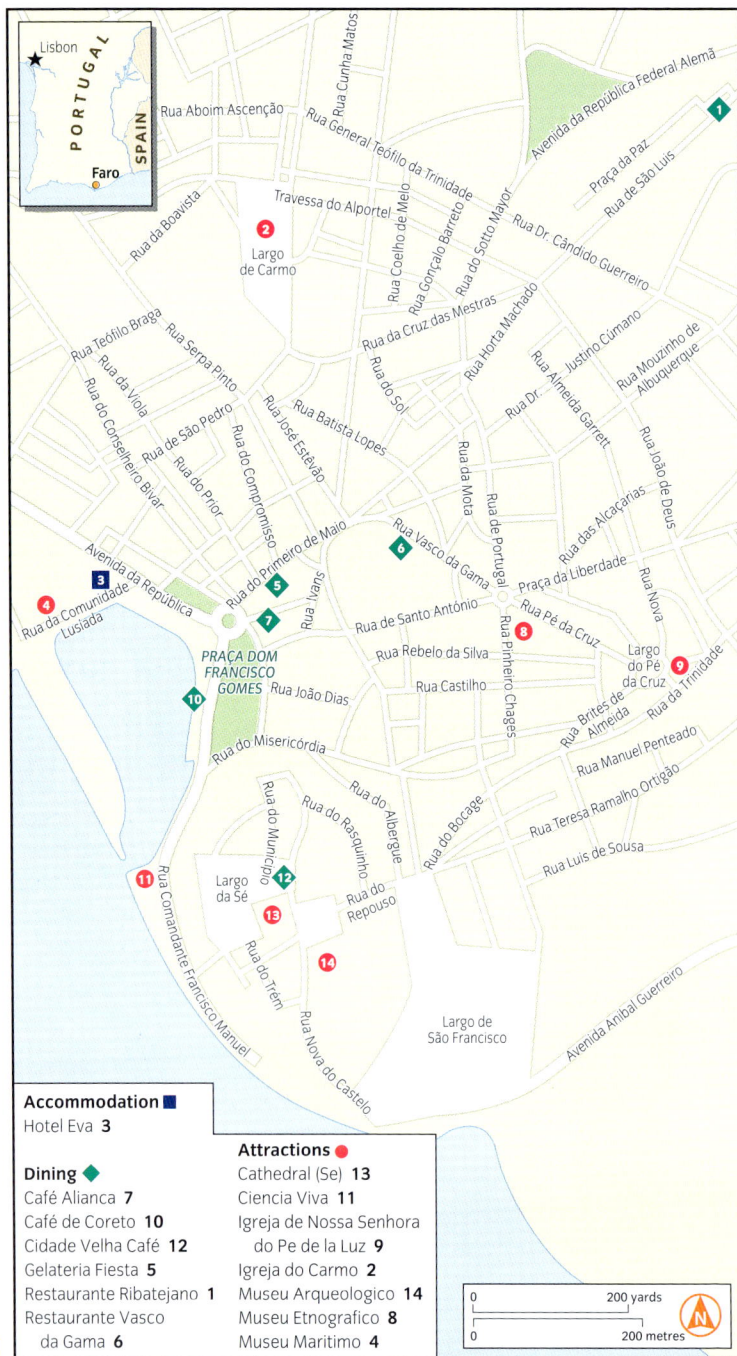

# FARO

Lisbon

PORTUGAL

SPAIN

Faro

Rua Aboim Ascenção

Rua Cunha Matos

Rua General Teófilo da Trinidade

Avenida da República Federal Alemã

Praça da Paz

Rua de São Luis

**1**

Travessa do Alportel

Rua da Boavista

Largo de Carmo

**2**

Rua Coelho de Melo

Rua Gonçalo Barreto

Rua do Sotto Mayor

Rua Dr. Cândido Guerreiro

Rua da Cruz das Mestras

Rua Horta Machado

Justino Cúmano

Rua Mouzinho de Albuquerque

Rua Teófilo Braga

Rua Serpa Pinto

Rua da Viola

Rua do Conselheiro Bivar

Rua de São Pedro

Rua do Prior

Rua do Compromisso

Rua José Estêvão

Rua Batista Lopes

Rua do Sol

Rua Dr. Almeida Garrett

Rua João de Deus

Rua da Mota

Rua das Alcaçarias

Rua do Primeiro de Maio

Rua Vasco da Gama

**6**

Rua de Portugal

Praça da Liberdade

Rua Nova

**5**

Avenida da República

**3**

**4**

Rua da Comunidade Lusiada

**7**

Rua Ivans

Rua de Santo António

Rua Pé da Cruz

**8**

Largo do Pé da Cruz

**9**

Rua da Trinidade

PRAÇA DOM FRANCISCO GOMES

**10**

Rua João Dias

Rua Rebelo da Silva

Rua Castilho

Rua Pinheiro Chagas

Rua Brites de Almeida

Rua Manuel Penteado

Rua do Misericórdia

Rua do Município

Rua do Rasquinho

Rua do Albergue

Rua do Bocage

Rua Teresa Ramalho Ortigão

Rua Luis de Sousa

**11**

Rua Comandante Francisco Manuel

Largo da Sé

**12**

**13**

Rua do Repouso

**14**

Rua do Trém

Rua Nova do Castelo

Largo de São Francisco

Avenida Aníbal Guerreiro

## Accommodation
Hotel Eva **3**

## Dining
Café Alianca **7**
Café de Coreto **10**
Cidade Velha Café **12**
Gelateria Fiesta **5**
Restaurante Ribatejano **1**
Restaurante Vasco da Gama **6**

## Attractions
Cathedral (Se) **13**
Ciencia Viva **11**
Igreja de Nossa Senhora do Pe de la Luz **9**
Igreja do Carmo **2**
Museu Arqueologico **14**
Museu Etnografico **8**
Museu Maritimo **4**

| 0 | 200 yards |
|---|---|
| 0 | 200 metres |

N

**F**aro is the gateway to the Algarve for thousands of families every year, and many of them head straight from the airport (which is on the outskirts of town) to their resort hotel or villa. Surprisingly few make the effort to discover Faro's pretty hinterland – which is, admittedly, hidden behind a certain amount of suburban sprawl created by five decades of tourism. And surprisingly few people stay in Faro itself, as most visitors are lured to the Algarve by the promise of sunshine and sandy beaches. The Algarve region covers less than one-tenth of Portugal's total territory, but nevertheless has more resort hotel rooms, villas and self-catering apartments than the rest of the country put together. With around three million visitors arriving by way of Faro's toytown airport, it's easy to be caught up in the holiday bustle and forget that there is more to see than the resort, the beach and the pool. East and west of town, families are spoilt for choice when it comes to beaches and resorts, with a range of accommodation and facilities to suit all budgets. However, Faro itself repays investigation with a mixture of old and new charms, and its hinterland is equally attractive.

Some of the Algarve's most popular resorts lie west of Faro. Vilamoura, set between a marina where enviable yachts and motor cruisers lie at anchor and lush, green foothills that have been landscaped by some of the world's best-known golf course designers, is an upmarket haven. From here there is a sharp contrast with the fish-and-chips ambience of Quarteira, where cheap and cheerful holiday apartment complexes spread to either side of a fishing harbour where boatmen still unload their haul every morning. Inland lie towns dominated by medieval castles around which young readers of sword-and-sorcery epics may weave their own legends, such as Silves – one of the region's classic landmarks, with its brooding, red-stone battlements – and Loulé, whose castle has been carefully restored and dominates one of the region's prettiest towns. And immediately south of Faro and its airport is one of the Algarve's pockets of undeveloped coastland, the Parque Natural da Ria Formosa, where dune-fringed lagoons and islands will entrance young travellers with an interest in nature and the environment.

# ESSENTIALS

## Getting There

**By Plane** The Algarve is a year-round destination and scheduled and charter flights operate from most main British airports at least weekly even in winter, with more frequent flights from April to October. Flying time from London is 2 hours 30 minutes. Faro International Airport (📞 *00 351 289 800 801; www.ana. aeroportos.pt*) is 8 km from the town centre. Many of those arriving on a package holiday will be transferred to their resort by a pre-booked company coach, but if you are travelling with impatient children and are eager to get to your accommodation without waiting there are several affordable alternatives.

Self-drive car rental is the best bet for families, allowing you not only to get from the airport to your accommodation under your own steam, but also to explore at your own pace once you have settled in. Car rental companies with desks at the airport include all the major car rental brands and several local companies. There is often little to choose between them in terms of price – but you may find more competitive rates if you book well in advance, and you may feel more comfortable booking with a major rental chain with offices in the UK than with a less well-known Portuguese outfit. Travelling with children under 10, you will need to book child seats (specifying the age of your children) in advance unless you are bringing your own.

Faro Airport Transfers (*www.faroairporttransfers.com*) offer minibus transfers, bookable online, to destinations throughout the Algarve, with prices starting at €32 for a family of four from the airport to downtown Faro. If you're staying in Faro itself, you'll find the bus stop for EVA public bus services (☎ *00 351 289 899 700; www.eva-bus.com*) just outside the airport terminal (turn right as you leave the arrivals hall). Hang on to your airline ticket or boarding pass, as it entitles you to a free bus trip downtown. Buses run 7.10am–8.40pm on weekdays, 8am–7.30pm at weekends and on public holidays, leaving approximately every 30 minutes and taking about 15 minutes to EVA's city centre terminus.

The airport taxi rank is immediately outside the arrivals hall and families in a hurry can use taxis not just to points near the airport but also to resorts and towns throughout the Algarve and even as far as Spain. A taxi to downtown Faro costs around €12, and the longer trip to Lagos costs around €80. There are plenty of taxis to greet every arriving flight, but for longer trips it's a good idea to book in advance (☎ *00 351 289 827 203*; E: *faro@antral.pt*). Like almost everyone involved in tourism in the Algarve, most taxi drivers speak adequate English.

The airport has currency exchange facilities, but it is easier and quicker to use one of the ATMs in the arrivals hall, from which you can withdraw cash using your UK chip-and-pin debit or credit card. It also has a handful of restaurants and cafés, most of which are in the departure area and are open from 7am—11pm, serving a basic menu of snacks and soft drinks. They're not especially child friendly.

## VISITOR INFORMATION

### The Algarve Tourist Board

(☎ *00 351 289 800 400*; *www.visitalgarve.pt*) The main source of information for the region, with a website that includes accommodation listings and links to booking sites, restaurant recommendations and a calendar of events.

### Faro Tourism Board

8–11 Rua da Misericordia (📞 00 351 289 803 604; E: turismo.faro@ rtalgarve.pt)

**Open** Mon–Fri 8.30am–1pm and 2pm–5pm, Sat 8.30am– 1pm, closed Sun.

### Radio

Tune to KissFM Algarve 95.8 and 101.2 FM from Thursday to Saturday for Guillermo Gonzalez's English language show – it's a goldmine of information about what's on, where to go and where to eat.

### Faro Airport Tourist Office

(📞 00 351 289 818 582; E: turismo. aeroporto@rtalgarve.com)

## Orientation

Positioned roughly midway along the Algarve's southern coast and within spitting distance of some of the finest beaches, holiday resorts and golf courses, Faro is the natural gateway to the region. The N125 highway connects the city with all points east and west along the coast, from Sagres in the far west to Vila Real de Santo António, the River Guadiana and the border with Spain in the east. Sagres is 108 km west of the airport, and Vila Real de Santo António is around 60 km to the east. The A22 motorway, running a short distance inland from and parallel to the N125, allows faster but less scenic long-distance driving. Heading north from Faro, the N2 highway winds its way

through the Algarve's hilly hinterland into the Alentejo, the region of wide prairies and cork oak forests that spreads from southern Portugal as far as the Spanish frontier and the River Tejo (Tagus) far to the north.

## Getting Around

Faro's historic centre is compact. Navigating and parking in its maze of narrow streets is tricky, even without children in the back seat, so don't even think about driving in the old town – there is plenty of metered parking space around the harbour, but bring loose change for the parking meter. Parking costs 50 cents per hour.

Faro's sights are within easy walking distance of each other, even for younger children. Taxis are plentiful and affordable, and by far the best way of transporting children from place to place over medium distances, such as from your resort to central Faro. Many family attractions also offer mini-bus pickup from your hotel as a means of enticing you to visit. Further afield, renting a car on arrival is the most seamless and easiest way of getting around the region.

For non-drivers, those with environmental qualms or parents who don't feel happy navigating on unfamiliar turf, there is a menu of mix-and-match alternatives. Combine taxis (for short hops) with buses and trains and you can easily explore Faro, its surroundings, and the wider Algarve region without renting your own wheels.

Caminhos de Ferro Portugueses (Portuguese Railways) trains (📞 00 351 808 208 208; *www.cp.pt*) trundle several times a day from Faro west to Lagos and east to Vila Real de Santo António, stopping at every point en route, and can be a relaxing way to explore the coast. EVA buses (see p. 48) are fast, clean and efficient, and link virtually every part of the Algarve with Faro and the rest of Portugal.

Ferries sail from Faro's harbour (departing from the jetty just south of the Science Alive Centre) to Praia de Faro, the nearest beach to town, on a long, sandy peninsula; and from Olhão, around 6 km west of Faro, to other beaches on offshore islands, including Praia de Farol, Praia de Culatra and Praia da Armona. Within town, a miniature 'tourist train' leaves every hour from the north end of Jardim Manuel Biver, and follows a route through the historic centre, stopping at all the main points of interest. It's a bargain, and ideal for families with tots (see p. 62).

# WHAT TO SEE & DO

## Children's Top 10 Attractions

**1 A day at the beach** anywhere between Praia de Faro and Praia de Farol (don't mix them up!) in the east to Quarteira and Vilamoura in the west. There are endless kilometres of sand near the city, but the further east or west you go the emptier the beaches become. Pack sunscreen, sun umbrellas and plenty of water (see p. 66).

**2 Aquatic fun** for mums, dads, brothers and sisters at Atlantic Park, with its pools, rides and water chutes – there are activities and play areas for all ages from toddlers upwards (see p. 63).

**3 Meeting shaggy, friendly dogs** at the Portuguese Water Dog Kennels, near Faro (see p. 67).

**4 Taking a trip into the wild wetlands** and empty sand dunes of the Ria Formosa Natural Park (see p. 67).

**5 A sunset cruise** along the coast from Vilamoura's bustling marina, followed by a late-night fireworks display.

**6 Travelling into the depths of the galaxy** at the Science Alive Centre observatory in Faro (see p. 60).

**7 Finding out about the not so distant past** at Faro's Museu Etnográfico (folklore museum) (see p. 61).

Quinta do Lago, Ria Formosa

**8 Watching boats unload** and taking an eye-opening look at seafood that isn't shrink-wrapped at the Quarteira fish market. Not for the squeamish (see p. 56).

**9 The view of old Faro** from the Cathedral bell-tower – where in spring you may encounter a brood of fledgling storks (see p. 59).

**10 A trip round town** on Faro's miniature tourist train (see p. 62).

## Towns & Resorts

**Faro – the Harbour Area** Don't be put off by the approach to Faro from the airport. The historic city centre is surrounded by extensive, modern suburbs, but these conceal a charming historic centre, a pedestrian area packed with shops and open-air ice-cream cafés, and a view over a wide river estuary patrolled by storks, spoonbills and fishing boats. Children with a taste for dread will love to hear that Faro – like so many cities in Portugal – was devastated by the 'Great Earthquake' of 1755, a seismic event that could re-occur at any time. It also suffered from an early English visit by the Earl of Essex, whose troops sacked the city in 1596 (it was then in Spanish hands, and Spain and the England of Queen Elizabeth 1 were at war).

Comfortingly, most of Faro's solidly constructed 17th- and 18th-century buildings still stand. The town centre is fairly pedestrian friendly, despite the Portuguese habit of using every metre of pavement space for car parking (except in the pedestrian zone) and there are plenty of cafés and restaurants. Accommodation-wise, the town is less promising – for family-friendly places to stay close to Faro, the string of beaches west of town, from Praia de Faro to Quarteira, is a better bet.

Faro's harbour is the focal point of the town and nowhere is more symbolic of the Algarve in the 21st century. The vessels anchored here range from shiny new yachts and motor cruisers to a sizeable fleet of working fishing boats which still use the port as a base for inshore fishing – you can

The Marina, Faro

watch them zooming through the islands and channels of the estuary at all times of day. In spring, look up to find cheeky storks nesting right in the middle of town, on top of lamp posts, chimneys, church bell-towers and historic buildings. When they're not roosting on nests that look like big piles of sticks, you'll see them wheeling overhead.

Next to the port are two of Faro's top attractions for families – the **Museu Marítimo** (see p. 60) and the **Ciência Viva** centre (see p. 60). The **Café Aliança,** on Praça D. Francisco Gomes, is a nice place to take a break – it's an elegant old-style teahouse, just over a century old, and its walls are hung with quaint prints and photographs of Faro in days gone by. There's a children's play area, with see-saws, swings and a wooden locomotive, a few steps away beneath the palm trees on **Jardim Manuel Bivar,** and the **Café de Coreto,** overlooking the harbour (see p. 73) has outdoor tables and miniature rides for smaller children.

**Faro – Cidade Velha (Old Town)** The rest of modern Faro is less than thrilling, but the old part of town has some more interesting sites. Enter through the unique and ornate Arco da Vila gateway (the city tourist office is immediately to your left as you enter), which leads from an attractive public garden, the Jardim Manuel Bivar. Inside is a collection of broad squares and hidden corners lined with orange and lemon trees, overlooked by a complex of lovely medieval religious buildings, with the 13th-century Cathedral towering above them all. Heading east, the Rua de Reposo passes through another arched gateway and south of here the last surviving stretch of old Faro's medieval walls extends southward to the river. West of Largo da Se and the Cathedral, the 16th-century Porta Nova leads to the waterfront. Ferries leave from the quayside opposite this landmark for Faro's offshore beaches and islands.

*Tourist office: 8–11 Rua de Misericordia (☎ 00 351 289 803 604;* E: turismo.faro@rtalgarve.pt)

**Faro – Pedestrian Zone** East of Jardim Manuel Bivar, with its miniature bandstand, is the Zona Pedonal (Pedestrian Zone). This is the main shopping area in the older part of town, and a good place to look for a family-friendly café or restaurant. The streets are cobbled, but present no major obstacles to baby buggies. From Jardim Manuel Bivar, it's a short walk up Rua de Santo Antonio to Praça da Liberdade and the **Museu Etnográfico** (see p. 61). If you have time to kill, the pretty 17th-century chapel of **Nossa Senhora do Pé de la Cruz** *(Largo do Pé de la Cruz, opposite the Museu Etnográfico)*, is worth a quick peek for its rather comic paintings of Biblical scenes.

**Olhão** Olhão, a 15-minute bus ride from Faro, is a bit uninspiring – it's a working fishing port, with few redeeming features. However, it is the jumping-off point for the wild wetlands of the region's prime nature reserve, the Ria Formosa Natural Park, and there are also ferries to beaches on offshore islands. Its market – in two covered halls on the waterfront – is a great place to do your shopping if you're self-catering or planning a picnic. It throbs with colour and the sound of local housewives and stall-holders discussing the merits of their produce, and is at its best on a Saturday, when it sells more than just fruit, vegetables and fish.

*Tourist office: 8A Largo Sebastião Martins Mestre ( 00 351 289 713 936; E: turismo.olhao@rtalgarve.pt) 8 km east of Faro.*

**Loulé** ★★ The best thing about this attractive small town in the hills inland from Quarteira is that it's a complete contrast to the somewhat relentless tourism of the Algarve's coast, but only minutes away. Loulé is famous as a centre of traditional crafts – and has been for more than 700 years (see p. 66). Loulé's **weekly market**, held every Saturday morning between around 9am and 2pm *(Praça da República)*, is one of the most colourful in the region – and it's a very different experience from a weekend trip to Tesco, with heaps of fresh fish,

FUN FACT ▸ **English Bad Boys** ◂

**Not all the damage to the old towns of the Algarve can be blamed on** natural forces. Quite a bit of it is down to the English. During the reign of Queen Elizabeth 1 – the time of the Spanish Armada – Portugal was unfortunate enough to be ruled by Philip II of Spain, which made the Algarve a fair target for English freebooters including Elizabeth's boyfriend, the Earl of Essex, who turned up in 1596 and burned the old part of Faro to the ground (after looting the treasures of its Cathedral, palaces, monasteries and convents) on his way to seize Cádiz from the Spanish. He had a disagreement with Queen Elizabeth a few years later, and in 1601 she had his head chopped off. Most people in Faro probably think it served him right.

FUN FACT **White Elephant**

**You can't miss the massive, modernistic Estádio Algarve as you drive** past Faro and Loulé on the motorway – its spaceship-like silhouette looms over the local landscape, and signs point to it proudly from all along the motorway and from the centre of Faro. Sadly, it's a real white elephant. Built for Euro 2004, it has been empty (apart from one-off events) ever since – none of the 16 local teams can afford the running costs.

fruit and vegetables, ropes of garlic, whole hams, strings of sausages and bundles of dried and fresh herbs and sachets of spices. Loulé's older part surrounds the medieval castle inside which the dinky **Museu Municipal** (see p. 61) features more down-to-earth domesticity, with a recreation of a traditional local housewife's kitchen, complete with pots, pans, crockery and other kitchenware. Loulé's newest claim to fame is just outside the town centre. You can't miss it, perched on a hilltop above the highway – but you may not believe that what you're seeing is a church – it looks more like a flying saucer. **Nossa Senhora da Piedade** is a buttressed white dome with porthole-like windows all the way around. At the very least, it makes a change from the lookalike architecture of most of the region's places of worship, and it also has fab views.

*Tourist information: 9 Avenida 25 do Abril ( 00 351 289 463 900; E: turismo.loule@rtalgarve.pt)*

*16 km northwest of Faro*

INSIDER TIP

Loulé's annual Carnival, held each year over three days in the run up to Easter *(March or April, contact tourist office for annual dates)* is the most colourful in the Algarve and one of the liveliest in Portugal, with a parade of fancy-dressed floats, folk music, fireworks and dancing from dusk until dawn.

**Estói** Pretty little Estói, with its whitewashed walls and red-tiled houses, gives you a glimpse of what the Algarve's sleepy villages looked like before tourism arrived, but its main attraction is a grandiose pink folly, the **Palácio de Estói**. The story goes that work on this over-the-top

Painted Houses, Estoi

confection of wedding-cake architecture began in 1840 and wasn't finished until 69 years later – which must be a record. Estói's other sight is also described by some sources as a 'palace' but don't get your hopes up. Less than 100 metres from the village centre, this is in fact the site of a 3rd-century AD Roman villa, but it takes quite some imagination to picture what it must once have looked like from the stumps of columns, slabs of stone and fragments of mosaic tiling that have been unearthed. This isn't the most wildly exciting spot, but if your children are studying the Romans at school they may find it worth a quick look. Unlike other such sites, you can scramble all over most of the ruins and there is an air-conditioned visitors' centre with toilets and a small exhibition of finds from the site.

*IPPAR Visitor Centre: Milreu, Estói ( 00 351 289 997 823)*

## Beaches & Resorts

**Praia de Faro** ★★★ Faro's best-known beach is on the Ilha de Faro, an immense sandbar that stretches for almost 8 km west, where it merges with Praia do Ancão (see below). Despite its length, it can get very crowded, especially on summer weekends when locals compete with visitors for an empty spot. It's also brilliantly handy for a last-minute swim or paddle before you catch your home-bound flight – the airport is less than a five-minute drive away, and hanging out here is a lot more fun for children than hanging around the airport. Cheaper, too.

*5–12 km west of Faro*

**Praia de Farol**, ★★ FIND This marvellous beach of soft yellow sand is on a slightly more distant island, and the 45-minute ferry ride from Faro Harbour means it is never as crowded as Praia de

## Football Crazy

**The Portuguese are nearly as soccer-mad as the British and the** Algarve boasts no fewer than 16 teams in its regional league. The youngest is Algarve United – a joint British–Portuguese effort, launched in 2004 by Scottish football agent John McGovern and his Italian son-in-law Corrado Correggi. The Loulé-based club's first manager was Paul 'Gazza' Gascoigne and in 2006 they signed Emilio Peixe, ex-Benfica and Portuguese national player, as coach. When this book was written, he had failed to work wonders – the Lynxes, as they are known, languished second from the bottom of the Algarve table. To follow their fortunes, click onto *www.algarvedesporto.pt*.

Faro. Perfect for beachcombers, it's on the edge of the Ria Formosa Natural Park – look out for storks and many other water-birds on the way there. For a day here, plan to arrive early and leave late, because the children will want to stay as long as possible. A small chilly-bin full of snacks and cold drinks is a must-have accessory here, as facilities are limited.

*6 km east of Faro*

**Praia do Ancão** ★ ★ ★ Praia do Ancão is for all practical purposes a western extension of Praia de Faro, but this long stretch of yellow sand is usually a good deal less crowded and families can usually find plenty of space. In turn, this beach merges with Praia do Vale do Lobo to the west – the strand of one of Portugal's snootiest holiday resorts, and a magnet for water sports operators, beach sports, and summer-time snack kiosks and beach restaurants.

*12–15 km west of Faro*

**Vale do Lobo** ★ ★ ★ This huge, purpose-built resort has a worldwide reputation as a centre of excellence for golf and tennis coaching and other sports and family activities and is one of the flagships of tourism in the Algarve. Vale do Lobo is a vast enclave that combines several hundred villas, luxury hotel accommodation, manicured golf courses and state-of-the-art tennis facilities and a health and beauty spa that pampers those who can afford it. This cocoon of comfort may not suit all tastes, and it's certainly not for those on a limited budget, but it is the most luxurious place to stay in the Algarve (see p. 68). Opened in 1961, it welcomes 750,000 visitors annually (more than some entire countries!). It overlooks the 2 km, long sandy beach of Praia do Vale do Lobo, framed by striking red rock cliffs.

*Vale do Lobo information (☎ 00 351 289 353 261; www.valedolobo.com)*

*23 km west of Faro*

**Quarteira** ★ There is plenty of contrast between Vale do Lobo and Quarteira, its down-market neighbour some 5 km to the west. Quarteira's harbour is still in business, and watching the boats unloading their scaly catch at the lively Largo do Peixe fish market in the morning is good fun, but this formerly sleepy fishing village is now a full-blown holiday resort, with accommodation mainly in high-rise self-catering apartment complexes, lots of bars catering to the tastes of British holidaymakers and a weekly 'gipsy market' – the biggest in the Algarve. For some, Quarteira may epitomise mass tourism, but for families looking for no more than a relaxing holiday in the sun it offers excellent value for money, user-friendly facilities and a super beach with plenty of sand and warm shallow water that make it excellent for small children. It's also popular with Portuguese families, so it must be doing something right.

*Tourist office: Praco do Mar (☎ 00 351 289 389 209; E: turismo.quarteira@rtalgarve.net)*

*22 km west of Faro*

**Vilamoura Marina** ★★ Less than 2 km west of Quarteira (a 15-minute walk along the beach), the coast turns posh again as you reach Vilamoura Marina with its vast yacht basin crammed with enviable yachts and speedboats – more than 1,000 of them. Don't come here looking for authenticity – this huge resort complex was built from the ground up in the mid-1970s, and looks more like Miami than anyone's idea of a Portuguese fishing village (the original community of Vilamoura lies a couple of kilo-metres inland from the coast). That said, its facilities for fami-lies are top notch, with two beaches (Praia da Falesia and Praia da Marina) and a big choice of places to stay. Golf is the big deal here (there are five top courses nearby) but there's a good choice of water sports too, including jet-skiing and paras-cending. Boys and dads can book a deep-sea fishing trip at one of the kiosks on the marina, where you can also buy tickets for a variety of gentle cruises along the coast. On most sum-mer evenings, the marina comes alive to the snap, crackle and pop of a late-night fireworks display. Vilamoura isn't really a sightseeing destination, but it does have one of the region's bet-ter ancient relics in the **Museu Cerro da Vila** *(Avenida do Cerro da Vila,* 📞 *00 351 289 312 153)*. This is an excellent reconstruc-tion of a Roman villa site, with mosaics, sunken baths and a museum stuffed with Roman and Visigothic relics.

*Tourist office: Edificio BPA, Praça do BPA (📞 00 351 289 321 137; www. vilamouraalgarve.com)*

*29 km west of Faro*

## Nature Reserves, Parks & Gardens

### Ria Formosa Natural Park

★★★ **ALL AGES** 'Ria Formosa' means 'beautiful river' and the park is a super experience for children with an interest in nature and wildlife. It's a broad expanse of lagoons, sandy islands and narrow river channels, which you can explore aboard a converted fishing boat, by bicy-cle, or on foot. The centre is also the home of the **Portuguese Water Dog Kennels,** where you can meet the friendly, shaggy and uniquely web-footed *Cão d'Água,* a rare breed which in the old days helped fishermen with all sorts of tasks – including driving tuna into fish traps and rescuing drowning sailors. You can also visit the **Centro de Educação Ambiental de Marim** and spend a day working with park volunteers on a range of jobs, from walking water dogs and maintaining the centre's fish and reptile aquariums to caring for sick and injured wild birds.

*Visitor Centre, Quinta do Marim, Parque Natural da Ria Formosa (📞 00 351 289 704 134). Reserve open daily, 24 hours. **Admission**: adults €2.50, children free.*

*2 km east of Olhão*

# Almond Blossom

**In February and early March, gardens, parks, roadsides and orchards** across the Algarve are covered with drifts of white almond blossom. You might even think it was snowing. And that's the point of one of the Algarve's sweetest legends – the story of a Moorish prince of the Algarve who, once upon a time (the Moors were here from 711 AD until 1266 AD), married a princess from the far north. Some versions of the tale even say she was the daughter of a Viking earl. But the princess, in the sunny Algarve, grew ill, and the prince realised that she was pining for the winter snows of her homeland. So he planted vast groves of almond trees, and in spring their falling blossom reminded her of home. She recovered, and they lived (of course) happily ever after. Soppy or what?

"Brilliant! It's really like exploring – we saw flamingos, storks and spoonbills so it was a bit like being in a wildlife documentary, only for real. But the shaggy water dogs were the best bit."
*William, age 10*

## Palácio de Estói Gardens,

**Estói** ALL AGES When this book went to press, you could stroll, picnic and play hide and seek in the lush gardens of the fairytale pink palace, with their fishpools, broad flights of steps and array of statues, but the Palace itself was closed to visitors.

The palace at Estói is being converted into a pousada and is due for completion late 2008, when it will have 49 rooms, three suites, swimming pool, tennis court and very extensive gardens. Like the other pousadas, it can be expected to be family friendly as well as opulent (with touches such as chocolate milk and Smarties on the breakfast buffet for children) and the gardens with their trees, fountains and statues will be excellent

for hide and seek. However, anyone planning to stay here as soon as it opens should check the website **www.pousadas.pt** for confirmed opening dates. *Free admission*

## Historic Buildings

### Sé (Cathedral) Faro ★ ALL AGES

If you are a rationalist, secular parent, this 13th-century building – like every other cathedral

Faro Cathedral

in Portugal, with its pious martyrs and gory crucifixion – is an object lesson in the gilded excesses that elsewhere in Europe prompted the Reformation. If, on the other hand, you wish to put the fear of God into your children, there are few better places in which to do so!

That aside, the cathedral, on which work commenced in 1221, is still an impressive architectural achievement. Your children, accustomed to a 21st-century world in which towering buildings appear as if from nowhere, will be fascinated to be told that this, like all cathedrals, took centuries to construct – and that the whole thing had to be rebuilt all over again after the earthquake of 1755. The altars date from the 17th and 18th centuries, as do its *azulejo* tiles – which are typical of Portuguese churches – and its many statues of saints and martyrs.

They'll also begin to understand a medieval Christian world in which the shadow of the cathedral, and the hand of its prelates, touched every aspect of everyday life – a world that is in sharp contrast with some of the hedonism that is so typical of the rest of the Algarve.

The climb up the 68 steps to the top of the bell-tower is much more exciting than the staid museum on the second floor, with its displays of ecclesiastical robes, statues and other religious paraphernalia. Keep hold of younger children as the steps are narrow and there are no child-proof guard rails. The climb is rewarded

by fantastic views of old and new Faro and the river (you can see as far as the airport and watch holiday jets taking off and landing, and occasionally a Portuguese Air Force fighter zooms past at rooftop height). In spring, you will probably find a family of storks in their messy nest on top of the largest bell-arch.

To the right of the cathedral courtyard, a strange open-air chapel comprises a 'wall of bones' – slightly less gruesome than the more famous chapel at the Igreja do Carmo (see below) but still likely to provoke squeals of horror from younger family members.

*Largo da Se* (📞 *00 351 289 870 870).* **Open** *Mon–Sat 10am–6pm.* **Admission**: *€1.50.*

**Kid's Quote**

"The wall of bones was a bit scary, but not as scary as the stairs to the top of the bell-tower! I didn't think the museum or the cathedral inside was very interesting, but I liked the storks nesting on the roof". *Louise, age 7*

### Igreja do Carmo and Capela dos Ossos, Faro FIND ALL AGES

For a touch of the gruesome (too gruesome for tots, unless you want them to have nightmares) visit this landmark church, which you'll find on its own square around 400 metres north of the Zona Pedonal. With its two massive bell-towers, it is a prominent landmark, and within is Faro's most spine-chilling sight, the 19th-century **Capela dos Ossos** ★★★ (Chapel of Bones), with its walls lined with the skulls and bones of hundreds of long-dead local monks. Definitely not for the squeamish.

*Largo do Carmo (☎ 00 351 289 870 870).* **Open** *Mon–Fri 10am–1pm and 3pm–5pm, Sat 10am–1pm.* **Admission***: €3.*

### Loulé castle ★ AGES 9 AND UP

Loulé's medieval **Castelo** is in good shape, as a result of a top-to-bottom restoration begun in the 19th century, and offers good choice for most families. The ramparts open on to fine views of Loulé and the hills around, and will inspire the imaginations of young fans of sword-and-sorcery adventures. The castle's walls once surrounded the whole of the old town. What's left is the castle keep, with three towers, a turret, and walls surrounding an inner courtyard.

*17 Rua Dom Paio Peres (☎ 00 351 289 400 600).* **Open** *Mon–Fri 9am–5.30pm, Sat 10am–2pm.* **Admission***: €3, under 5s free.*

## Top Museums

### Museu Maritimo Almirante Ramalho Ortigão ★ ALL AGES

With its collection of model ships, paintings of storms at sea and costumes worn until only a generation ago by Faro's fisher folk, this is a good rainy-day option. From here, head round to the south side of the harbour to discover a more modern vision of life in the Algarve at Ciencia Viva.

*Doca de Faro (☎ 00 351 289 894 990).* **Open** *Mon–Fri 2.30pm–4.30pm.* **Admission***: €3, under 5s free.*

Loulé Castle

### Ciencia Viva (Science Alive)

★★ ALL AGES This is one of the better places in Faro for lively-minded children, and has something for most ages, from a rock pool stocked with small sea creatures to interactive displays demonstrating the power of the sun and – for older children – a flight simulator. Ciencia Viva is part of a chain of educational venues run by the Portuguese government – there is another one in Tavira. Each centre focuses on different aspects of the natural world and the local environment. The Faro centre's main theme – chosen as appropriate for the sunniest part of Portugal – is the sun and solar power.

*Doca de Faro (☎ 00 351 289 890 920).* **Open** *8th–30th June Mon–Fri 10am–5pm, Sat–Sun 11am–6pm; 1st June–15th Sept Wed–Sun 3pm–8pm; 16th Sept–30th June Wed–Fri 10am–5pm and Sat–Sun 11am–6pm.*

## Museu Etnográfico `ALL AGES`

This collection of old-fashioned household and kitchen equipment will astonish children who have grown up with 21st-century appliances and its collection of old photographs reveals a way of life that may seem prehistoric but which died out only recently – donkey and ox carts were still in regular use in rural Portugal only 30 years ago. There are cute, Action Man-sized rag dolls in traditional costume, scale models of brightly painted old wooden carts and carriages, and life-size mock-ups of old homes and shops, complete with mannequins in old-fashioned outfits. There's also a fascinating scale model of a *bicheiro* – a maze of nets which was used to catch tuna by driving them into a central corral. The real-life version would have been almost 2 km long, held down by 500 anchors and an amazing 70 km of rope. Unfortunately all the information posters are in Portuguese, but this is a great little museum, and not just for a rainy day (in summer it's nice and cool inside).

*Praça da Liberdade* ( 00 351 289 870 870. **Open** *Mon–Fri 9am– 12.30pm and 2pm–5.30 pm.*

*Admission: adults €2, children (13–18) €1.50, under 12s free.*

## Museu Arqueologico/Museu Municipal ★ `ALL AGES`

This is the place to go to reveal more of the Algarve's past. It's more inspiring for youngsters than most such museums – housed in the cloisters of the old Convento de Nossa Senhora da Assuncão it's decorated with monstrous stone gargoyles that will entertain fans of the *Harry Potter* stories or *The Lord of the Rings*, and there's a pretty Roman mosaic floor. There are also wooden figures of a Roman, a Moorish woman and King Afonso III – they have holes through which children can pop their heads to have their photo taken. A massive statue of King Afonso stands outside the museum.

*Largo Dom Afonso III* ( 00 351 289 897 400). **Open** *15th Oct–15th Mar Tues–Fri 9am–6pm, Sat–Sun 11.30am–6pm; summer Mon–Fri 10am–6pm, Sat–Sun 1.30–8pm.* **Admission**: €2, under 5s free.

## Children-Friendly Tours

### City Walks in Faro `AGES 8 AND UP`

A good way to introduce older

---

**FUN FACT** ❯ **Earthquakes** ❮

**The Algarve was shaken up by its most recent earthquake in February** 2007. It registered around 5 on the Richter scale in the west, but was barely noticeable in Faro. And it was a mere tremor compared with the great 'quake of 1755', which knocked down most of the medieval city – so that although the cathedral and the other great religious buildings around it were founded as early as the 13th and 14th centuries and still stand where they were originally built, the buildings you see today mostly date from the 18th and even 19th centuries.

Tourist Train, Faro

children to Faro's chequered past, from its foundation as a colony of Carthage through to its conquest by the Moors, reconquest by King Afonso II of Portugal in 1249 and devastation in 1755, is to take one of the daily free walking tours around the historic centre.

*Daily, year round, starting at the Municipal Museum, Praça Afonso III (📞 00 351 289 897 400 for times). Free*

**Faro Tourist Trains (Comboios Turisticos)** ★ ★ ★ `ALL AGES` The 'mini-train' that runs round the older parts of Faro – three dinky carriages pulled by a toy locomotive – is an instant hit with children and the perfect way for the family to explore the historic centre. Trains leave from Praça D. Francisco Gomes, (next to the Jardim Manuel Bivar bandstand and opposite Café Alianca) and loop through the narrow streets of the old town, stopping at the cathedral and other strategic points. The whole trip (at not much more than walking pace) takes around two hours, with stops for sightseeing, but if the

children get bored it's always possible to get off at any stop and walk back to the start point, which is never more than 10 minutes away on foot. Buy tickets from the driver before boarding.

*Daily, year round, on the hour from 10am–midnight, operated by Delgaturis (📞 00 351 289 389 067; www.deltrain.com). Admission: €3.*

**Sunset cruises from Vilamoura** ★ ★ `ALL AGES` The **Condor de Vilamour**, a replica of a 19th-century fishing schooner sails on daytime and sunset cruises from Vilamoura marina – it's a fairly pricey experience, but children under six go free.

Look out for gliding storks and flamingos over head, and keep older children busy with binoculars scanning the horizon for dolphins and maybe, if you're very lucky, a cruising pod of killer whales.

*25 Cais 1, Vilamoura Marina (📞 00 351 289 314 070; www.condorde vilamoura.com). Daily departures. Admission: adults €40, under 15s €20, under 5s free.*

## Folkfaro

**Launched in 2003 by an enterprising group of young Algarvean** musicians, Groupo Folklorico de Faro, Folkfaro has grown into a fun nine-day party and celebration of international goodwill that fills the streets of Faro with music, musicians and dancers from all over the world (mostly, so far from Portugal, Spain and Latin America, but the list keeps growing every year). There are parades, gala nights, dance workshops and open-air performances, and it's not too noisy or crowded an event for younger children. *Folkfaro, Apartado 271, 8001-904 Faro (📞 00 351 966 049 355/ 00 351 962 556 599;* **E: grupofaro@hotmail.com***; www.folkfaro.com).*

## For Active Families

**Atlantic Park** ★ **ALL AGES** The first (and smallest) water park in Portugal, this family fun destination on the outskirts of Quarteira has 15 water slides, six pools for all ages, a 'Rio Grande' rubber raft ride, bouncy castle and quad bikes and has its own snack bar. A free barbecue lunch is thrown in if you buy a full-day ticket including transfers from your hotel. There are coach pick-ups from all points between Via Real de Santo António and Lagos.

*Quatro Estadas, Quarteira, N125 highway (📞 00 351 289 397 948; www.aspro-ocio.es).* **Open** *28th* *May–14th Sept 10am–4pm.* **Admission***: adults €17.50, children (4–10), €14.50.*

**Aquashow** ★ **ALL AGES** This water park has slides and tubes, wave pools, swimming pools and whirlpools as well as a collection of colourful tropical birds, falconry displays and the unique Wax Museum of the History of Portugal, produced by the creator of the animatronic waxworks at Madame Tussaud's in London, so you could claim that it is an educational experience as well as a great family day out. If you really like water parks, you might want to consider buying the seven-day

Aquashow

## FUN FACT ▶▶ Water Dogs ◀◀

**Black, strong, shaggy and web-footed, the Portuguese water dog has** been around for at least 2,000 years. They were trained to retrieve fishing nets and to help drive shoals of tuna into the huge fish traps called *bicheiros*, and some claim that they could even spot sharks, tuna and other large fish deep under water with their keen eyesight. Fishermen treated them as part of the crew, and it is said that they earned the same share of the day's catch as the men did. They were even used to carry messages by swimming from boat to boat. The breed started to die out as old-fashioned fishing methods were replaced by larger, more modern boats, and by the 1930s there were not many water dogs left. The Water Dog Kennels in the Ria Formosa Natural Park have played a big part in preserving the breed, and at the kennels (near the park visitor centre) visitors can meet and stroke the dogs, talk to their handlers and learn more about the breed.

pass, which costs only as much as three one-day tickets.

*Quarteira, N396 highway (☎ 00 351 289 389 396; www.aquashowpark. com). **Open** 1st June–30th June and 1st Sept–15th Oct 10am–5.30pm; 1st July–31st Aug 10am–6.30pm; 15th Oct–5th Apr 10am–5pm. **Admission**: adults €20, children (5–15) €15, under 5s free. Seven-day tickets: adults €60, under 15s €45.*

### Quinta dos Amigos ALL AGES

This three-acre farm and guest house just outside Almancil (see p. 64) also has a riding centre with qualified instructors and offers guided horseback tours for children and adults, beach rides and riding lessons for all age groups.

### Exploring Ria Formosa

AGES 8 AND UP For families with older children, there are one to two-hour self-guided walks along signposted trails starting from the visitor centre. The going can get too rough for buggies, so it's not ideal for toddlers. It is also important to make sure

everyone wears sunscreen (and, preferably, a hat too) and to take plenty of drinking water, but there's no risk of getting lost – this is a very soft adventure.

Viagens Cebola, 117 Rua Antero de Quental, Faro (☎ 00 351 289 827 822) organises boat trips around the reserve.

### Almancil Karting AGES 8 AND UP

This is definitely one for the Jeremy Clarkson fans in the family, with a full-blown circuit that is a faithful copy of the Jacarepaguá circuit in Brazil. On the big boys' circuit, karts available range from nippy 120cc junior jobs to twin-engined 400 cc monsters. There is also a gentler circuit for younger children, with mini Formula 1 electric karts, and a boating lake with mini-electric speedboats. The track is surrounded by a 'Western' theme park with mechanical bull rides (how long can dad stay on?), and other good stuff including bungee trampolines, table-top games

Almancil Karting

and computer games. There's a snack restaurant (not great) and a picnic area too.

*Kartódromo de Almancil, Sitio das Pereiras, Almancil (☎ 00 351 289 399 899; www.mundokarting.pt). Mini Formula 1 karts €5 for five minutes; mini-boats €3 for five minutes; junior karts €11 for 10 minutes; 400cc karts €25 for 10 minutes.*

### Roma Golf Park ALL AGES

Vilamoura takes golf very seriously. Roma Golf Park doesn't, and is the perfect antidote to the pomp of the big-deal courses that surround it. This 18-hole putting course is embellished by fake-Roman columns and monuments, fountains, lakes and landscaped gardens, there's a play area for younger children and a free miniature golf course for under 10s. The design of the clubhouse, it is claimed, 'reflects the architecture of ancient Rome' – that's if a Roman villa came equipped with miniature football and other table games and an ice-cream terrace. It's family fun in a gently silly way –

not worth making a special trip, but if you are staying nearby it's a pleasant way of wasting an afternoon.

*Central Vilamoura, about a five-minute walk from the Marina (☎ 00 351 289 300 800; E: romagolfe@mail. telepac.pt.) Closed from 25th Nov–25th Dec.*

## Shopping

For one-stop shopping in Faro, look no further than **Forum Algarve,** which claims to be Europe's largest shopping mall. It's on the outskirts of Faro (off the N125), and has more than 100 shops and a huge hypermarket – ideal for stocking up if you are in self-catering accommodation. Another big mall is **Shopping Algarve,** just outside Albufeira at Guia on the N125 highway, which has around 130 outlets of all kinds, including a supermarket – more than Forum Algarve, but because they are not all under one roof the Faro mall retains its 'Europe's largest' title.

Faro's **Gypsy Market** takes place on the first Friday and Sunday of each month. Don't expect to see flocks of authentic travelling folk, but do go in search of baskets, pottery and carved wooden toys, dolls and ornaments as well as more day-to-day items. Although billed as Faro's market, it is actually a 15-minute drive from Faro at Estói, and is held next to the municipal market close to the town centre. For dates and locations for this and other gypsy markets around the Algarve, see the website **www.algarve-portal.com/en/shopping/markets**.

These are more like car boot sales than the picturesque flea markets you may have been expecting, but are good family fun nonetheless (and also good places to pick up everything from T-shirts and cotton socks to nappies and underwear at knock-down prices).

Most shops in Faro and the Algarve in general are open from 9am–1pm and 3pm–7pm Monday to Saturday. Many smaller shops close on Sunday, but the malls are good for emergency shopping as they are open all week until midnight.

In Faro town centre, **Rua D. Francisco Gomes and Rua de Santo António,** running through the middle of the Zona Pedonal, comprise the main shopping thoroughfare, though there's nothing here that you would not find in the UK at a similar (or cheaper) price.

**Boy's and Girl's** at 13A Rua de Santo António has a reasonable choice of clothes and footwear for children up to around age six. **Trakinas,** at 10 Rua de Santo António, has baby clothes and formal clothing for under 10s, including communion dresses for girls and suits for boys. The Zona Pedonal's other main shopping thoroughfare is **Rua Vasco da Gama,** which is also the eastern boundary of the pedestrian zone. **Belmondo,** at 14 Rua Vasco da Gama, has quite attractive clothes for babies, children and pre-teens, but nothing that is likely to impress the average style-conscious British sub-adolescent. You'll find British and Irish newspapers such as the *Times, Daily Mail, Daily Telegraph, Daily Record* and *Irish Independent* at **Tabacaria Vasco da Gama,** 49 Rua Vasco da Gama. You'll also find English-language newspapers and a few magazines at the **Quiosque Farense** kiosk on **Praça Ferreira de Almeida,** just past the north end of Rua Vasco da Gama.

A smart new shopping complex, **Atrium Faro,** was due to open at 27–35 Rua Vasco da Gama in early 2007. At the time of writing, however, none of its units had yet attracted a tenant.

In **Loulé,** things to look out for include colourful, hand-stitched rag dolls, colourful pottery, straw hats, mats and baskets, metalwork and turned-wood bowls and platters. The best place to find these is along **Rua da Barbaca,** next to the walls of the medieval castle, which is lined with the workshops of lace-makers, metal-workers, saddle-makers,

**Go West**

**The Moors – who lived here for 500 years – gave the Algarve its name:** *'Al-gharb'*, which in Arabic means 'the West'. They also named many of the big rivers in the Algarve and southern Spain, like the Guadiana and the Guadalquivir – *wadi* is the Arabic word for river.

potters and wood-turners. Even if you don't intend to buy, watching these artisans at work is a new experience for most children. Rather sadly, it's also a last chance for them to see such skills still being used – most of the crafts-men and craftswomen are elderly, and few of their children want to take over their businesses.

## FAMILY-FRIENDLY ACCOMMODATION

Few families will want or need to stay overnight in Faro, given that there are dozens of places to stay on the beach nearby, at Praia de Faro (which is even closer to the airport than Faro itself) and other neighbouring resorts. However, the town has a few acceptable family hotels that are adequate for an overnight stay at the begin-ning or end of an independently organised holiday.

### Faro

**MODERATE**

**Hotel Eva** ★★ If for any reason you do need a room in town, the eight-storey Hotel Eva, right on the harbour, is a decent option, with convenient parking, views of the harbour and the river, large, uniform but well-equipped

en-suite bedrooms with baths as well as showers, and all the Faro attractions are virtually on the doorstep.

*Av. Da República (☎ 00 351 289 001 000; www.eva.tdhotels.pt). 148 rooms. Rates: doubles from €90. Amenities: rooftop pool and restau-rant, 24-hour room service, babysit-ting (must be booked in advance).*

### Ilha de Armona

**INEXPENSIVE**

**Parque de Campismo Ilha de Armona** ★ There are only a few places to stay on the Algarve's offshore islands, and this bunga-low site next to a 200-metre stretch of beach on Ilha de Armona is probably the most accessible, and a good pick for would-be castaway families look-ing for a beach holiday on a shoestring budget. The bunga-lows are on the small side, but then again you are unlikely to be spending much time indoors except when asleep, and each has its own private veranda, with plenty of space around. There's a fairly basic children's play-ground, with a seesaw and swings. No pool, but with a warm, shallow, sheltered natural lagoon just a few steps away you can live without one. There are cafés and restaurants along the beach which are open through the summer months, and in shoulder season the shops and facilities of Olhão are just a 15-minute ferry ride away.

*Ilha de Armona (📞 00 351 289 714 173; www.orbitur.pt). Rates: from €70 for a bungalow sleeping 6 people. Amenities: basic children's playground with seesaw and swings.*

## Vale do Lobo

VERY EXPENSIVE

**Vale do Lobo** ⭐ Covering 400 hectares of groomed grounds and set on a 2-km stretch of beach, Vale do Lobo is a resort destination in its own right. It's probably the most expensive and luxurious place to stay in the entire Algarve, and if it has a downside (apart from the price) it is a certain inevitable lack of local colour.

There are several hundred gorgeous privately owned villas and apartments (available to rent by the week or month) and most guests never feel the need to stray off the complex, which has its own supermarket and designer boutiques as well as 15 very

upmarket restaurants. Around half of the villas and apartments are British-owned, so you'll be meeting plenty of other British families. What Vale do Lobo really excels at is sports, with 14 tennis courts, two 18-hole golf courses, and other activities ranging from lawn bowls to volleyball, yoga, aerobics and top-spinning.

Facilities include babysitters and nannies on request, a large children's village with animators, child-minders and its own pool and mini-golf course and a tennis academy where your budding Wimbledon stars can be coached by world-class tennis aces.

Football fans in your family will like to know that the England 2006 World Cup squad used Vale do Lobo as their training camp. There's a very wide range of accommodation, from moderately priced one-bedroom 'comfort apartments' that sleep two adults and one child up to luxury villas where the sky's the limit. If you stay in the cheaper accommodation, you still have access to all the resort facilities, but you'll

Vale do Lobo

have to pay – albeit at reduced rates – to use some of them (such as the main pool, tennis courts and golf courses).

The resort is self-catering, but they do provide a welcome basket of breakfast basics when you arrive, and a maid comes in daily to tidy up and make the beds, while bed linen is changed three times a week.

*23 km west of Faro on N125 ( 00 351 289 353 261; www.valedolobo.com). 1,500+ rooms. **Rates**: one-bedroom comfort apartment €110–265, two-bedroom €160–420. **Amenities**: children's village, outdoor and indoor pools, mini-golf, tennis academy, tennis courts, golf courses, supermarket, beach, hairdresser, travel agency, car rental service, 15 restaurants, shops. **In room**: satellite TV, DVD player, Internet access, maid service, fully equipped kitchen.*

## Quarteira

MODERATE

**Hotel Dom José** ★★★ This is a typically functional but comfortable three-star Quarteira hotel, just across the esplanade from the beach, where the Dom José has its own sun-loungers and umbrellas. It also has a pool (but not a children's pool) and a nine-hole mini-golf course. Breakfast is buffet-style, which suits families – as does its location only 20 minutes from Faro airport. Babysitting is available.

*Av. Infante de Sagres 143, Quarteira ( 00 351 289 302 750; www.domjose-hotels.com). 154 rooms. **Rates**: doubles from €70. **Amenities**: pool, nine-hole mini-golf course, babysitting. **In room**: TV.*

MODERATE

**Pinhal da Marina Apartments** This village of holiday apartments – from compact studios that would be OK for a couple with a baby or solo parent and child to three-bedroom apartments that are (somewhat ambitiously) described as sleeping up to eight people (two on a sofa bed in the living room) – is close to the centre of things at Vilamoura and is an affordable compromise between hotel accommodation and basic self-catering. It has services including regular cleaning and bed-linen change, and rates include breakfast in a decent self-service cafeteria. All the apartments have fully equipped kitchens with cooker, fridge, dishwasher and microwave oven as well as satellite TV (though here, as in even the most luxurious Algarve hotels, the choice of English channels is limited). There are three pools, one of which is reserved for children, as well as a children's playground but babysitting is not available.

*Pinhal da Marina, Vilamoura ( 00 351 289 303 230; www.pinhaldamarina.com). 128 rooms. **Rates**: three-bedroom apartments from €130. **Amenities**: children's pool, adults' pools, playground, mini market, football, basketball, beach volleyball courts, snooker room, tennis court. **In room**: full kitchen, cooker, fridge, dishwasher, microwave oven, satellite TV.*

**Hotel Quarteira Sol** ★★ This is about as good value as you will get for your money in a hotel in the centre of Quarteira. All things considered, it's as cheap as chips – the rooms are (as usual in three-star hotels) none too inspiring, but there's a fair-sized pool surrounded by a terrace with loungers and umbrellas, and facilities including baby cots, high chairs and babysitting are available by arrangement. The restaurants (choice of à la carte or buffet style) offer children's menus. The only fly in the ointment for those hoping for an early night is the nightly 'entertainment' in the hotel bar.

*Av. Francisco Sa Carneiro, Quarteira ( 00 351 289 381 460). 108 rooms. **Rates**: doubles from €85–105, extra bed €12.50, under 4s free, 50% discount for children (5–12) sharing parents' room. **Amenities**: pool. **In room**: TV.*

**Parque de Campismo de Quarteira** ★ The Orbitur company operates a number of sites around Portugal, with accommodation in tents, motor-homes, caravans or self-contained chalets. The Quarteira site is among pine trees, set about 600 metres back from Quarteira's beach and about 1 km from the town centre, so it's relatively peaceful. The trees provide plenty of shade and there are around 100 chalets, offering space for 2–6 people. The site also has a choice of pools – some with slides – for everyone from toddlers to grown-ups. Budget accommodation in guesthouses and hotels below three-star rating in Portugal, and especially in resorts like Quarteira, is far from

ideal for families – rooms tend to be cramped and often noisy and services are minimal in cheaper hotels – so this comfortable campsite is a great solution for families on a tight budget.

*Estrada da Fonte Santa, Av. Francisco Sa Carneiro ( 00 351 289 302 826; www.orbitur.pt ). Approx. 100 bungalows. **Rates**: bungalow sleeping up to six from around €70. **Amenities**: three pools. **In room**: basic kitchenette.*

## Almancil

**Quinta do Lago** ★★★ Quinta do Lago is the acknowledged queen of Algarve hotels. Don't be deceived by the Almancil address – it actually spans some 2,000 acres of gardens, greens, lakeside and pinewoods running down to the sea close to Praia do Ancão. If you have the money (and you'll need plenty) this must be the best family address in the region, and one of the best in the world. As well as run-of-the-mill services such as babysitting and child-minding there is an all-summer programme of activities (mostly water-based) for children aged three and up. Windsurfing, windsurfing lessons, sailing dinghies, sailing lessons, swimming lessons, hobbiecats, toppers, canoes, kayaks, rowing boats, tractors, pedalos and fishing rods are available on a private lake, and parasailing, jet-skiing, waterskiing, waterskiing lessons, bronco, windsurfing lessons, hobbiecats, Laser II, canoes, pedalos, ringos, knee boards, body boards, motorboat rides to nearby caves and scuba diving are available at the beach for beginners as well as experienced practitioners.

The sybaritic Royal Suite – with two bedrooms, two bathrooms, kitchen, sitting room and dining room, wraparound terrace and private pool – is strictly for lottery winners and City bankers with big bonuses, but the garden-view double rooms are much more affordable, and a range of generous discounts for children and teenagers takes even more of the sting out of the price.

*Quinta do Garrao, Almancil ( 00 351 289 350 350; www.quintadolago hotel.com). 141 rooms and suites. Rates: Royal Suite €2,000–3,000 depending on season, garden view doubles from €200 per room, children under 12 sharing parents' room free on bed and breakfast basis, extra bed in parents' room free, 50% reduction for children (13–16) sharing parents' room; 25% reduction for 13–16 year olds in own room, 50% reduction on half-board and full-board supplements for under 12s. Amenities: sports as above. In room: satellite TV and DVD player, mini-bar, safe, 24-hour room service.*

## Vilamoura

**INEXPENSIVE**

**Algamar Apartments** ★ This complex of bright, clean apartments in the middle of Vilamoura is only 300 metres from the marina and beach. All apartments have private balconies, and there is a shared pool surrounded by a grassy courtyard. These are one- and two-bedroom apartments, so it's stretching a bit to claim, as they do, that some of them sleep 6–8 people but the rates are very attractive. Extra services are minimal (no babysitting) but laundry service can be arranged. This is comfortable, no frills accommodation for the family that prefers self-catering to a full-service hotel.

*Vilamoura ( 00 351 289 389 998; www.garvetur.pt). Rates: from €80 (for 6–8 people) in low season to €180 in high summer. Amenities: pool. In room: basic kitchen.*

## Inland

**MODERATE**

**Quinta dos Amigos** ★★★ Just off the highway at Almancil, 15 km west of Faro, this former farm is a great family base if you don't mind being away from the beach (to compensate, there are two pools, one for children). The property spreads over three acres of gardens and meadows, so with only 14 rooms in a collection of former farm buildings there is plenty of room for everyone – it's much more like staying with friends than staying in a hotel. The Quinta has its own riding stables, and offers riding lessons, beach rides and guided trail riding. Breakfast and dinner are not included in the price, but can be arranged on request, as can babysitting. You can choose between two-person studios and one-, two-, and three-bedroom apartments (the largest sleep up to seven people). They're all on the ground floor and each has its own terrace and comes complete with a fully equipped kitchen, bed linen, towels, TV and central heating. You can choose between daily and weekly rates, and it's really excellent value for money and an excellent compromise between self-catering and hotel-style accommodation.

*15 km west of Faro on N125 (☎ 00 351 289 395 269; www.quintados amigos.com). 14 rooms.* **Rates**: *two-bedroom apartments from €350 per week (€60 per night), three-bedroom apartments from €430 per week (€74 per night), no credit cards.* **Amenities**: *adults' and children's pools, gardens, riding stables.* **In room**: *kitchen, TV.*

**Quinta da Belgica** ★ FIND This is the best little place in the Faro area for families, bar none. The only problem is, it has so many fans already that you need to book way in advance. The Belgian owners, Mieke Everaert and Jef Cloots have two children of their own, so they know the score and make children very welcome with a playroom full of toys, a big garden with an old fishing boat on which to play at being Johnny Depp (or Keira Knightley) in *Pirates of the Caribbean* – even a 'dressing-up' box full of old clothes and costumes. There's a fair-sized pool, a ping-pong table, table footie and more pragmatically they also provide cots, baby chairs, baby baths and potties. There's even a kid's page on their website so younger family members can

check it out in advance. The nearest beach (Sotavento) is 5 km away, a drive of less than 10 minutes, and the airport is only 15 km away, so you can be there only minutes after your luggage comes off the carousel.

*Sitio da Formalha, Moncarapacho (☎ 00 351 289 791 193; www.quinta-da-belgica.com).* **Rates**: *double or twin €65, bed and breakfast (half board also available), under 3s free, children 3–5 years €5, 6–11 years €10; 11–18 years €20 (all when sharing room with two adults).* **Amenities**: *pool and ping pong, cots, baby chairs, baby baths and potties.*

> **Guest book comment** »
>
> "An oasis of kindness and serenity in the middle of the crazy Algarve."

# FAMILY-FRIENDLY DINING

It's fair to say that virtually all restaurants in Algarve resorts – bar a few formal spots favoured by local executives for business lunches, and one or two rough-and-ready fishermen's taverns – are family friendly, in the sense that children are welcome everywhere. That said, very few eating places except for those within resort hotels – go out of their way to offer such amenities as high chairs for tots or specially priced menus for children. On the other hand almost every restaurant offers starters and snacks that are child-sized and affordable, and there is no objection to ordering these smaller dishes without a main course. It is unusual to find a restaurant which does not offer an English translation of its menu, and in most resorts you'll find that restaurants offer an array of British dishes – from bacon and eggs to burger and chips to beans on toast – in tandem with Portuguese favourites. Note that alcohol is sold in all cafés and ice-cream parlours, so it's perfectly possible for parents to have a glass of wine or beer while children enjoy ice cream or pancakes. Outside many cafés you'll see miniature coin-operated, fairground-style rocking horses and other mini-rides for younger children. The Algarve's climate means families can sit outside virtually all year round, which helps to keep children from getting restive.

## Faro – Old Town & Zona Pedonal

**Café de Coreto** ★ This spruce, modern café-restaurant right on the harbour is a good spot to take a breather after a walk round town, or to wait for the mini-train (which leaves from the opposite side of the gardens, just a minute's walk away). Next to the outside tables there are coin-operated rides – including a rocking horse and a helicopter – to keep tots occupied, and the menu has plenty of familiar comfort food, including burgers, kebabs and sticky desserts.

*Doca Faro*

*Burgers from €2.75, kebabs from €7.25, ice-cream pancakes from*

€4.80. No credit cards. No reservations required. **Open** daily 9am–11pm.

**Gelateria Fiesta** ★ Despite the rather forbidding looking elderly local ladies who loiter over coffee and pastries in the indoor section, this ice-cream parlour is a good place to rest tired little legs, with tables outside on a pedestrian street lined with shops. At the last count, Gelateria Fiesta offered no fewer than 24 kinds of ice cream and sorbet, from toxic-looking, bright blue bubblegum flavour to more natural tastes such as lemon, green apple and peach.

*26 Rua de Santo António*

*From around €3.50 per dish. No credit cards. **Open** all day.*

**Cidade Velha Café** ★ This cheap and cheerful café-restaurant behind the cathedral is the most family-friendly spot within the old town walls (where there are only four places to eat or drink). It has tables inside and outside and a menu that includes omelettes, sweet crêpes and banana splits, salads, burger and chips, sandwiches and a healthy choice of freshly squeezed juices including apple, pear, melon, peach, pineapple and mango.

*19 Rua Domingos Guieiro/Largo da Se.*

*Omelettes and burgers from €5.50, sandwiches from €1.50, fruit juices €3.00. No credit cards. **Open** all day for snacks, drinks and light meals.*

# It Came from the Sea

**The most exciting fish markets in the Algarve are at Quarteira and Olhão,** and each is an education for children who think fish comes in handy shrink-wrapped fillets. The Portuguese will eat just about anything that comes out of the sea, so as well as more familiar offerings like sardines they'll see conger eels, huge tuna, swordfish, long, black scabbard-fish with rows of needle teeth and even the occasional shark – all with the head still attached, and many still alive and wriggling.

## Restaurante Vasco da Gama

★★ This restaurant close to the north edge of the Zona Pedonal is a good place to introduce older, bolder children to the delights of Portuguese seafood – most of what is available is prominently displayed on ice outside the front door. It's a long way from the supermarket fish counter, and expecting them to be turned on by local delicacies such as slimy-looking lampreys, baby cuttlefish and weird goose-necked barnacles may be expecting too much, but there are plenty of less threatening offerings such as grilled sardines.

*Rua Vasco da Gama 47*

*From around €10 per person. Credit cards accepted. Reservations not essential.* **Open** *for lunch and dinner.*

## Restaurant Ribatejano ★★

Ribatejano is as far as we know the only vegetarian restaurant in the Algarve and although it sells itself as vegetarian it bends the rules a bit – since when was *bacalhau* (dried salt cod) a vegetable? The rest of the menu is slightly old-fashioned, with vegetable rissoles, tofu omelette and soya burgers, but vegetarian

families trying to keep the faith will find few other options in Faro.

*Rua de S. Luís 32 A (☎ 00 351 289 812 110; www.ribatejano.net).*

*From around €7.50. Credit cards accepted. Reservations not essential.* **Open** *for lunch and dinner, take-away service available.*

## Quarteira

**Fernando's Hideaway** The menu here is mainly meat and the portions are vast, with enormous steaks (T-bone, fillet, stone-grilled, rump and sirloin) as well as Sunday roasts and fish and chips. The children's menu should please – it features familiar favourites and some vegetarian specials. Friendly, English-speaking owner and staff, and high chairs are usually available if you book in advance.

*Rua Mestre Luís, Loja 13, Quarteira (☎ 00 351 289 315 628). €10–20. Credit cards accepted. Reservations recommended.* **Open** *for lunch and dinner.*

**Irish & Co** ★★ This is more like a family pub than a restaurant, with Guinness, Tetleys,

Kilkenny, Carlsberg and Strongbow on draught and a plentiful choice of soft drinks for children. There are tables on a sunny wooden deck beside the marina and the restaurant is family-pleasingly familiar to British and Irish visitors alike. Full Irish breakfast is served all day and a full lunch and dinner menu is served from 11am to 1am. Main dishes are meaty, and include such delights as tenderloin steak sizzler with Guinness sauce, breast of Cavan chicken and steak with Irish whiskey and cream sauce. For smaller appetites, there's a good selection of snacks and sandwiches.

*Centro Commercial, Marina Vilamoura ( 00 351 289 395 216).*

*Around €15. Credit cards not accepted. Open all day.*

## Almancil

**Henrique Leis** ★★★ This intimate restaurant is only for special occasions – and only if you can find a babysitter. The atmosphere is relaxed and elegant, but even the best-behaved children are likely to feel a little out of place. Still, for couples looking to inject a little *romance à deux* into a family holiday, this is the place to be if your credit limit will stand it. As you would expect from a Michelin-starred restaurant, the service is discreetly professional and the food is beautifully presented. The menu combines Portuguese influences and local produce with international flair, as evidenced in starters such as salad of quails or scallops and langoustine starters and mains such as crispy breast of guinea fowl stuffed with wild mushrooms and pata negra ham.

*Vale Formoso, Almancil ( 00 351 289 393 438).*

*Around €50. Credit cards accepted. Reservations essential. Open for dinner only.*

**Pig & Whistle** ★★ The Pig and Whistle is an oddly charming combination of Portuguese inn and English pub, with tables in cosy nooks and alcoves in the low-ceiling rooms of an old-fashioned Algarve house. Families are welcome, child portions are available, and the menu is reassuringly familiar, even old-fashioned, with dishes like liver and bacon with mustard mashed potato and onion gravy.

*Almancil ( 00 351 289 395 216)*

*Around €20–22. Credit cards accepted. Reservations recommended. Open for lunch and dinner.*

**Restaurante Van Gogh** ★★★ This family-friendly restaurant has a large bar, off-street parking and can usually offer high chairs and children's portions if you give them some advance notice. It's an all-year, all-weather spot – they have recently added a conservatory for cooler evenings. The menu

Olhao Market

is varied and imaginative and offers a wider than average choice of vegetarian options. Some of the mains may be a bit complex for finicky children, but there are simpler choices too and the desserts are luscious.

*N 125, Maritenda, Boliqueime, near Vilamoura (📞 00 351 289 360 721).*

*Around €20–25. Credit cards accepted. Reservations recommended. Evenings only.*

# 4 Albufeira & Around

**I**t's easy to see why the stretch of coast west from Praia da **Vilamoura and the Ribeira de** Quarteira to Portimão and Alvor has become the Algarve's family holiday heartland.

Apart from miles of sandy beaches and splendid weather year round, it has an enviable portfolio of purpose-built attractions, almost all of them developed in recent years with British families in mind.

The British have taken this part of the world to their hearts in a big way, and almost half the people who holiday along these fabulous beaches are British. Huge numbers have been seduced by a mellow climate and congenial surroundings into buying a second home in the sun or a retirement villa here, too.

So: gorgeous, safe, toddler-friendly beaches with lifeguards (in summer, anyway)? Check. Golf, tennis and water sports for families with older children? Check. State-of-the-art water parks and activities such as karting and bowling? You got it. And to back that up, the central Algarve has a vast choice of accommodation, from big resort hotels offering services such as children's clubs, child-minding, babysitting and sports coaching to self-catering studios and apartments, new-built luxury villas or farmhouse conversions with pools tucked away in the hills a few miles inland.

If your children quickly hanker for the familiar taste of burgers, chicken masala, baked beans or fish and chips, that's not a problem either – this part of the Algarve has more British-accented pubs, cafés and restaurants than you can shake a stick at. Family members (probably male) who suffer withdrawal symptoms if they can't follow the footballing fortunes of their favourites will also be relieved to know that Albufeira has far more than its fair share of sports bars boasting wide-screen TV (again, if you really *need* it).

But the central Algarve is more than a beach-holiday enclave for British expatriates. A short drive inland brings you to Silves, one of Portugal's most picturesque medieval castles, haunted by the ghosts of Moorish princesses and Templar knights. Cruise, or paddle your own canoe, on the tidal estuaries of the Ribeira de Arade and the Ria de Alvor, which are refuges for storks, flamingos and other wild birds, go scuba diving or shark fishing, or spend a day at the zoo.

And food-wise, it's not all curry and chips. There are some excellent gourmet restaurants along the coast, and Portimão's riverside waterfront has more than a dozen restaurants – some funky and traditional, others gleaming new – serving fresh-caught sardines, snapper, prawns and other delicious seafood.

# ESSENTIALS

## Getting There

**By Car** For information on arriving at Faro airport, see p. 47.

The N125 highway connects the towns and resorts of the central Algarve with Faro and points east and west. The A22 motorway, running a few miles inland from and parallel to the N125, allows faster driving from point to point, ending just north of Lagos.

**By Rail or Bus** The Algarve regional railway line connects Portimão and Albufeira with Loulé, Faro, Tavira and Vila Real de Santo António (eastbound) and Lagos (westbound). There are several trains daily.

Caminhos de Ferro Portugueses (Portuguese Railways) trains (☎ *00 351 808 208 208;* *www.cp.pt*).

EVA buses (see p. 48) are fast, clean and efficient and link virtually every part of the Algarve with Faro and the rest of Portugal.

# VISITOR INFORMATION

## Orientation

As far as this book is concerned, the central Algarve starts at the mouth of the Ribeira de Quarteira – just west of Quarteira and Vilamoura – and ends at the west end of Praia de Alvor, on the Baia de Lagos. That said, these boundaries are pretty arbitrary. The villa and golf course developments and apartment complexes inland of Albufeira merge imperceptibly into those that fringe Vilamoura, and Portimão and Lagos reach out towards each other between the Ria de Alvor and the A22 motorway and will eventually merge into one big suburban sprawl.

From east to west, it's an almost unbroken stretch of sand, sand, sand until you reach Praia do Carvalho. From here, just for variety, the coastline becomes spectacularly rocky until you reach the mouth of the Ribeira de Arade.

Albufeira, the biggest, brashest resort in the Algarve, lies roughly midway along the central Algarve coast, with great beaches stretching off to both sides. On the west bank of the Ribeira de Arade, Portimão sprawls inland, virtually merging with its smaller neighbour, Alvor, to occupy the entire peninsula between the Arade and the Ria de Alvor, with a stretch of golden sands and rugged cliffs between the two river mouths. A couple of miles inland, a soaring suspension bridge spans the river – it's an engineering marvel and a sight in its own right.

### Main Tourism Offices

**Albufeira Tourist Office** Rua 5 de Outubro (☎ *00 351 289 585 279;* E: *turismo.albufeira@ rtalgarve.pt*)

**Alvor Tourist Office** Rua Dr Afonso Costa 51 (☎ *00 351 282 457 540;* E: *turismo.alvor@rtalgarve.pt*)

**Armação de Pêra Tourist Office** Avenida Marginal ( 00 351 282 312 145; E: turismo. Armaçãodepera@rtalgarve.pt)

**Carvoeiro Tourist Office** Praia do Carvoeiro ( 00 351 282 357 728; E: turismo.carvoiero@rt algarve.pt)

**Portimão Tourist Offices** Cais do Comercio e Turismo ( 00 351 281 416 556) and Avenida Zeca Afonso ( 00351 282 470 732; E: turismo@cm-portimao.pt)

**Praia da Rocha Tourist Office** Avenida Tomas Cabreira ( 00 351 282 419 132; E: turismo. praiadarocha@rtalgarve.pt)

**Silves Tourist Office** Rua 25 de Abril ( 00 351 282 442 255)

## Getting Around

Beyond the main resorts of Portimão and Albufeira, renting a car on arrival is the most seamless and easiest way of getting around the region.

Non-drivers can mix and match taxis (for short hops in resorts) with buses and trains. Most of the purpose-built visitor attractions and water parks lay on coach transfers with pick-up/set-down points at all the main resorts at a nominal extra cost – see individual attractions for details. In short, unless you have chosen to stay in a country-side villa some way inland, a car isn't essential.

## WHAT TO SEE & DO

### Children's Top 10 Attractions

❶ **FIESA Sand Sculpture Festival** Areias de Pêra. Awesome sand art on an equally awesome beach, all summer long (see p. 83).

❷ **Bella Vista** Fun park for the littler ones with bouncy castles and unscary rides (see p. 99).

Beach Art

**3** **Praia da Rocha** Legendary, busy but well maintained and spectacular scenic beach with lifeguards and excellent family facilities (see p. 95).

**4** **Praia dos Barcos** Painted boats, gnarled fishermen, golden sand – and right in the middle of Albufeira (see p. 92).

**5** **Castelo dos Mouros, Silves** The most spectacular castle in the Algarve, with massive walls, pretty gardens and spooky dungeons (see p. 105).

**6** **Slide and Splash** If you only visit one of the Algarve legendary water parks, this is the one to go for. Mental (see p. 96).

**7** **Krazy World** Robot dinosaurs, crazy golf, live crocodiles and giant pythons. What are these guys like? Outstanding (see p. 98).

**8** **Aqualand** The oldest of the region's water parks is still a great day out, with lots of rides for all ages (see p. 97).

**9** **Zoomarine** Swim with dolphins and learn more about the Algarve's marine life (see p. 97).

**10** **Ria do Alvor Canoe Trips** Can I canoe you up the river? Yes, and the children can come too. A great active day out from Alvor (see p. 100).

## Children-Friendly Events & Entertainment

The central Algarve has a calendar packed with family-friendly events – some traditional, others invented to entertain visitors.

Albufeira is an especially lively spot, with musicians and entertainers playing in the streets and squares of the old town centre every evening from June until the end of August, and teams of 'animators' bringing fun and games (everything from beach volleyball and tennis to sandcastle competitions) to the nearby beaches through the summer. Annual events in Portimão for big boys include the Portuguese P1 Powerboat Grand Prix, where a new motor sports circuit, scheduled for completion in 2008, will bring a new dimension to the resort for petrolheaded fathers and sons. Contact the tourist offices in Albufeira or Portimão for the latest update on what's on where while you are there.

### February: Albufeira

**Carnival** Albufeira takes its mid-February carnival less seriously than most other Portuguese towns, with a special children's carnival parade on the Friday closest to 14th February – floats, children in costume, and baby, toddler, pre-teen and teenage carnival princesses and princes. For dates, times and details of parades, contact the tourist office in Albufeira or the regional tourist office (*www.rtalgarve.pt*).

### August: Portimão

**Sardine Festival** Children who think sardines come straight from the shops will be mesmerised and

## Buying a Place in the Sun

**Everybody dreams of buying their own place in the sun, and more** than 40,000 Britons have already done so in the Algarve. If you are looking for a family-friendly second home there are few better places – but the days when you could snap up an old house to be restored for a song, or buy a purpose-built villa or apartment off-plan at a bargain price, are long gone. Realistically, you're not going to get much change out of €300,000 for a ready-to-use two- or three-bedroom family apartment. If you do decide to go prospecting for a second home while on holiday, there are plenty of estate agencies to help (mostly run by British expatriates who have moved out here themselves). Foreigners have the same legal property rights as Portuguese nationals, inheritance tax has recently been abolished and tax on house purchases has been reduced. Buying is straightforward provided you don't cut any legal corners. Use a licensed estate agent and deal only with a fully qualified lawyer. Never use a lawyer who is also acting for the seller. Just as in the UK, you must have a land registry search done to make sure the vendor has clear title, and you will also need:

- Numero de Contribuente (fiscal number). This is supplied by your local tax office for payment of rates.
- Caderneta Predial. This official tax document must be provided by the vendor. Make sure the description of the house matches the land registry description.
- Licenca de habitacão (habitation licence). Make sure the description on this matches the documents above.
- Contrato promessa (promissory contract). Includes all the terms and conditions of sale. You pay a 10% deposit when this is signed by you and the seller. If you later back out, you lose the deposit, but if the vendor pulls out he has to pay you double the deposit.

*Destination Algarve* magazine (£2.95 in newsagents in the UK) comes out six times a year with listings of thousands of apartments, villas, houses and plots for sale in the Algarve, so it's useful for pre-trip planning if you're hoping to buy.

shocked by Portimão's celebration of the sardine, which has grown into a week-long party in mid August (dates vary) where the sardine is honoured, praised and finally grilled (with the head on) and eaten.

The old town streets and waterfront are a family-friendly and mainly car-free setting for this happy street party every evening, with fireworks, live music, market stalls and many other attractions. For dates and event timings contact the Portimão tourist office or see *www.rtalgarve.pt*.

## August: Silves

**Silves Medieval Fair** This is one for the Dr Who fans in the family, when the Castle of the Moors and the old town of Silves are transported back to the Moorish Middle Ages.

Everybody dresses in Moorish costume, and musicians, dancers, knights and veiled damsels, snake-charmers, jugglers and jesters roam the streets and everyone can join in. For dates and event timings contact the Silves tourist information office or see *www.rtalgarve.pt*.

## June–October: Areias de Pêra

**FIESA giant sand sculpture competition** FIESA has to be the Algarve's top family fixture. Every year, 'sand artists' from all over the world descend on this stretch of beach near Albufeira to create a 'city' of gobsmacking, colossal wonders of the world, from gigantic idols and copies of famous statues to castles, dragons, temples and monsters.

There is a different theme each year. Everybody loves this one, and children are inspired to even greater sandcastle-building efforts of their own.

(📞 *00 351 969 459 261; www.pro sandart.com*). **Open** *daily 7th June–7th Oct, 10am–midnight.* **Admission**: *adults €7, 6–12s €4, under 5s free.*

## 14th August: Albufeira

**Festa da Ourada** The religious procession, which begins Albufeira's biggest summer festival, is as solemn as it gets around here, with local fisher folk heading for church to beseech the help of the Virgin Mary in her role as *Stella Maris* – the 'Star of the Sea' and protector of fishermen.

Things loosen up and become more tourist-accessible after mass at Albufeira's main church, with a procession of fishing boats, and reach a crescendo with a phenomenal fireworks display on the beach. Small children will find the crowds, the noise and the flash-bangs a bit much, and dads should be willing to carry children shoulder high so they can get a decent view of the pyrotechnics. For dates and event timings contact the Portimão tourist office or see *www.rtalgarve.pt*.

## Towns & Villages

**Albufeira** Albufeira was the first of the Algarve's fishing villages to explode into a full-blown tourist resort in the 1960s. It is now the largest holiday hot spot in the Algarve – and, indeed, in Portugal – but despite its hundreds of hotels, villas, apartment complexes, pubs, bars and restaurants it still remains true to its roots, with bright-painted fishing boats hauled up onto its golden sands and gnarled fishermen mending nets on the beach next to the series ranks of sun-loungers

# ALBUFEIRA

Rua Antero de Quental

N526

Rua Miguel Torga

Rua Camilo Castelo Branco

Rua Dunfermline

Rua Almeida Garrett

Avenida Infante Dom Henrique

Rua Vasco da Gama

**8**  **7**

**9**

Avenida Infante Dom Henrique

Rua Columbano

Bordalo Pinheiro

Rua do Município

**4**

Rua do Estádio

Rua do Atlantico

Rua Pedro Alvares Cabral

Rua Flórbela Espanca

Rua dos Bombeiros Voluntários

**5**

Rua Almirante Gago Coutinho

Estrada de Vale Pedras

Avenida dos Descobrimentos

Rua do Município

Rua Gil Vicente

Bairro dos Pescadores

Rua da Encosta

Rua do Marpique

Rua António Aleixo

Rua do MFA

Rua Alves Correia

Avenida 25 de Abril

Rua dos Caliços

Rua do Cerro

Rua da Bateria

Rua da Bateria

**6**

N395

**1**

**2**

**3**

N526

Rua Bernardino de Sousa

Av. da Liberdade

Rua 5 de Outbro

1/5 mi

0.2 km

0

0

SPAIN

PORTUGAL

Lisbon

Albufeira

**Accommodation** ■
Albufeira Camping **2**
Club Med da Balaia **8**
Vila Gale Cerro Alagua **5**

**Dining** ◆
Susan's Cabaret **7**
Tasca d'Alkhaz **3**

**Attractions** ●
Bella Vista Leisure Park **4**
Praia da Oura **9**
Praia dos Barcos **6**
Rock 'n' Bowl **1**

and beach umbrellas. The big selling point for many of the hundreds of thousands of Britons who come here every year is self-sufficiency – there's enough within shouting distance of Albufeira to keep the whole family occupied for a full fortnight, and most of it is likely to be within walking distance of your resort. To east and west, the beaches merge into 1 km-long strips of golden sand, getting less crowded as you get further from the centre of things.

Albufeira certainly isn't a sight-seeing destination, but it has chunks of history (such as Silves castle) and purpose-built visitor attractions (water parks and zoos) within easy reach, the beaches are conducive to enjoying your holiday, and it has managed its brand of cheap and cheerful tourism with considerable aplomb. The old-town streets are still clean, trim and charming, (even if every second building seems to be a souvenir store). Sophisticated it isn't, but for a family resort holiday staying here is a good option. Through the summer months, there's always something to see and do in the old town, with mimes, street artists and entertainers – including the inevitable troupe of Peruvian pan-pipe musicians wandering the cobbled streets and squares.

## Orientation

Just inland from Praia dos Barcos, also called 'Fishermen's Beach', Praça da República is the centre of the old part of town on the site of the medieval castle – there's hardly a trace of it left, but the little white Capela da Misericórdia on Rua Henrique Calado on one side of the square is the town's oldest building, dating from the 16th century.

Most of the old-town streets between Praça da República and Largo Engenheiro Duarte

Sandy Beach, Albufeira

## Living Statues

**Watch out for 'living statues' in the squares and gardens of central** Albufeira during the summer. Dressed as film stars, celebs, mythical characters or people from history, these actors stand motionless for minutes on end, with a mesmerizing effect on smaller children, who can't decide whether they are real people or not – until they suddenly move, which produces squeals and giggles from small spectators.

Pacheco are pedestrian only, though cobbles, café tables, and some steepish inclines can make them a tough proposition for baby buggy pushers. Extensive renovation work was being carried out in the old-town area in 2006–7. When complete, this pretty district will be even prettier, but it's hard to say when the job will finally be done – so bear in mind when planning a visit to Albufeira that parts of the centre may resemble a building site. East of town, Avenida Infante Dom Henrique, generally known to most visitors as 'The Strip' is a solid mass of restaurants, bars and souvenir shops leading all the way to the more modern resort of Praia da Oura. Vast suburbs of holiday apartments stretch a long way inland here – it's short of character but the beach is hard to beat and it certainly has plenty of user-friendly places to eat, drink and shop. Families with tots, though, will want to find accommodation well clear of this part of town, as its nightlife is legendary, raucous and goes on until dawn in summer. Albufeira's Marina Nova is 1.5 km from the old town centre, with moorings for more than 400 yachts and

cruisers, and a quayside lined with cafés, restaurants and shops painted in Miami art deco-style pastel pink, blue and green. Leaping dolphin statues painted in psychedelic rainbow colours line the harbour.

**Porches** Midway between Albufeira and Portimão, Porches has long since lost any real village identity of its own but is renowned for its beautiful ceramics – very much a cut above the cheap and cheerful bowls and plates exhibited by shops all along the N125 highway, which at times looks like one big pottery outlet shop. Olaria de Porches (see p. 108) uses high-quality paints and glazes to produce richly coloured and finely designed majolica ware.

**INSIDER TIP** ▷

In Albufeira, beware of timeshare touts who infest the town and can be very persistent when trying to sweet-talk you into attending one of their 'presentations'. Just say no.

**Silves** ★★ Silves is by far the prettiest town in the central Algarve and is steeped in fascinating history. Its red sandstone castle, the **Castelo dos Mouros**

(see p. 105), is a knockout. Its battlements and towers surround a hilltop above the town, looking out over red-tiled roofs and narrow cobbled streets. Silves also boasts a lovely 13th-century **Cathedral** and a **Museu Arqueologia** though there is nothing in either to captivate younger visitors. The arched bridge over the Arade river is around 800 years old. More exciting for children is a night at the **Fabrica do Ingles**, a former 19th-century cork-processing works that has been turned into a large indoor and outdoor entertainment venue with bars, six restaurants, coloured fountains, jugglers, clowns and street entertainers. The only downside to a family night out here is that the best part of the Aquavision spectacular, featuring fountains illuminated by coloured lasers, doesn't kick off until 11pm, which could mean tears before bedtime.

*Castelo dos Mouros, Silves (📞 00 351 282 445 624). Open daily 9am–5.30pm (until 7pm in summer). Admission: €1.25, under 11s free.*

*Fabrica do Ingles, Rua Gregorio Mascarenhas, Silves (📞 00 351 282 440 440; www.fabrica-do-ingles. pt). Admission: free until 6pm.*

**Lagoa** There is little reason to stop in Lagoa unless you have relatives among the large number of British expatriates who have bought houses in the surrounding area, where new-built villas and leisure complexes mingle with the vineyards of the Algarve's largest wine-producing area. The vineyards have been to some extent the saving of the Lagoa region, as the owners have been understandably unwilling to sell out their profitable land to property developers – unlike those who owned the unprofitable areas of scrubby sheep-grazing that have long since been ceded to tennis resorts and golf courses in neighbouring areas.

**INSIDER TIP** 〉

By all means sample the local red, white and rosé wines at the Lagoa Wine Cooperative, on the Portimão road, but don't expect to be wildly impressed. The emphasis around here has until recently been on quantity rather than quality.

**Portimão** The eye-catching scenery of Praia da Rocha, with its sandstone crags and creamy yellow sand, has made it a picture-postcard favourite since the 1930s, and Portimão owes its place on the tourism map almost entirely to this beach.

The heart of Portimão is the old town, a clutter of narrow streets stretching inland from the west bank of the Ribeira de Arade. The crescent of waterfront between Largo do Dique at the southern end up to Largo Francisco A. Mauricio at the north end, and the string of sardine restaurants on Cais da Lota, beyond the arches of the Ponte Velha road bridge is a pleasant enough place for children to hang out. The Jardim Manuel Bivar is a wide expanse of pedestrianised

# PORTIMAO

Lisbon

PORTUGAL

SPAIN

Portimao

Rio Arade

| 0 | | 200 yards |
| 0 | | 200 meters |

N

**Accommodation** ■
Boca do Rio Resort **1**
Hotel Bela Vista **10**
Le Meridien Penina **5**

Forte y Feio **3**
Meco a Flor Sardinha **2**
O Ancora **8**
Restaurant Dockside **7**

**Dining** ◆
Castelo **9**
Dona Barca **4**

**Attractions** ●
Praia da Rocha **6**

To inset
(1 mile)

Portimão Marina

river-front squares with pools and fountains, gardens shaded by palms, lots of outdoor cafés (several of which have euro-in-the-slot rides for young children) and – along the riverside – a parade of modern statues, some of which are likely to provoke rude sniggering from younger family members.

Praia da Rocha is undeniably one of the best-equipped and most attractive of the region's beaches, but it is no place for families after dark during the summer high season, when its esplanade tends to overflow with mobs of younger British and Irish visitors intent on drinking as many cheap happy-hour cocktails as possible.

**KID'S QUOTE** ❯❯

"We liked the headless naked lady and the giant seahorse, and the sardines were OK once you got used to the little bones."
*Fraser, age 7*

## Orientation

South of the town centre, there's a long, dull sweep of commercial docklands leading down to the mouth of the river, but the Estrada da Rocha bypasses this to lead you to Portimão's real tourism honeypot, Praia da Rocha, 3 km from the old town centre. Avenida Tomas Cabreira runs the full length of the beach and onward to Praia dos Três Castelos, an even longer and more spectacular strand that extends westward all the way to Alvor. A road bridge carries the N125 highway across the Ribeira de Arade, past an unpromising look-ing industrial stretch after which a side road to the right brings you to pretty Ferragudo, on a sandy creek lined with fishing boats.

**Ferragudo** ★ Although it's just a hop and a skip from Portimão and surrounded by the usual fringe of newly built villas, Ferragudo is one of the Algarve's

**Albufeira has a miniature road train that does the rounds of the town** and outlying resort suburbs every day from 8am until 1am. It's a great way of getting around, and a one-day unlimited journey pass costs just €3.00 for adults and €1.50 for children. It takes about 40 minutes to complete the circuit from the Strip to the old town, and travels in a clockwise direction, with departures every 20 minutes. There are only three stops: one at the Strip, one in the old town, and one midway.

surprisingly well-kept secrets. It's on a small creek on the east bank of the Arade estuary, facing the open sea. Painted fishing boats are hauled up on the scruffy beach opposite the village or moored on the creek, and the stretch of wasteland on the west side of the creek is an informal camp-ground for a motley international crew of motor-home dwellers, with battered hippy-surfer VW vans parked next to enormous motor-homes with all mod cons including satellite TV. Ferragudo's white-painted waterfront reminds some visitors of the Greek islands, and the village houses are smartly maintained, with red, blue and green doors and window shutters, pots of plants and red-tiled roofs. There are half a dozen family-friendly cafés with open-air tables on the pretty main square, and a miniature 17th-century castle – which is now an enviable private home – looks out over the harbour mouth. Beyond this is the western end of Praia Grande, and a string of other beaches that get less busy (and less family friendly, with few if any facilities for children) as you head east (see p. 94).

**São Bartolomeu de Messines**
This attractive market town in the foothills is a little bit (but not too far) off the beaten track and escapes most of the ever-present tourism of resorts and villages on and near the coast. It has the usual array of white-washed buildings and cobbled streets radiating from a central square and a baroque 16th-century church. Not mind-boggling exciting, but an attractive enough spot for a break on a self-drive tour of the hinterland, maybe followed by a picnic and a swim on the shores of the nearby Barragem do Arade (see p. 104).

**Alte** You'll read the claim that Alte is the prettiest village in the Algarve again and again in tourist board leaflets, guidebooks and holiday company brochures. If you repeat something often enough, most people will believe it, and judging by the vast numbers who disembark from their tour coaches here every morning in summer most of them do. To be fair, Alte is gorgeous, with its immaculate whitewashed cottages, pots of flowers everywhere, and caged songbirds on pretty balconies and terraces.

But it does get very crowded, and may be a bit overwhelming for toddlers and tedious for older children – particularly because in their terms there is nothing very exciting here and finding a seat at a café table is far from easy. Many people like to combine a trip to Loulé's famous 'Gypsy Market' (see p. 66, Faro chapter) with lunch in Alte, so on Saturdays the place is usually absolutely heaving.

> **INSIDER TIP** ❯
>
> To get away from the crowds and keep the children happy, follow the signs to the *fonte* (spring) – it's a five-minute walk from the village centre, beside a chuckling stream which is a cool and pretty spot for a family picnic. If you forgot to bring cold drinks, you can buy them in the village and chill them in the stream.

## Beaches & Resorts

Beaches are, above all, what the central Algarve is all about – and they are stunners, as well as being extremely family friendly. Water sports abound, most stretches are watched over by lifeguards in the summer months and have first-aid stations too. Sun-loungers and umbrellas are available to rent by the day and half day (some restaurants offer them free to patrons) – but you certainly need to get there early to bag one in July and August. The more popular beaches also have a plethora of summer kiosks selling ice creams, snacks and cold drinks.

For convenience, we have listed the main beaches of the central Algarve from east to west, starting at Falésia just west of Vilamoura and ending at Alvor. You're very much spoilt for choice along this fabulous stretch of coast, and families who are prepared to do a bit of exploring can find smaller, less crowded bays and coves. Many of these have car parks, and few are without at least one restaurant or café-bar, but not all have sun-loungers, umbrellas or lifeguards.

> **INSIDER TIP** ❯
>
> The website *www.travel-portugal.com* has a comprehensive list, with descriptions of facilities and pictures, of just about every sandy patch in the central Algarve.

**Falésia** At the eastern end of this stretch of coast – closer, in fact, to Vilamoura than Albufeira – Praia da Falésia is a 6 km length of sand. This is the perfect beach for families looking for room to breathe, as it is probably the least crowded of all the beaches in this part of the Algarve. There is parking space near the eastern end of the beach, but space is sometimes hard to find here, so try to arrive before the rush. Steps lead from the car park down to the beach, and they are quite steep, so toddlers will probably have to be carried (especially on the return journey). Near the foot of the stairs is a children's playground with swings and a seesaw, and next to this are several cheap and cheerful beach restaurants and a couple of water sports kiosks offering windsurfer and pedalo rental.

**Olhos d'Àgua** Olhos d'Àgua is one of the smaller, more pictur-esque beaches in the central Algarve. It's a small sandy bay between steep red cliffs. Behind the beach, pine trees offer some shade for summer picnics and there are restaurants within walk-ing distance. Older, more active children may get bored here, but it is one of the better choices for families with toddlers.

Olhos d'Àgua is about 8 km east of Albufeira, west of Falésia.

**Praia da Oura** At the east end of Albufeira's 'Strip', this is under-standably one of the most popu-lar – and therefore also one of the most crowded – beaches in the central Algarve. In high summer you can barely see the sand for sun-loungers and umbrellas. The beach is accessed by a steep hill from the Strip, which can make getting there a bit of an issue for baby buggies, and parking is also a nightmare from June to August. On the positive side, this is a friendly, well-serviced beach with lots of places to buy drinks, ice cream and snack lunches and a

particularly good range of water sports including parasailing, banana-boat rides, rubber-ring rides and jet-ski rental. Prices vary from year to year and season to season, often depending on how much competition there is, and there is no need to book – just turn up and go. That said, if you don't want to wait your turn for up to an hour, it's best to turn up early.

**Praia dos Barcos** ★ They don't come any more conveniently located than 'Fishermen's Beach' – it's right across the road from the Albufeira tourist office on Praça da República and there is a pedestrian tunnel, so you don't have to challenge the local traffic to get there. Praia dos Barcos is naturally very popular, but oddly enough it doesn't seem to get as overwhelmingly crowded as Praia da Oura – perhaps because not so many people stay right in the centre of Albufeira these days. Fishermen mending nets and tin-kering with boats and engines add a slice of real life here, and when the beach gets boring there are shops, cafés and restaurants just the other side of the tunnel, in the new town.

**TIP** ▶ **Beach Flags** ◀

**Blue flags (*bandeiras azuis*) fly proudly over many Algarve beaches to** show that their water, sands and facilities meet the highest cleanliness and safety standards. Other flags to watch out for:
Green flag: It's OK to swim
Yellow flag: No swimming
Red flag: Do not swim or go into the water
Chequered (blue and white) flag: No lifeguard on duty

Praia dos Barcos

### Praia de São Rafael ★

Heading west from Albufeira (about 6 km from Praia dos Barcos), São Rafael is pleasantly uncrowded compared with beaches closer to the core of the resort. There is a reason for this – it's not so easily accessible for smaller children, as it's reached by a somewhat steep and bumpy path off the coast road. To compensate, it has fantastic views, clean sand, and at least one small restaurant open in the summer months.

### Praia do Castelo

Praia do Castelo is around 8 km west of Albufeira. It's a pretty bay of fine yellow sand, and it is easily accessible, with a car park atop the cliffs a short walk from the beach, and a well-surfaced, buggy-friendly pathway leading to the sand. There's a restaurant between the car park and the beach. Both these assets mean it's popular with local week-enders from around Portimão

and Albufeira, as well as British holidaymakers, so don't expect to have much space to yourselves here in the high holiday season.

### Praia da Galé/Praia de Armação de Pêra

Praia da Galé has to be one of the top recommendations for families, combining the best of several worlds. It's separated from Praia do Castelo by a stretch of steep sandstone cliffs, and at the west end it merges with Praia Grande de Armação de Pêra and Praia do Salgado – they're marked on most maps as separate spots, but there's really no telling where one stops and the other begins. Together, the two beaches form a strip of soft sand and occasional rocky outcrops that stretches for almost 8 km, so there is plenty of space and plenty of parking, with car parking areas at both the Galé and Pêra ends. For families with smaller children, there is a demarcated swimming zone with life-guards and first aid station roughly midway between Galé and Armação de Pêra, and there are also waterskiing, windsurfing shacks located on this stretch. For cafés, restaurants, shops and more water sports, the Armação de Pêra end is the best bet. Praia de Pêra (Areias de Pêra) is also the venue for the fantastic International Sand Art Festival (FIESA) held every year from June to October, when sand sculptors create an amazing array of colossal wonders. For families, this is an absolute must (see p. 83)

### Carvoeiro and Carvalho

Carvoeiro is a small seaside village that has blossomed into a medium-sized resort with a choice of hotel, villa and apartment accommodation, and with sandy beaches both east and west of the town centre. Sadly, these are among the least family-friendly spots along this stretch of coast. Just east of town, Praia do Carvalho is teeny compared with other nearby strands – less than 100 metres long and hemmed in by sandstone cliffs – but has the advantage that you can drive right to the beach, through a road tunnel. The cliffs are honeycombed with small caves that were once used by smugglers to hide their contraband.

Carvoeiro's own beach is slightly larger – a full 200 metres long – but that isn't enough to stop it getting very overcrowded in July and August. On the plus side, it is accessible and has several beachside bars and cafés where mums and dads can take a break while keeping an eye on swimming and paddling offspring. Paraiso beach, a tiny bay just west of Carvoeiro, offers some refuge from the crowds in summer but steep steps leading to the sand make it hard for smaller children to get to, there are rocks that can easily stub an unwary toe at low tide, and at high tide the beach is reduced to a tiny patch of sand.

### Praia Grande de Ferragudo

More than one beach in the Algarve is dubbed 'Praia Grande'.

Carvoeiro

It just means 'Big Beach'. Ferragudo's version isn't, in fact, all that vast compared with some of the strands to east and west. This is a better spot for active teenagers than for smaller children. Despite a modern sea wall which protects it from the surf, it is quite exposed and windswept – which means it is also a favourite beach for windsurfing, and boards can be rented by the hour, day or half-day from at least one kiosk in the beach from June to September.

**Praia da Rocha** ★ Along with Lagos's Doña Ana, Praia da Rocha is one of the most photographed beaches in the Algarve. It's easy to see why it has captivated visitors since the 1930s, with looming sandstone promontories separating it into two long sandy crescents, natural rock arches and rocky outcrops that children love to scramble over. Arguably it was a lot prettier before the beach was dwarfed by the parade of high-rise hotels that tower along the cliff top, but nothing can spoil the view out to sea. Massive commercialisation has its upside, too – Praia da Rocha is probably the most family-friendly beach in the region, once you have negotiated the steep wooden stairs from the cliff-top to the beach. A well-maintained boardwalk stretches for its full length, making it easy to push a baby buggy, and every hundred yards or so along it there are concession cafés and restaurants housed in modern, quite stylish wooden

pavilions. They all have tables on decks outside. The beach shelves very gently and is not usually pounded by surf, and there are lifeguards on duty throughout the summer. It's not an 'away from it all' experience, but Praia da Rocha has a lot to recommend it.

**Praia do Vau** Locals will tell you that Praia do Vau, about 3 km west of Praia da Rocha, is the Algarve's answer to St Tropez – a jet-set haven where Portuguese celebs go to see and be seen. Unfortunately, you won't have heard of any of them (this is, after all, a country that imports its soaps from Brazil). The beach, however, is excellent and kept spotless, with calm warm water in a sheltered bay and plenty of beach kiosks and restaurants. One downside: it is very popular with Portuguese visitors, who hate to walk anywhere if they can drive, so finding a place to park is murder.

**Praia dos Três Irmãos** This wonderful beach starts a few kilometres west of Praia do Vau and stretches most of the way to Alvor – almost 16 km of gleaming golden sand, interspersed with rocky headlands that are pierced by natural tunnels and arches through the soft sandstone. There's great snorkelling around the rocks at low tide, the water is clear and blue, and there is a car park at the top of the beach road, about 11 km from Portimão and 4 km from Alvor. Below the car park is a beach restaurant, and this stretch of the beach also has lifeguards in summer.

**Alvor** ★ Portimão has spread all the way across the peninsula between the Arade and Alvor estuaries, engulfing Alvor in the process, so that what used to be a separate community has become virtually a suburb of its bigger neighbour. Never mind – this is still one of the best spots for families looking for a quiet holiday on a great beach, with plenty of activities nearby (see also the West Algarve chapter for fun family outings within a short distance of Alvor, including Lagos Zoo p. 132). It has, however, managed to hang on to its original fishing village identity, and it is fun to watch little fishing boats being unloaded at the quayside on the river. Some of the catch will be recognisable by British children, but they are likely to look at some other squirming specimens with horrified fascination. Octopus, anyone? There are several really good fish restaurants on the quayside (including the Fisherman's Rest and the Irish-owned Captain's Table) and the owners meet the boats to buy the pick of the catch.

The original village centre faces west, across the wide Ria de Alvor estuary, where you have a good chance of seeing storks, spoonbills, egrets and herons stalking across the sandbanks at low tide and where you can take the family on a canoe adventure upriver with a visit to a tropical palm grove and lunch on a desert

island. Most of the holiday accommodation, however, is along Praia do Alvor, 1 km south. This wide, 6-km long stretch of sand is great for families, with unchallenging shallow waters (though do beware of strong ebb-tide currents at the far western end of this beach, where the Ria de Alvor flows into the sea), lots of water sports including snorkelling and windsurfing, easy access and plenty of parking spaces.

## Water Parks & Theme Parks

The central Algarve has enough purpose-built visitor attractions to keep even the choosiest children happy, from parks designed with the youngest in mind to water parks with death-defying flumes that make even the boldest dad shake in his Speedos.

Most open in early April and close for the winter in mid to late October. All of them offer at least a couple of places to eat and drink, usually serving up snacks that will be familiar to British children, and most have picnic areas for families who prefer to bring their own packed lunch and drinks.

> **INSIDER TIP** ⟫
> All the Algarve's theme parks add new rides and attractions almost every summer so visit their websites for the latest developments and all-inclusive family offers.

**Slide and Splash** ★ **ALL AGES** If you only have enough time (or money) to visit one water park in the Algarve, it has to be Slide and Splash. It's the biggest, it's the best, and it has rides and slides for everyone. For under 10s, there is a children's area with its own mini-flumes and games and a pool with a maximum depth of 16 inches. Also for under 10s there are soft slides – including a multi-lane slide where they can race mum, dad or older siblings to the splashdown. For grown-ups and over 10s, there are more challenging adventures such as the Black Hole, a high-speed plunge in total darkness. Slide and Splash also has a full Olympic-sized pool for adults and teenagers who want to put in their full daily complement of lengths and with two full-service restaurants, three snack bars and an ice-cream parlour nobody is going to go hungry.

*Vale De Deus, Estombar, Lagoa ( 00 351 282 341 685; www.slidesplash. com). **Open** 2nd Apr–31st May and 22nd Sept–31st Oct 10am–5pm; 1st–30th June and 1st–21st Sept 10am–5.30pm; 1st July–31st Aug 10am–6pm. **Admission**: adults €17.50, children (5–10) €14.50, under 5s free. Add €5 for transfers from Albufeira and Portimão.*

## Aqualand ★ ALL AGES

Aqualand, at Alcantarilha (just inland from Armação de Pêra) has been around longer than any of its water-park rivals. It has a pool and play area especially for younger children, but is not too soft for daring older children or teens – the 92-metre Kamikaze is the longest speed chute in the Algarve, and the 23-metre

Banzai Boggan (Portugal's highest water slide) will take their breath away.

*Sítio das Areias, Apartado 11, Alcantarilha ( 00 351 282 320 230; www.aqualand.pt). **Open** 28th May–14th Sept 10am–6pm. **Admission**: adults €17.50, children (4–10) €14.50. Add €5 per person for bus transfers from Albufeira, €4 for transfers from Portimão or Carvoeiro.*

**INSIDER TIP**

All the parks listed offer coach transfers to and from resorts, with pick-up points at major hotels, so you don't need a car to enjoy them. Budget around €5 per person on top of the admission price for coach transfers to and from your resort. In high season there are often long queues for the most popular rides at all the water parks.

## Zoomarine ★ ALL AGES

Zoomarine, off the A22 motorway near Guia, seems to get rave reviews from everyone who visits, especially those who take the opportunity to swim with tame dolphins. This Dolphin Interaction experience lasts for 90 minutes (including time to change into your wetsuit) and allows groups of up to 12 to stroke and play with two dolphins in a large pool for half an hour. Other attractions include a dolphin show, when trainers lead the dolphins through a stunning series of leaps and tricks, and a 'Peter Pan' seal and sea lion show – though quite what sea lions have to do with Captain Hook and dancers dressed as Peter and

Zoomarine

Wendy remains a mystery. Tropical birds, eagles, crocodiles and sea turtles are among Zoomarine's other denizens and it also has three big lagoon pools – for adults, children and toddlers – a big wheel, flume ride and a mini-rollercoaster that isn't too terrifying for children and timid adults. Some eco-conscious parents may find Zoomarine's animal shows off-putting, but the attraction does at least try to polish its green credentials with assorted conservation and education efforts, including Portugal's first rehabilitation centre for sick, injured or lost sea creatures, where animals such as marine turtles and seals are nursed back to health before being released into the open sea.

*Km 65, Guia (☎ 00 351 289 560 306; www.zoomarine.com).* **Open** *Oct–Mar 10am–5pm, Apr–Sept 10am–7.30pm.* **Admission**: *Dolphin Interaction experience €135, DVD and book of five photos €25. Price includes two spectators per participant. Minimum age 8 years.*

### Krazy World, Algoz ★ ALL AGES

Krazy World (formerly Krazy Golf) can only be described as delightfully cheesy. For harassed parents, however, it's a bit of a godsend. There's a petting zoo, where children can meet llamas, wallabies, camels and deer, and ride miniature ponies (small enough even for the smallest hobbit in the family). There's an 18-hole mini-golf course through a fake Jurassic swamp where robot dinosaurs lunge out to put you well off your stroke. The Amazonia section of the park has alligators, Nile crocodiles and Burmese pythons (some geographical confusion there, as younger pedants will probably point out) and in summer there's what is billed as an 'exciting live show' in which an unfortunate young alligator gets pulled around by its tail. Children: don't try this at home. When they are tired of all that, there are pools with sun-loungers and umbrellas for exhausted parents, play areas with swings, seesaws and climbing frames, several bars and an unchallenging pizza and pasta restaurant. It may not be very environmentally correct, but it is very hard not to like this daft family-friendly attraction.

*Lagoa de Viseu, Algoz (☎ 00 351 282 574 134; www.krazyworld.com).* **Open** *Jan–June and Sept–Oct Wed–Sun 10am–6pm; July–Aug 10am–7.30pm.* **Admission**: *adults €9.50, under 14s €4.50.*

### Bella Vista Leisure Park ★

ALL AGES FIND This is one theme park where children under 12 are not an afterthought but the main audience. For the littlest people, there's a Fun Factory space – in fact two, one area for babies and tots under three years old and another for 4–11 year olds, with bouncy castles, ball pools, slides, baby changing rooms and a DVD library. Parents who want to catch up on their e-mail while the children are playing have free Internet access. For slightly older children, there's mini-golf and a mini quad-bike circuit (which costs extra, for 10 or 20 laps). Every Monday, Wednesday and Friday from 10am to 2pm there is a children's club with child-minders where parents can leave children under adult supervision and enjoy a few hours off. And if one of your offspring is celebrating a birthday on holiday, Bella Vista can even lay on a party. All you have to bring is the cake and the guests.

*Quinta da Bella Vista, Apartado 2101, Albufeira (☎ 00 351 289 570 064; www.bellavistaleisurepark.com).* **Open** *Mon–Sat 9am–6pm.* **Admission**: *€20.*

### Rock 'n' Bowl ALL AGES

This gleaming games centre is part of the Algarve Shopping complex between Albufeira and Guia, so you could combine it with a shopping splurge or a visit to Zoomarine, nearby. It has bowling – of course – but it also has an array of arcade games and X-Box favourites, including (as of April 2007) Forza Motorsport,™ Halo® 2, Project Gotham Racing 2, and Dead or Alive®: Ultimate. By the time you read this, they will almost certainly have rolled out a bunch of later-generation games. If you can tear the children away from the consoles, there's also good old-fashioned bowling in air-conditioned, hi-tech comfort, with bargain rates for family groups at weekends.

*Algarve Shopping 10A, N125, Guia (☎ 00 351 939 712 415; www.rock-bowl.com).* **Open** *daily 11am–11pm. Family bowling Sat and Sun 11am–2pm, €10 per hour for up to six people. Console games: one player €2.50 per hour, two players €4 per hour.*

## For Active Families

For water babies of all ages, and their parents, this part of the Algarve is holiday heaven.

Most of the family activities on offer are water-based, and all the main beaches have every water sport you could want in summer. There are too many jet-ski, waterski and surfboard rental shacks to list in this book. The best way to book these water sports is through your hotel, but you don't in fact have to book in advance – just turn up and go. If you are staying in or around Portimão or Alvor, there are also lots of boat trips and other activities starting from Lagos, which is just a few minutes' drive away, and even if you're staying as far east as Albufeira some of the Lagos-based trips may tempt you – it's only a half-hour drive from Albufeira to Lagos (see p. 124 for details of more Lagos-based activities).

### River Canoeing ★ AGES 11 AND UP

Messing about in boats is always fun, and this is a great river trip from Alvor – it starts with a quick lesson in how to paddle your own Canadian-style canoe (children under 10 share a boat with parents) then heads upriver for a visit to the biggest palm plantation in Portugal and a desert island picnic (for more information, see West Algarve chapter p. 138).

*Outdoor Tours, Alvor (☎ 00 351 916 736 226; www.outdoor-tours.net). Departures mid June–mid Sept 10am. Rest of year Fri and Sun 10am. Trip lasts three hours. Adults €22.50, under 10s accompanied by two adults €5.00. Lifejackets (for adults, children and babies), guide and support boat included.*

> **INSIDER TIP** >
> Bring swimsuits, flip-flops, sun-block, sun hats and plenty of water.

### Learn to Sail AGES 13 AND UP

You don't have to stay at the Boca do Rio Resort on the shores of the Arade to use its yacht club. It's an excellent choice for families with active teenagers who love water sports (powered and unpowered), with classes and individual coaching in dinghy sailing, waterskiing, wake-boarding, canoeing and kayaking. The Naval Club is one of Europe's leading centres for water sports coaching and is used by a number of Portuguese school and college teams.

Boats available include Optimist (perfect for young beginners), Laser, Laser Pico, 420 and Raquero.

*Boca do Rio resort, Mexilhoeira da Carregação, Estombar, Lagoa (☎ 00 351 282 402 500; www.bocadorio resort.com). Beginners' group dinghy sailing courses (for 6–9 year olds, separate courses for over 9s) €35. One-on-one courses start at €30 for 90 minutes. Dinghy rental starts at €10 per hour (free to hotel guests). Open 7.45am–sunset daily.*

## TIP > New Attractions

**Portimão will have several new attractions by 2009, including a** planetarium, an aquarium and a 3-km waterside parade of new restaurants, bars, shops and green spaces extending north of Ponte Velha and 'Sardine Row'. At least, that's the plan – in March 2007 the council was still trying to drum up €40 million from private investors to pay for the project.

# Scuba

## Scuba Diving: Indigo Divers

**AGES 16 AND UP** Scuba diving is a very big adventure, but for older children who are already confident swimmers it is a very safe and incredibly exciting experience. Indigo Divers is a PADI (Professional Association of Diving Instructors) registered operation. For beginners of all ages (minimum age 11 years old) there are 'Discover Scuba' courses lasting three hours, during which you learn how to use the equipment and breathe underwater in a swimming pool. Even in just a few feet of water this is magical. The next step up is a 'Discover Scuba Diving' course which includes mastering basic skills in the pool, then a shallow dive in the open water close to shore (with divemasters to hold your hand).

For qualified divers, the coastline of the Algarve offers some super dive sites, including overhangs and caves, wall dives, rocks and reefs and even the wreck of the *Ipimar*, which sank offshore in 1995 at a depth of 22–30 metres. There is plenty to see in depths of 10–20 metres – ideal for beginners and less experienced divers – and a profusion of marine life including octopus, crayfish, big conger eels, morays, trigger fish and lots of smaller sea creatures.

*Indigo Divers, Rua Alexandre Herculano 16, Areias de São João, Albufeira ( 00 351 289 587 013; www.indigo-divers.pt). Contact Indigo Divers direct for times of dive trips and PADI dive courses.*

**Angling** **AGES 13 AND UP** This is probably one for the boys, but there are black bass, carp and perch for the taking in the huge Barragem do Arade, near Silves, and other dams. The Portuguese aren't enthusiastic freshwater anglers, so the lake hasn't been depleted and there's a very good chance of a result. It's also a pretty picnic spot – so family members who can't understand the thrill of the chase can also enjoy a pleasant day out and a swim in the freshwater lake, and with a bit of luck you may even have an on-the-spot barbecue with your catch. Fresh water anglers do need a licence, which costs €6 at the town hall in Silves (bring your passport).

If your lads are more serious about fishing, local rod and line expert John Bate will arrange your licence, provide accurate maps of his favourite fishing spots, impart tips on the best times to fish and baits to use and brief you on the local fishing rules for €37. He also rents full sets of angling equipment (€74 per week) and leads guided fishing trips.

*John Bate, c/o Cero de S. Miguel, Lot 2 R-C ESQ 8300-033 Silves (☎ 00 351 282 343 261; www.tight lines-portugal.com). Contact John Bate direct for departure dates and times.*

## Sea Angling AGES 13 AND UP

Lagos is the main centre for blue-water fishing for shark, marlin and tuna – see West Algarve p. 137 for details.

## Jeep & Canoe Safaris ★★

AGES 11 AND UP Young adventurers love these open-top four-wheel-drive trips into the back of beyond. This is quite a demanding day out, though – both physically and in terms of the time you spend on the road – and not really for the under 10s, though all ages are welcome. For older children who love the outdoors, it's brill.

Portitours offers a whole range of mix-and-match trips, but the top of the line experience is a combination four-wheel-drive convoy, followed by a canoe trip on a calm, gentle river and an unchallenging walk

in the woods before lunch at a local restaurant. In the afternoon, there's another off-road drive, fording streams and bashing across rolling meadows, with time out for a swim in the river.

*Portitours, Edifício Portimar, Alto do Quintão, Portimão (☎ 00 351 282 470 063; www.portitours.pt).* **Admission**: *adults €47, children (5–11) half price, under 4s free. Contact Portitours for departure dates, times and details of pick-up points.*

## Cruises & Boat Trips

AGES 11 AND UP If you love the idea of seeing dolphins but don't want to see these beautiful wild things in captivity, think instead about meeting them in the wild. The narrow sea between the Algarve and Morocco is a natural highway for whales and dolphins migrating between the Mediterranean and the Atlantic, and several kinds of dolphin are often seen in the waters close inshore.

Several companies offer dolphin-spotting cruises from Portimão, Alvor and Lagos and some offer to give you your money back if you don't see at least one. Most advertise their trips as suitable for families – but in practice children under 10 may not like the experience of speeding around in a noisy open boat. These are really trips for older children.

## Dolphin Seafaris ★

AGES 10 AND UP Dolphin Seafaris claims its high-speed, high-tech rigid inflatable boats (the same as the ones used by Greenpeace and HM Coast Guard) are 'sea-sickness free'. They are certainly fast and as comfortable as an open boat can get (but they don't have toilet facilities, so go before you sail). There is seating reserved for families, lifejackets are provided for all ages and there is no minimum age (but this is not a lot of fun for under 10s). The 90-minute trip goes a fair way off shore, and with luck you may see basking sharks, whales and even orcas (killer whales) as well as dolphins. This is a real family adventure, and very memorable.

*Year round from Lagos Marina, Easter until end Oct from Portimão and Alvor. Seven departures daily (first sailing 8.30am, last 6pm) in high season from Marina de Portimão (Praia da Rocha), Lagos Marina and Alvor harbour (☎ 00 351 282 799 209; www.dolphinseafaris.com).* **Admission**: *adults €40, under 12s €30, under 5s free.*

## Sealife Ocean Safaris

`AGES 10 AND UP` Sealife boasts that it has a better than 90% success rate for spotting dolphins, with fast boats that cruise at up to 30 knots and a free ticket for a second trip if the dolphins don't show up. The day starts with a slow cruise down the river from Alvor or Portimão, then a high-speed search for dolphins in the open sea. The knowledgeable guides speak English and are clearly enthusiastic about their job. The trip lasts a maximum of two hours, depending on the weather and sea conditions, and weather-proof jackets are stored on the boat in case it gets wet and windy – which isn't likely but is possible even in summer. You can also charter a boat to go wherever you like (Morocco, they say, is not an option).

*Sealife Ocean Safaris, meeting point: Alvor (☎ 00 351 919 919 966); main office, Marina de Portimão (Praia da Rocha) (☎ 00 315 919 919 200; www.sealife.pt)* **Admission**: *adults €30, children (4–12) €15. Contact Sealife direct for departure dates and times which vary according to season and weather.*

Dolphin Spotting, Sealife Ocean Safaris

## Banana Boat Arade River Cruises ALL AGES

Vikings attacked the Algarve in the 8th century and rowed their long-ships up the Arade to besiege Silves. You can imitate them on a boat trip from Portimão, aboard a wooden Portuguese river boat.

The Banana Boat is a fun family day out aboard a Portuguese longboat (with an engine and a canopy to keep off the sun), starting at Portimão and going all the way up the Arade to Silves, where there is time for a visit to the castle. It's easy to see why Silves is no longer a river port – even this little vessel only just manages to avoid running aground on the very shallow river. On the way you sail beneath the suspension bridge and pause for a look at the shrine of Santo António (St Anthony) in a grotto beside the river.

*Arade Mar, Rua Serpa Pinto, 19, Portimão ( 00 351 282 419 998).*

## Cave & Coast Cruises ALL AGES

The *Santa Bernarda* is a 23-metre replica caravel sailing from Portimão on several different trips along the coast, including visits to the sea-caves of Carvoeiro and the dramatic rock formations and grottoes at Algar Seco. Cruises start and finish at the Cais Vasco da Gama quay on the Portimão waterfront, and last for 3–4 hours. There are toilets on board, and the price includes cold drinks.

*Santa Bernarda Cruzeiros, Rua Judice Fialho 11, Portimão ( 00 351 282 422 791; www.santa-bernarda. com). Departures at 9.45am and 2.15pm. Admission: adults €25, under 10s €15.*

## Bom Dia Sailing Trips & Dolphin Cruises ALL AGES

These wooden sailing boats, each with bar and toilet, sail twice a day from Lagos to Sagres (see p. 124) with great views of the coast and barbecue lunch or dinner. Bom Dia also runs dolphin-watching trips in RIBs (rigid inflatable boats, also known as 'rubber ducks') and guarantees that you'll see dolphins. Other fun things to do with these guys include family fishing trips, beach barbecues and grotto trips to the more scenic bits of the coast.

*Bom Dia ticket booth, Lagos Marina ( 00 351 282 764 670; www. algarve-dolphins.com and www. bomdia-boattrips.com). Departures hourly 9am–5pm. Admission: adults €40, children €20. No credit cards.*

## Beauty Spots

### Barragem do Arade FIND

This long artificial lake with its many

---

**FUN FACT**    **St Anthony**

**St Anthony is a popular saint in these parts, and a patron of pets and** families – he is traditionally in charge of blessing happy marriages. He started life as a swineherd, and when he became a hermit in the Egyptian desert he took the smallest of his pigs with him for company. In the English West Country, the smallest pig in a litter is still sometimes called a tantony pig.

**See the beaches, rivers and hills of the Algarve from the air on a** sightseeing flight from Portimão's small aerodrome. The shortest trip is a 25-minute hop over the Ria de Alvor to Praia da Luz and back, but there are eight different panoramic air-tours to choose from. Flights are in four- and five-seater light aircraft. Prices start at €125 per person, no child discounts.

*Aero Vip, Hanger 3, Aerodromo de Portimão (☎ 00 351 282 496 593; www.aerovip.pt).*

bays, created by damming the Arade river around 10 km east of Silves, is the biggest stretch of fresh water in the central Algarve. It's big enough for water sports, and pedaloes, canoes and jet skis can be rented in summer. It's safe and calm enough for children to swim, and a day here makes a nice change from the heat of the coast – it's just that little bit cooler up here and during the week it's a good deal less crowded, though picnic spots fill up with local families at weekends. The lake is also stocked with fish, including black bass, carp and perch.

**Algar Seco** This dramatic stretch of rocky coastline has been carved by thousands of years of wave action into a series of caves, grottoes and natural arches. Bolder grown-ups scramble across the rocky ledges and into some of the more accessible holes in this honeycomb of yellow sandstone, but this is certainly too risky for younger visitors. In any case, the best way to see Algar Seco is from the sea, and there are family-friendly scenic boat trips from nearby Armação and Carvoeiro to help you do so.

## Castles & Historic Buildings

**Silves** ★ **FIND** **ALL AGES** The Castelo dos Mouros (also known as the Castelo de Silves) is a marvel, and if you only visit one historic building on your holiday in the Algarve this has to be it. The castle is more than 1,000 years old – it was built by the Moors, who were driven out finally in 1249 by King Afonso III.

Toddlers may not be all that impressed, but older children will be – and all will need to be kept well in hand as the castle's walkways and parapets mostly lack guard rails. From below, the looming red sandstone battlements are truly intimidating. Put yourselves in the sandals of a medieval soldier ordered to scale these ramparts against defenders armed with bows, arrows, boiling oil and nasty sharp swords, and be afraid. It's no wonder the Vikings who rowed up the Arade in search of easy pickings in the 8th century just gave up and went home to Denmark (or, quite likely, Yorkshire, which was full of Viking freebooters in those days).

The Portuguese finally conquered this Moorish stronghold in the 13th century not by

TIP ## Watch the Skies

**Watch the skies over the Ria de Alvor for colourful parachutes –** Portimão's aerodrome, at Penina just south of the N125 highway, is very popular with sky-divers and at weekends you can often see them floating earthward from small planes.

storming its walls but by cutting off its water supply. The Moors surrendered, and the Christian Portuguese promptly slaughtered every man, woman and child within the walls.

Today, the pretty, sunny gardens within the huge ring of towers and battlements are filled with flowers and orange trees, but beneath them lie grim stone dungeons and a maze of tunnels where the last Moorish defenders of the castle were massacred. It's spooky down there.

(📞 00 351 282 445 6240). **Open** daily 9am–6pm, 15 July–15 Sept until 6.30pm, closed Mon. **Admission**: €1.25, under 5s free.

### Shopping

Albufeira is awash with shops supplying visiting families with everything from sunblock to swimwear and souvenirs, but it has to be admitted that this part of the Algarve is not rich in imaginative holiday shopping. Chunky cotton knitwear, woven baskets, wood carvings and painted pottery are the main stock in trade of most souvenir shops. There's a giant Algarve Shopping mall just outside Albufeira (on the way to Guia on the N125) with almost 100 shops on two levels, plus a Rock 'n' Bowl family entertainment

centre, an FNAC supermarket, a cinema showing the latest English-language blockbusters, restaurants and cafés. Algarve Shopping is open 9am to midnight. Albufeira's other big mall is Modelo, on Rua de Municipio about 500 metres north of the town centre, open from 10am–10pm. In the centre of Albufeira, Rua 5 de Outubro is the main shopping street.

At Portimão, an enormous open-air market takes place on Rua de Comércio, next to the railway station, on the first Monday of every month. Portimão's main shopping streets are Rua Comércio and Rua Vasco da Gama, both of which are traffic-free and crammed with shops selling cotton knits and porcelain that is advertised as hand-painted but that is mainly mass-produced.

At the end of 2006, the French Carrefour hypermarket chain opened its first Algarve branch at Vale Arrancada on the outskirts of Portimão. You can buy just about anything here, and it has a very wide range of baby foods and baby products, and a comprehensive pharmacy.

Portimão Retail Park Urbanização Vale Arrancada (📞 00 351 282 008 000; www.carrefour.pt). **Open** Mon–Fri 9am–10pm, Sat 9am–11pm, Sun and holidays 9am–1pm.

Souvenirs

Shops around the region that stand out from the run of the mill include:

**The Infante Dom Henrique House** Pretty painted ceramics from all over Portugal, woven baskets and carved wood.

*Rua Cândido do Reis, Albufeira 30 ( 00 351 289 513 267).*

**Apumanke** Attractive, imaginative silver jewellery and watches using turquoise, coral, opal, jet and other semi-precious stones.

*Rua 5 de Outubro 3, Albufeira ( 00 351 289 512 420).*

**Abracadabra** Pretty handcrafted jewellery and colourful hand-painted clothing.

*Rua 5 de Outubro 8 Albufeira ( 00 351 289 513 405).*

**Adega do Cantor** Buy your wine and take a tour of this winery near Guia, in which Sir Cliff Richard is a partner.

*Quinta do Miradouro.*

**Charles Jourdan** Mothers and daughters with a taste for flash footwear and accessories will find bags, purses and shoes here at around half the UK price.

*Rua do Comercio 33 Portimão; Av. Tomas Cabreira, Praia da Rocha.*

**Julie's 2nd Hand Books** Save money on holiday reading here, with a very wide choice of used books in English and in good condition, for children and adults.

*Rua Igreja Nova 6, Albufeira ( 00 351 965 129 482).*

**Papa Figo** This small family run shop (he's Scottish, she's Portuguese) in Alte makes and sells pretty, sweet-smelling soap using locally produced almond and olive oil, lavender, thyme, rosemary and other herbs and aromatics. Their soaps are kind and gentle enough even for sensitive baby skin.

*Rua da Fonte 11, Alte ( 00 351 962 069 140; www.papa-figo.com).*

**Olaria de Porches** For pottery that stands out from the masses of cheap and cheerful stuff sold all along the N125 highway, visit this pretty pottery, founded in 1962 by Irish potter and painter Patrick Swift, whose daughters Julie and Stella now run it. It also has a pleasant café terrace.
*EN 125 Porches*

**Olaria Pequena** Opposite Olaria de Porches, Scottish expat Ian Fitzpatrick makes boldly colourful pottery adorned with images of lemons, oranges and other fruit, and fish and other sea creatures. They are excellent value and as they are of better quality than the mass-produced stuff they are less likely to become chipped on the way home. (closed lunchtimes from 1pm to 3pm and Sundays).
*EN 125 Porches*

# FAMILY-FRIENDLY ACCOMMODATION

There is a bigger selection of accommodation in the central Algarve area than in any other part of the region. Options for families range from five-star hotels with lavish facilities to cheap and cheerful self-catering apartment complexes, luxury villas with private pools, converted farmhouses, family-run guesthouses and riverside campsites.

The two big accommodation clusters are around Albufeira and Portimão, with Albufeira offering a huge portfolio of cheap and cheerful accommodation while the beach resorts near Portimão are a little more upmarket.

## Albufeira

**INEXPENSIVE**

**Albufeira Camping** ★ There may be cheaper places to stay in the Albufeira area but they certainly won't come with the facilities that this campsite offers: a children's play park, three pools (one especially for children), on-site supermarket, car rental agency, restaurant, self-service café, tennis courts, bar and disco (though, happily, the noise is turned off at midnight). And you don't need a tent – there are comfortable mobile homes, each with its own patch of private garden, or wooden chalets with terraces. Both types of accommodation have air conditioning, TV and reasonably well-equipped kitchens (with basic gadgetry including blenders, microwaves and electric kettles as well as fridge and cooker). Bed linen and bath towels (changed weekly) are included. For families on a tight budget, this is a much better deal than some of the cheap and nasty older apartment blocks on Albufeira's Strip. You are, however, some distance from the beach as the site is located on the northern outskirts of Albufeira, around 1.6 km from the centre of town.

*Parque de Campismo de Albufeira, Estrada Ferreiras, Albufeira (📞 00 351 289 587 629; www.camping albufeira.net). Rates: two-bedroom mobile home (sleeping up to five people), from around €50 in Jan to*

## Renting a Villa

**The no-sweat way to plan a villa holiday is to book a package** including car hire and flights off the peg with a UK-based holiday company. Cosmos, for example (☎ *0871 622 4763*; *www.cosmosvillas.co.uk*), has a wide choice of affordable family-friendly properties and also offers cots and highchairs for a small extra charge, beach packs for children and free child places, with car hire included in the package. Cosmos also has villas for larger families (with 4–5 bedrooms) and for families and friends it also has villas next door to each other.

For a full list of specialist villa companies featuring the Algarve, see the Association of Independent Tour Operators website *www.aito.co.uk* or contact the Portuguese National Tourist Office in London. However, with cheap, Internet-bookable flights and car rental you may want to seek out your villa independently, even though this can be a more lengthy process, in which case the first place to look is in *Holiday Villas* magazine, which has dozens of villas and apartments to rent direct from the owners (£2.95; ☎ *01458 274447*; *www.villaseek.com*). There are also lots of Algarve villas available on the website *www.ownersdirect.co.uk.* Most of the owners are British, and are very knowledgeable about what to see and do in their area.

---

*€80 in Aug.* **Amenities**: *play area, children's pool, supermarket, restaurant, self-service café, tennis courts, bar and disco, car rental.* **In room**: *air conditioning, TV, kitchen with blender, microwave, electric kettle, fridge and cooker, bed linen and bath towels.*

**Hotel Bela Vista** ★★ Perched above Praia da Rocha – and dwarfed by the high-rises behind it – is a building that looks like the Addams Family's summer villa, all towers and turrets and arched windows. This is the Hotel Bela Vista. Built as a millionaire's home in 1916, it was turned into a hotel in 1934. Inside it's like the setting for a *Poirot* episode, with a winding staircase, grand lounge with baronial fireplace and lots of colourful *azulejo* tiles and crystal chandeliers. There's a rooftop terrace with great views, and although there is no pool, steps lead down to the hotel's own semi-private sandy cove. The Bela Vista is surrounded by its own palm gardens, and from July to September there's a tropical cocktail party every evening, with musicians. The whole scene could hardly be in greater contrast to the cheap-as-chips ambience of Praia da Rocha. But it's not a pompous place; children are made welcome and with just over a dozen rooms it sometimes feels more like an extended family house party than a hotel.

*Av. Tomas Cabreira, Praia da Rocha (☎ 00 351 282 450 480; www.hotelbelavista.net). 14 rooms.* **Rates**: *doubles €90–125, baby bed €5–10,* *extra bed €25–35.* **Amenities**: *roof terrace, palm garden, beach.* **In room**: *TV, fridge, telephone.*

Hotel Da Balaia

### Club Med Da Balaia ★★★

This big resort (almost 400 rooms) is really three hotels combined, sharing the same super facilities but with slightly different styles of accommodation (visit the website **www.clubmed.co.uk** for all the details). The Pyramide, a four-floor building with low-rise two-storey wings, is perhaps better for families than the high-rise La Tour or the six-storey Golf. The hotels are on a 21-hectare park overlooking the beach, with eight tennis courts, golf course, pitch and putt and three restaurants. What makes it stand head and shoulders above everywhere else in the Algarve, though, is its great range of services and facilities for families with children from age zero and up. The Club Med Baby Welcome service, included in the package price, includes baby cot, nappy-changing mat, baby bath, bottle-heater and high chair available in your room on request and babysitting service by arrangement as an extra. There's a dedicated baby restaurant, with jars of sweet and savoury baby food, utensils for preparing meals, high chairs and/or booster seats, and

the on-site shop stocks replacement baby care articles, toiletries, nappies and milk.

As part of the Baby Club Med service (an optional extra), instructors will take babies and toddlers off your hands for a day of gentle games, naps and educational activities. Petit Club Med is for toddlers from 2–3 years old, with one specially trained supervisor for every six children and big outdoor Happy Gym sessions, early learning sessions, pool activities and games. Meals are tailored to children's needs and instructors even take care of children during lunch, though you are welcome to join them. The fun even goes on in the evening, with family dinner at the Baby Restaurant accompanied by songs and story-telling until 9pm. Mini Club Med is for 4–11 year olds, with a similar level of supervision but with a bigger range of more adventurous activities. For grown-ups, older

**FUN FACT** ⟩ **Bela Vista** ⟨

**The Hotel Bela Vista is the oldest hotel in Portugal and has welcomed** such exiles as ex-King Umberto of Italy and Flugencio Batista, former dictator of Cuba, after he was ousted by Fidel Castro. Take a look in the visitor's book for the comments of other famous guests.

children and teens, there are pools, a fab beach with water sports and on-site activities, eight tennis courts, table tennis, golf, mini golf, achery, volleyball and *petanque* (bowls) all included in the package. Package prices also include all meals and some drinks, including a ration of wine or beer with lunch and dinner.

*Club Med da Balaia, Praia Maria Luisa Albufeira ( 00 351 289 510 500; www.clubmed.co.uk). 392 rooms and suites. **Rates**: prices for one week including flights from the UK start at around £450 per adult and £325 per child. **Amenities**: several pools, baby, toddlers' and children's clubs, water and land sports. **In room**: TV, air conditioning, safe.*

### Vila Galé Cerro Alagoa ★★

This hotel claims to be 'next to' Albufeira's Praia dos Pescadores. In fact, it's a good 700 metres from the beach. This can be forgiven in view of its two outdoor pools (one for children) and a heated indoor pool, choice of self-service buffet and à la carte restaurants, pool bar and the Dog and Duck pub. Renovation of the hotel, starting from the top down, was scheduled for completion in 2007 but make sure you ask for one of the new rooms – some work may still be continuing on the lower floors.

The buffet breakfasts are generous, with a big choice of fresh fruit (varying according to season, but including such treats as melon, pineapple, grapes, peaches and kiwi fruit) and several varieties of yoghurt. There's the usual platter of ham, sausage and cheese, along with buns,

pastries and croissants and if you insist on a cooked breakfast there's a hot buffet too, with scrambled eggs, sausages, beans, tomatoes and so on. Breakfast is served until 10.30am.

Children with British appetites may find the lure of the McDonald's and KFC outlets immediately opposite the hotel hard to resist. The lounge area has a large flatscreen TV (and the in-room TV has some British movie channels, evenings only) and a library of holiday paperbacks to borrow. The Dog and Duck, with its evening programme of bingo, karaoke, dancers and accordionist, may not be to everyone's taste, but it's friendly enough. Outdoors, the pool has an ample supply of sun-loungers and the grounds are well kept.

In theory, the hotel has a free shuttle bus to take you to the old town (a 10-minute walk) or to the Algarve Shopping mall. Reception staff seem oddly reluctant to publicise this service, but it is available on request.

*Rua do Municipio Albufeira ( 00 351 289 583 100; www.vilagale.pt). 310 rooms and suites. **Rates**: doubles from €60. **Amenities**: bar, restaurant, TV lounge, pool, shuttle bus. **In room**: TV, safe.*

## Portimão

**EXPENSIVE**

### Boca do Rio Resort ★★★

You wouldn't guess that this stylish resort and yacht club, on the Arade river midway between Portimão and Lagoa, used to be a sardine factory. This is not a

## Markets Calendar

**Supermarkets are handy for one-stop shopping in comfortingly** familiar surroundings, but every family should visit the local market at least once, if only to marvel at the range of things on sale, from fruit and vegetables to live chickens, ducks and rabbits, bread and cheese, textiles and household goods. The local flea markets can be a good laugh too, with local vendors (and expats) hopefully displaying complete junk as well as some real bargains.

Albufeira: 1st and 3rd Tuesday each month, flea market 3rd Saturday
Alcantarilha: 1st Friday each month, flea market 4th Sunday
Lagoa: 2nd Sunday each month
Portimão: 1st Monday each month, flea market 1st and 3rd Sunday

spot for tots, but for families with active teenagers who love water sports (powered and unpowered) it could be perfect. There are classes and coaching in sailing, waterskiing, wake-boarding, canoeing and kayaking, and the Naval Club has a reputation as one of Europe's leading centres for water sports coaching – it's used by a number of Portuguese school and college teams. Canoes, kayaks, yachts and motor cruisers are available for hire, and the hotel health club has a heated indoor pool to complement the outdoor one, so it's a true year-round resort, perfect for winter breaks.

It's also very Portuguese – British guests, for once, are in a minority, but the staff are attentive and speak good English. Rates include breakfast, which is lavish by anyone's standards, with eggs and hot breakfasts cooked to order as well as a spread of fresh yoghurt, fresh fruit and juices, cold cuts and cheeses. It's served from 7.45am until 11.30am,

which is perfect for parents whose offspring can't wait to hit the water – they can linger as long as they like. Or, if you prefer you can skip breakfast and opt for a buffet brunch between midday and 2.30pm instead.

The hotel's own catamaran shuttles guests up and down the river to Portimão and the beaches, and the deal also includes an hour's use of the tennis court and an hour's use of non-powered boats (dinghies, cats and canoes) every day. This certainly isn't the cheapest place in the area, but considering what you get for the money, it's a bargain for families with older children.

*Mexilhoeira da Carregação, Estombar, Lagoa (📞 00 351 282 402 500; www.bocadorioresort.com). 120 rooms. **Rates**: doubles from €100. **Amenities**: pool, sailing, water sports. **In room**: air conditioning, TV, safe, minibar.*

### Le Méridien Penina Golf Hotel
★★★ If you follow Chelsea, you might as well follow them all the way here. Chelsea (along with

many other top sides) have used Le Méridien Penina's FIFA-sized football field for winter training, and this really is a top-whack spot for sports-mad families. As well as the footie pitch, there's an 18-hole Championship Course, a 9-hole Academy Course and a 9-hole Resort Course, a Golf Academy, driving range, practice holes and putting greens. There are six floodlit tennis courts and a 3-km jogging circuit with 12 exercise stations for families who want to burn off flab or excess energy. Mountain bikes and an archery academy are also available (but cost extra). There's a free shuttle service to and from the beach all summer, and the hotel's own Beach Club offers windsurfing, sailing, pedaloes, waterskiing, sun-loungers, towel service and a restaurant.

Accommodation is also family friendly – there are family rooms for those with smaller children, but if yours are too grown up to want to share a room the Méridien also has interconnecting rooms so they can be out of sight but not entirely out of mind. The other huge family bonus is the Penguin Village for toddlers and under 10s, which has a safe adventure play area, swimming pool and slide and crèche. Film shows and a bouncy castle are further facilities for children.

*Penina, Portimão ( 00 351 282 420 200; www.starwoodhotels.com). (Penguin Village open Easter to 31st Oct and over Christmas 9.30am–6pm and during July and Aug 9.30am–9.00pm, seven days a week).* **Rates:** *doubles from €145; various special offers and seasonal discounts*

*available – see website.* **Amenities**: *football pitch, golf courses and driving range, tennis courts, jogging circuit, toddlers' village, play area.* **In room**: *minibar, TV, air conditioning, direct-dial telephone, Internet access.*

## Armação de Pêra

**MODERATE**

**Casa Bela Moura** FIND Staying with Christophe and Sofie is like staying with friends in a private home, with the advantage that they don't expect you to muck in and help with the washing up after dinner. Set in pretty gardens a good way from the highway (but still very easy to get to), Casa Bela Moura is half hotel, half villa, inland from the coast highway but only 1 km from the beach of Armação de Pêra (with its giant sand sculptures in summer). There are 14 rooms, all with air conditioning and TV with DVD player, so bring a stack of favourites or new releases. For families, a room in the main building has an adjoining children's room with twin beds and its own shower. A special self-catering suite overlooking the pool has a separate lounge which can sleep two more children, a large kitchenette, a modern bathroom with shower, hairdryer, individually controlled air conditioning in both rooms, TV and DVD player and a private terrace and separate parking space. There's a great buffet breakfast with fresh fruit and freshly squeezed juices and you can order your favourite sandwiches to be served by the pool around midday. In the afternoon, there's complimentary coffee or tea and home-baked cake. Sofie and Christophe seem to know everything there is to know about what to do and see in the area. They don't, however, offer babysitting or child-minding.

*Estrada de Porches 530, Alporchinhos, Porches (☎ 00 351 282 313 422;* www.casabelamoura.com*). 14 rooms. **Rates**: doubles €75–160, baby beds free on request, children under 18 in separate room €35–70; weekly rates including car hire available, see website. **Amenities**: pool. **In room**: air conditioning, TV, DVD player, one suite with mini-kitchen.*

## FAMILY-FRIENDLY DINING

Restaurants right on the beach are the best of all worlds for families, allowing parents to linger over coffee while impatient children can head straight back to the sand after lunch. The central Algarve has plenty of beach restaurants along the boardwalks of the most popular resort areas. There's a very wide choice of purpose-built eating places in slightly futuristic-looking wooden cabins on Portimão's spectacular Praia da Rocha (while along the clifftop esplanade above the beach you can take your pick of Italian, Chinese and Indian restaurants as well).

Portimão wins hands-down when it comes to fish and seafood restaurants, with a string of half a dozen modern establishments serving fresh-caught sardines at sunny outdoor tables on the quayside north of Largo Francisco A. Mauricio, and another batch of more old-fashioned fish restaurants tucked away under the arches behind Largo da Barca, next to the Ponte Velha road bridge that crosses the river. Alvor, like its bigger neighbour Portimão, offers a choice between authentic Portuguese eating – with a small parade of restaurants overlooking the river in the centre of the old part of town – and a bigger array of cheap and cheerful restaurants catering mainly to holiday visitors in the resort part of town overlooking the beaches.

Albufeira is even more of a Little Britain when it comes to eating and drinking. The roster of

---

**TIP ▶ Cover Prices ◀**

**In every authentic Algarve restaurant, you'll be served a basket of bread** and butter, plus some *pratinhos* (little plates of snacks) – olives, chunks of octopus, ham, sausage or cheese. The bread is part of the cover charge and is automatically added to the bill (typically about €0.75–1.50) but there is an extra charge for the other snacks. If you don't want them, you can politely refuse them – on the other hand, they are a good way of keeping children occupied until the main course arrives and introducing them to local flavours. Typically, you'll find a bowl of olives adds €0.75 to the bill, a small pot of sardine pate €1.50 and a plate of octopus chunks (yummy) €2.25.

British-style pub restaurants serving all-you-can-eat Sunday roasts, fish and chips, pizza and pasta is ever-changing, though there are some long-established stalwarts (some of which are listed below). In and around Albufeira, you'll also find pizza and pasta restaurants and Indian and Chinese eating places, and for families in self-catering accommodation there are plenty of restaurants that will deliver a family-sized pizza, curry dinner or Cantonese feast direct to your villa or apartment. And if all else fails, the tourist train shuttling between the town centre and the Strip stops right outside McDonald's.

Pick up the free *Algarve Gastronomic Guide* (*Guia Gastronomico*) from tourist offices for a list of places to eat near your accommodation.

## Portimão

INEXPENSIVE

**Restaurante Meco A Flor da Sardinha** ★★ Outside this cheerful open-air restaurant by the river there's a big painted sign showing the cheerful owner, Meco, wearing a traditional boatman's wide straw sombrero. "That's me, 20 years ago," he says, and that's his old wooden boat high and dry at the end of the Portimão's 'Sardine Row', tempting children to clamber over it. Meco started out with a simple quayside shack, grilling sardines that he caught himself and now has a full-scale restaurant with tables outside for family dining (under awnings to keep

the sun off) and a mouth-watering display of seafood, some of which is usually still squirming.

*Cais da Lota, Loja no. 1, Junto a Ponte Velha (☏ 00 351 282 424 862). Lunch or dinner from around €10–15. Credit cards accepted. Reservations not essential. **Open** daily midday–4pm and 8pm–midnight.*

**O Ancora** ★ This is one of the string of cheap and cheerful purpose-built concession snack bars and restaurants that stretches all the way along Praia da Rocha beach, connected by a buggy-friendly wooden boardwalk. If all you're looking for is a decent selection of well-priced, unchallenging snacks and cold drinks in or out of the sun, this is a good option at this end of Praia da Rocha (there are clean public toilets and changing rooms nearby).

*West end of Praia da Rocha beach. Small beer €1, sweet crêpes from €2.80, salads from €10, pizzas €4.50–8.20. No credit cards. Reservations not essential. **Open** 11.30am–11 pm.*

MODERATE

**Forte y Feio** ★★ 'Forte y Feio' means 'strong and ugly' – in the Algarve, they believe that if you aren't born handsome, providence makes up for it by making you strong. This restaurant is one of a bunch of eating places that are well hidden under the arches behind the old fish market, next to the Arade road bridge. It has tables outside (sheltered under an awning in case of rain) and in a large and busy inside dining room. This is quite a well-kept secret, and you are likely to be

Forte y Feio

outnumbered by local diners at lunchtime or in the evening. Select your sea bass, bream or huge grouper from trays of crushed ice (strategically placed by the door to lure you in), or choose your lobster from those living beneath the aquarium-style dining room floor. You can spend as little or as much as you want here – a plate of grilled sardines is just €4.50 and is a small enough portion to be child-manageable. At the other end of the scale, the rich seafood casserole for two costs €30 and the special *cataplana*, also for two, is €40. If you visit in spring, look out for the storks nesting on top of

the old brick factory chimney at the end of the street.

*Largo da Barca, Portimão ( 00 351 282 418 854). From €8 per head for lunch. Credit cards accepted. Reservations recommended for dinner.* **Open** *daily midday–4pm and 8pm–11pm.*

**Dona Barca** ★★ Just across the hidden courtyard opposite from Forte y Feio, Dona Barca has won awards for its excellent fresh seafood, including of course its famous sardines. Served simply grilled, they are delicious (and cheap). Older and more daring children can (as at Forte y Feio) select their own fish from a bed of crushed ice by the entrance and watch it being grilled by the chef on a big open-air stove.

*Largo da Barca, Portimão ( 00 351 282 418 216). From €10 per head for lunch. Credit cards accepted. No reservation required.* **Open** *for lunch and dinner.*

**Restaurante Dockside** ★★
Make sure you get a table on the wooden deck by the river so you can watch the yachts, cruisers and fishing boats come and go while you eat. Dockside offers a children's menu and a good selection of snacks, but it doesn't fall over backwards to cater to British

**FUN FACT** ▶ **Oranges & Lemons** ◀

**Look out for farmers selling oranges and lemons by the roadside –** you'll be doing them a favour if you stop and buy some, because European Commission rules insist that fruit must be graded for size and quality to be sold in supermarkets. Unfortunately for many Algarvean citrus growers, their plots are too small for the grading scheme, so they have to sell their sweet juicy fruit to passers-by.

**The Algarve's fastest-selling wine is made by Sir Cliff Richard and fellow** Britons, Nigel and Lesley Birch and their son Max, on their family farm at Quinta do Miradouro, near Guia. They now make more than 180,000 bottles a year of their red, white and rosé Vida Nova wine – and when the first vintage was released in 2001 Tesco sold 500 cases online in 24 hours, setting a record for selling wine over the Internet.

tastes – the children's menu starts with cream of vegetable soup, followed by a choice of chicken and chips, fish and chips, Peruvian-style beef with rice or spaghetti Bolognese. *Pratinhos* ('little plates') include octopus salad, egg salad, grilled chicken and the famous Serpa cheese. If all of these are too challenging, Dockside also has a good selection of toasted sandwiches which should hit the spot.

*Marina de Portimão (☎ 00 351 282 417 268; www.restaurante dockside.com). From around €20 for a full meal, snacks from €5. Credit cards accepted. Reservations not essential. Open daily midday–4pm and 8pm–11pm.*

## Albufeira

**INEXPENSIVE**

**Tasca d'Alkhaz** ★ It's not exactly the most peaceful place on the planet, but this amiable sports bar does its best to please everyone with children's 'happy meals', English breakfasts and Sunday roasts, jacket potatoes, steak and kidney pie, kebabs, steaks, pizza and pasta as well as Algarvean dishes such as *cataplana*. For the sports fans in the family, there are two giant screens and two TV screens.

*Rua 5 de Outubro 37, Albufeira (☎ 00 351 289 514 793). English breakfast €8, Sunday roasts from €10–15. No credit cards. No reservations required. Open all day.*

### Susan's Cabaret Restaurant
★★ Yes, this is a rip-roaring, yee-ha fun night out for all the family, with country and western singers, Portuguese guitars, Moroccan belly dancers and statuesque showgirls. It's also great value for money. Three times a week there is a traditional all-you-can-eat English carvery offering at least three roasts from a rotating menu of lamb, ham, beef, pork and turkey, with all the trimmings. The rest of the time there's an à la carte menu, and a children's menu that should find favour with even the pickiest British appetites. Susan's is also open for breakfast.

*Hotel Oura Praia, 3 Trees Roundabout, Oura, Albufeira (☎ 00351 289 590 455; www.susanscabaretrestaurant. com). Traditional English carvery Sun, Wed and Fri evenings, €9.95 per person. Credit cards accepted. Reservations recommended. Open daily 9am until after midnight.*

**VERY EXPENSIVE**

**Hotel Vila Joya** ★★★ Two Michelin stars. Leave the children

# Red Green Wine

**'Red green wine' – what's that about? Although it comes from the north,** most Algarve restaurants sell *vinho verde* and a very refreshing summer drink it is, with an alcohol content of only 9%. It's a white wine, called 'green wine' because it's drunk 'young' – almost immediately after bottling – and it's mildly fizzy. In some restaurants you might even find *'vinho verde tinto'* or 'red green wine' – similarly fizzy and low in alcohol, but made from black grapes.

behind but remember to bring your credit card (preferably platinum) for a night at the Vila Joya's marvellous restaurant. Austrian chef Dieter Koschina runs the only restaurant in Portugal which has two Michelin stars. Koschina sources the finest ingredients – such as lobster, crayfish and turbot – from local markets and imports truffles, goose liver and caviar for superb combinations. From time to time, he also invites guest chefs from other Michelin-starred establishments around Europe to show their culinary skills here.

Vila Joya

*Praia da Galé, Apartado 1202, Albufeira (📞 00 351 289 591 795; www.vilajoya.com). Credit cards accepted. Reservations essential.* **Open** *8pm–midnight, closed Mon.*

## Guia

**INEXPENSIVE**

**Restaurante Ramires** ★ Jose Carlos Ramires is to the Algarve what Colonel Saunders is to Kentucky – he's the chicken king. Senhor Ramires served up his first grilled *piri piri* chicken in Guia in 1964 and the family are still hard at it. This is a great place to come for lunch or an early dinner after a day at Zoomarine or the other nearby fun parks, and the food is family friendly – simply grilled chicken, pork, chops, veal or fish, and this is also a good place to sample that Portuguese favourite, *bacalhao* (salt cod). The surroundings are clean, simple and unpompous – this is very much a place where Portuguese families come for a relaxed meal, and it makes a change from the quite formal atmosphere of many Algarve restaurants.

*Rua 25 de Abril 14, Guia (📞 00 351 289 561 232; www.frango-da-guia. com). Tourist menu (soup, choice of grilled chicken or fish) €10. No credit cards. No reservations required.* **Open** *daily midday–11pm.*

# 5  The West

# SOUTH WEST ALGARVE

Map of the South West Algarve region showing locations including: Vila Nova de Milfontes, Ourique, Odemira, Zambujeira do Mar, Aljezur, Monchique, Caldas de Monchique, Bordeira, Carrapateira, Silves, Portimao, Lagoa, Albufeira, Lagos, Luz, Burgau, D. Ana, Três Irmãos, Praia de Rocha, Pintadinho, Carvoeiro, Armação de Pêra, Galé, Oura, Vila do Bispo, S. Vicente, Martinhal, Baleeira, Mareta, Sagres. Inset map shows Portugal with Lisbon and Spain, marking the area of detail. Serra doe Espinhaço de Cão, Serra de Monchique, Rio Mira, Ribeiro de Odelouca. Roads: N390, N393, N120, N123, N263, N266, N264, N267, N268, N124, N125, A22, IC1, IP2, E01.

If your family includes teenagers or older children who love animals, the sea, wild landscapes and the great outdoors and have a
taste for excitement, this wild western shore of the Algarve is positively,
definitely for you. Equally, if you have tots and toddlers and want to
avoid the fish-and-chips ambience found in some of the spots of
Albufeira and Quarteira – go west. Lagos, and the beach resorts around
it, are a happy compromise between the two, but west of here full-scale
tourism development quickly peters out and you won't find the huge
villa resorts, landscaped golf courses and high-rise hotels that dominate
the central region. For active families, this is heaven, with everything
from surfing to shark fishing, parascending, scuba diving and dolphin
watching.

This western region of Portugal stretches from the big coastal lagoon of the Ria de Alvor in the east to Cabo de São Vicente – the southwest tip of mainland Europe – and the windswept reaches of the true Atlantic coast. Along the south coast, a chain of smaller resorts lies between Lagos – the only big town and the only really big and bustling resort in the region, with some excellent beaches on its doorstep – and the fishing port of Sagres.

Luz, which is almost a suburb of Lagos, is the only one of these that we can genuinely call family friendly – the rest, including Burgau and Salema, are small, fairly low-key spots with no outstanding places to stay or eat, few if any facilities for children, and beaches that are hemmed in by steep cliffs and often subject to surf that makes them less than toddler friendly.

Next to the Algarve's westernmost point, Sagres is a pleasantly ramshackle fishing port and low-key tourism resort, with an impressive clifftop fortress, surf beaches beneath steep cliffs, and a harbour full of brightly painted little trawlers. It mainly attracts two kinds of holidaymaker – dedicated surfers whose camper vans cram the car parks for much of the year as they wait for the best waves, and flocks of northern European retirees who arrive each winter in convoys of fully loaded motor homes, complete with luxuries such as satellite TV, to avoid the cold winters of Germany, the Netherlands and the UK. That said, it's a pleasant enough place for a quiet family holiday, with an excellent beach and a decent choice of places to stay and eat – and the sunsets are hard to beat.

North of Sagres and Cabo de São Vicente, the coast turns wild and empty, with long stretches of sand which remain (as yet) undeveloped, in huge contrast to the overwhelming tourism presence of the Algarve's south coast. This is a great part of the world for self-sufficient families who are happy with self-catering, beachcombing on huge uncrowded stretches of sand, sandcastle building, surfing, walking and exploring, but if you want lots of organised activities, purpose-built visitor attractions, hotels with pools and all the trimmings of a full-service resort, stick to the south coast.

Inland, the small market town of Monchique nestles on a hillside overlooking the wooded slopes and valleys of the Serra de Monchique, a region known for its cork oak plantations and hills covered in red-berried arbutus bushes, from the fruit of which the locals make the fierce spirit known as *medronho*.

# ESSENTIALS

## Getting There

**By Road** Lagos is around 80 km by road from Faro via the A22 motorway (which ends just north of Lagos at Bensafrim) or the slower N125, which continues west from Lagos to Sagres, 113 km from Faro. The N120 highway heads northwest from Lagos to Aljezur, and the N268 connects Sagres (via Vila do Bispo) with Carrapateira, Aljezur and points north along the west coast.

**By Rail** Lagos is the western end of the Algarve regional railway line, which connects Lagos with Portimão, Albufeira and Loulé on the way to Faro and carries on to Tavira and Vila Real de Santo António on the Spanish border.

# VISITOR INFORMATION

**Lagos Tourist Office** Rotunda Rossio de São Gonçalo, Rua Vasco da Gama, Lagos (📞 00 351 282 763 031; E: turismo.lagos@ rtalgarve.pt)

**Sagres Tourist Office** Rua Comandante Matoso (📞 00 351 282 624 873; E: turismo.sagres@ rtalgarve.pt)

**Aljezur Tourist Office** Largo de Mercado (📞 00 351 282 998 229; E: turismo.aljezur@rtalgarve.pt)

**Monchique Tourist Office** Largo São Sebastião: (📞 00 351 282 911 189; E: turismo.monchique@ rtalgarve.pt)

**INSIDER TIP**

The Lagos tourism information office is inconveniently located for those without wheels – it's a long way from the historic centre and the beaches, just south of the roundabout where the N120 leads you into town from the motorway. If you are driving, stop here on the way into town to pick up any information you need.

## Getting Around

If all your family wants is a holiday on one of the beaches near Lagos, with the occasional jaunt into town, boat trip, or a day at the zoo or a water park, it is perfectly possible to manage without a rented car. All package holiday companies include coach transfers from Faro airport to your accommodation as part of the deal. For those who are travelling independently, most larger hotels can arrange minibus or taxi transfers. For family outings, most of the purpose-built visitor attractions in the area (and further afield in the central Algarve) offer coach or minibus transfers from your hotel. That said, the cost of a taxi to and from the airport is not much less than a week's car rental, so for shorter stays there is no big saving.

If you plan to head west of Lagos, there is really no alternative to hiring a car from Faro airport. There are local buses, but they are geared to the needs of local schoolchildren, workers and shoppers so they tend to operate at times that do not suit holidaymakers. Don't even think about trying to drive in the narrow streets of Lagos's old quarter – there are plenty of car parks on the outskirts of the old town and along the waterfront. By British standards, car parking is cheap (around €0.50 per hour) but make sure you have some change for the ticket machine before you set off for a day's exploring.

# WHAT TO SEE & DO

## Top Family Attractions

❶ **Meia Praia Beach, Lagos** Meia Praia is one of the Algarve's best family beaches, with good facilities and miles of sand with space for everyone (see p. 131).

❷ **Lagos Zoo** Furry lemurs, tightrope-walking monkeys, funky gibbons and baby wallabies (see p. 132).

❸ **Forte de Ponte da Bandeira** This miniature castle is good for playing pirates (see p. 135).

❹ **Carrapateira Beach** This huge, shallow bay must be one of the most amazing patches of white sand beach in Europe and is a favourite with surfers – including absolute beginners as well as experts (see p. 129).

❺ **Fortaleza de Sagres** Death-defying local fishermen cast their lines from the awesome cliffs that surround this impressive fortress from which many of Portugal's 15th- and 16th-century explorers began their long voyages of discovery (see p. 133).

## Family-friendly Trips

**Aquabus** ALL AGES Although it's advertised as a 'submarine' the Aquabus doesn't really plunge into the depths – it's a glorified glass-bottom boat, with windows below the waterline that allow passengers to watch the undersea world going by without getting their feet wet.

*Marina de Lagos (📞 00 351 282 767 794). Daily trips from Lagos to Salema or to the grottoes of Ponta da Piedade. Up to six departures daily: 9am–5pm Mon–Sat, Apr–Oct.* **Admission:** *adults €15, under 10s €7.50, under 4s free.*

### Caravel Boa Esperança

AGES 2 AND UP A visit to the *Boa Esperança*, which is usually moored outside Lagos Marina, is an eye-opener for grown-ups as well as children. This wooden sailing ship is a faithful replica of the caravels that in the 15th century carried Portuguese explorers such as Vasco da Gama and Bartolomeu Dias across the Atlantic to Brazil and round Africa and the Indian Ocean to India and China. What really strikes you is just how little it is – just 23.8 metres long. That's smaller than many of the modern yachts in the marina. The *Boa Esperança* is owned by the local councils, and sails up and down the coast – and in 2003 she sailed all the way to London. The caravel does not make regular cruises – and only has room for 22 people – but if this is your kind of thing contact the

# Slave Market

**A plaque in one corner of Lagos's Praça da República is a reminder** of the dark side of Portugal's overseas empire, which by the 18th century stretched from Brazil to southern Africa, Goa, Timor and Macau. This was the site of the first slave market in western Europe, begun in 1444. The Marques de Pombal freed Portuguese slaves in 1773 – a full 34 years before the slave trade was banned in Britain.

Algarve Regional Tourist Board to put your name on the waiting list for the next trip. To take a trip on the *Boa Esperança*, you have to contact the tourist board (by e-mail, fax or in writing) with the names of your party, asking to be placed on the waiting list for the next departure. After that, it's just the luck of the draw, and there may not be a trip leaving at a date to suit your family. Just cross your fingers and hope for the best. Prices and the length of the trip vary, starting at €40.

*Embarcadero de Recepción, Marina de Lagos. Region de Turismo Del Algarve (☎ 00 351 289 800 400; www.rtalgarve.pt).*

**Bom Dia Cruises** ALL AGES Bom Dia has two traditional-style wooden sailing boats, each with bar and toilet on board, and makes two trips a day (half-day excursions or sunset cruises) from Lagos to Sagres with great views of the coast and barbecue lunch or dinner.

*Bom Dia ticket booth, Lagos Marina (☎ 00 351 282 764 670; www.bomdia.info). Departures hourly 9am–5pm. Admission: adults €40, children €20. No credit cards.*

## Towns & Cities

**Lagos** Lagos (say 'lah – goash'), like Faro and Portimão, shows all the signs of having grown up in a hurry, with an ungainly spread of new suburbs and apartments sprawling around the old town centre.

Lagos's old town is pleasant enough for wandering and a bit of shopping. It's short of big-ticket attractions, but look out for the bizarre, twice-life-sized modern statue of the boy-king Dom Sebastião on Praça Gil Eames. Close to the mouth of the river, on the west bank, the small Forte de Ponte da Bandeira looks like a toy castle with its miniature turrets looking out to sea. 100 metres further on, Praia da Batata, hemmed in by cliffs but with sheltered shallow water and plenty of sand, is the place to combine a swim, a paddle or a picnic with a morning in town.

### Orientation

The old town lies on the west bank of the river, surrounded by the ever-growing modern part of the city. Across the river lie the marina, full of smart yachts and

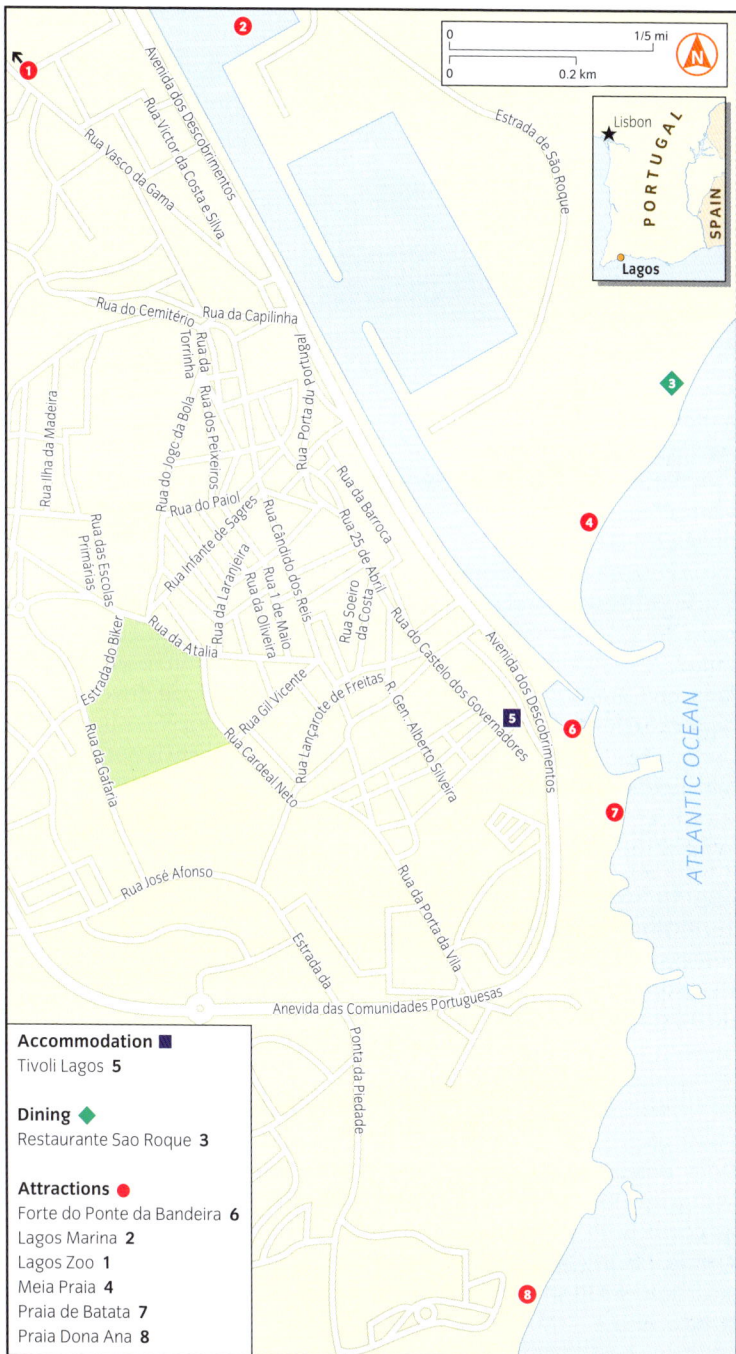

# LAGOS

Estrada de São Roque

Lisbon ★

PORTUGAL

SPAIN

Lagos

Avenida dos Descobrimentos

Rua Victor da Costa e Silva

Rua Vasco da Gama

Rua do Cemitério

Rua da Capilinha

Rua da Torrinha

Rua da Boa do João da Vegra

Rua dos Peixeiros

Rua Porta de Portugal

Rua Ilha da Madeira

Rua do Paiol

Rua das Escolas Primárias

Rua Infante de Sagres

Rua da Laranjeira

Rua Cândido dos Reis

Rua 1 de Maio

Rua da Oliveira

Rua da Barroca

Rua 25 de Abril

Rua do Sogeiro

Rua da Costa

Rua do Castelo dos Governadores

Avenida dos Descobrimentos

Rua da Atalaia

Estrada do Biker

Rua Gil Vicente

Rua Lançarote de Freitas

R. Gen. Alberto Silveira

Rua da Galeria

Rua Cardeal Neto

Rua José Afonso

Rua da Porta da Vila

Estrada da

Anevida das Comunidades Portuguesas

Ponta da Piedade

ATLANTIC OCEAN

**Accommodation** ■
Tivoli Lagos **5**

**Dining** ◆
Restaurante Sao Roque **3**

**Attractions** ●
Forte do Ponte da Bandeira **6**
Lagos Marina **2**
Lagos Zoo **1**
Meia Praia **4**
Praia de Batata **7**
Praia Dona Ana **8**

Fishing at Lagos

motor cruisers, and the commercial fishing harbour. Avenida dos Descobrimentos follows the west bank all the way into town from the A22/ N120 and carries on all the way south to the beginning of a string of beaches and resort suburbs: Praia de Batata, Praia do Pinhão, Praia Dona Ana and Praia do Camilo. Even better and bigger beaches can be seen across the river, where Meia Praia begins just beyond the breakwater and stretches off into the distance as far as the eye can see.

**Sagres** Sagres, close to the tip of a windswept peninsula that comes to a bleak point at nearby Cabo de São Vicente, isn't the prettiest of spots. It owes its existence to a sheltered harbour close to rich fishing grounds, and to a superb natural fortress that Prince Henry the Navigator made into the first base for the voyages of exploration that he sponsored in the 15th and 16th centuries. For some people, Sagres is idyllic. For others, it's boring. Once you've seen the historic Fortaleza and driven out to Cabo de São Vicente's lighthouse for the view there is nothing to do except go to the beach, play in the surf and in the evening go to one of the town's modest cafés or restaurants. Sagres is a good spot for teenagers, who enjoy its surfie buzz, and active older children. Those with babies and toddlers in tow may find the trek up and down steep hills to its

FUN FACT » **Dom Sebastião** «

**Dom Sebastião was only eight years old when he inherited the** Portuguese throne in 1557, so his mum ruled the country as regent until he was old enough to be crowned king in 1568. He made Lagos the capital of the Algarve, but things all went horribly wrong when he invaded Morocco with a great fleet of 400 ships in 1578. He was killed, and his army defeated, at the battle of Alcacer-Quebir.

# SAGRES

**Accommodation** ■
Nomad Surfers **4**
Pousada do Infante **7**

**Dining** ◆
Dromedario **3**
Pousada do Infante **8**
Raposo **5**

**Attractions** ●
Cabo de Sao Vicente **1**
Fortaleza de Sagres **9**
Praia de Mareta **6**
Praia de Martinhal **2**

Information ⓘ

PORTUGAL
SPAIN
Lisbon
Sagres

Ponta de Baleeira

Rua das Naus
Rua Jaime Conde
Rua Patrão António Faustino
Rua D. Sebastião
Rua da Mareta
Rua Comandante Matosos
Rua do Mercado
Rua das Cercas
Rua da Nossa Senhora da Graça
Rua de São Vicente
Rua da Fortaleza
Rua da Torral
N268
N268

ATLANTIC OCEAN

1/5 mi
0.2 km

beaches a bit tiring and should look for a place to stay at Martinhal, on the outskirts of town, right next to a good, uncrowded sandy beach.

## Orientation

Don't go to Sagres expecting to find a picturesque village of old-fashioned fishermen's cottages around a picturesque harbour. Although it hasn't been swamped by big hotels, this is a mainly modern small town of workaday homes, scattered over a wide area and without much in the way of a real focal point. Most shops and other facilities are strung out along Avenida Comandante Matoso, the main drag through the centre of town. The fishing port, with its covered fish market, is beyond the end of this thoroughfare, some distance from the town itself. At the other end of Avenida Comandante Matoso, Praça da República is where you'll find the main collection of modest bars, cafés and restaurants.

Sagres's original top-whack hotel, the Pousada do Infante, stands by itself, looking out to sea from the cliffs at the east end of Praia da Mareta, the most accessible beach, where you can rent pedaloes in summer and which has at least one family-friendly café bar and a slightly more formal restaurant. Off to the west is a long finger of land where sheer cliffs rise straight out of the sea, making it a perfect natural fortress. To complete its natural defences, a line of whitewashed battlements bars the narrow neck of land that connects it with the mainland.

**Aljezur** FIND This little riverside town is, let's face it, a bit of a nowheresville. But it's also a very pleasant, uncommercialised place for a stretch-your-legs stop or for lunch or a drink on the way between Sagres and the Monchique hills. And let's face it, everybody has to go to the loo sometime. There's plenty of places to park (free) and there's a very pleasant, sunny little café

Monchique Kid

(with resident child) away from most of the traffic on Largo da Liberdade, beside the Pont a Pé which crosses the Ribeiro do Aljezur. This little footbridge is perfect for a game of Pooh Sticks. On a hilltop just above the village (a steep walk for little legs) is the dinky little 10th-century **Castelo** – it's no more than a small ring of battlements and a little keep, but it is free and there are super views across the fields and farms to the Serra de Monchique.

### Monchique **OVERRATED**

Monchique, high in the hills, is less a destination, more of a lunch stop on a drive through the wooded hills of the Serra de Monchique which surround it. It is an unassuming small town (though there's a big livestock fair on the third Friday of each month, when the place is awash with sheep, goats, donkeys, pigs and cattle) that is best known for the panoramic views of the ruins of the **Convento da Nossa Senhora do Desterro**, a 10–15 minute walk from the town centre (or five minutes from the signposted car park).

The medieval convent is in ruins and a little ghostly, which may entrance young Dr Who fans, and its thickly wooded gardens are a good place for a family picnic where children can run wild.

**Caldas de Monchique**, a five-minute drive from town, just off the main Lagos road, has been famed for its natural thermal springs since Roman times – but if soaking in hot mineral water appeals to you, choose a nice package at one of the Algarve's modern spa hotels over a visit to this drab little town, where the hot springs are housed in grimly institutional buildings and you'll be sharing the waters with coachloads of elderly Portuguese folk seeking relief from their aches and pains. Just outside Caldas, however, **Parque da Mina** (see p. 133) offers a peek into an earlier era, with guided tours of a dignified old manor house where photos and portraits of former owners and their families hang on the walls along with rusting muskets, swords and pistols.

## Beaches & Resorts

### Carrapateira (Bordeira) ★★

Praia de Bordeira, 2 km from Carrapateira village, is one of Europe's great deserted beaches (though it's a lot less deserted in July and August than in spring, early summer and autumn). There is room for everyone on this huge delta of pristine yellow sand, from sandcastle-building toddlers to windsurfing teens. It's at least 2 km in length and stretches a good 800–1000 metres inland, where it is bounded by lines of dunes. You can drive most of the way to the beach, but to get to the sand you must wade across a shallow, clear stream – no big deal, but toddlers will have to be carried and pushchairs left behind. The beach shelves very gently so it's good for little children at low tide, but beware big waves when the tide is high. There are no services of any kind on the beach (and precious few in Carrapateira village) so you will need to be self-sufficient for a happy day here – at the very least, you'll need beach mats, a sun umbrella or folding shelter, and plenty of chilled drinks.

### Belixe, Cabo de São Vicente

It's a steep hike down to Belixe, a crescent of yellow sand hemmed in by steep cliffs, below the car park opposite the Forte do Belixe. This is a surf beach, and much of the time its waves are so crowded with wet-suited surfies that it looks like a wildlife documentary about some strange new form of sea life. The big waves make it unsuitable for tots and toddlers a lot of the time, but older children learning to surf with body-boards, or teens who already have the knack, will love it. There are no facilities of any kind, so you will need to bring a picnic.

### Praia da Mareta, Sagres This
is the closest beach to Sagres town. A winding road leads down to it from Praça da República, but in summer you will have to get there early if you

want parking space at the foot of the hill. It's a steep walk, but not a very long one, from the top of the hill. There's a laid-back beach bar which also serves basic snacks such as burgers, and where you can rent pedaloes. Toddlers may find the waves can be a bit intimidating at high tide.

### Praia da Batata, Lagos FIND

Praia da Batata is a local beach for local people. It's the closest patch of sand to the centre of Lagos, just a five-minute stroll down the riverside esplanade of the Avenida dos Descobrimentos. Walk past the little Forte de Ponte da Bandeira and the boathouses of the Lagos Sailing Club, cross a short stretch of sand, then duck through a natural rock arch to discover a sheltered sandy bay, surrounded by cliffs, that is more popular with local children than with visitors. Despite its proximity to town, it rarely gets as crowded as the bigger resort beaches nearby.

### Praia Dona Ana, Lagos

OVERRATED Lagos's most photo-graphed beach, with steep cliffs and rocky pinnacles cutting off a series of small sandy bays and coves from the main stretch of

## TIP ≫ Children's Kit ≪

**If you're heading for the Algarve's Wild West, you need to buy your** family's expedition kit before you leave. The Beach Factory (☎ *020 8332 7467*; *www.beachfactory.com*) stocks children's wetsuits, sun protection swimwear and rash shirts for babies through to teens and adults, pop-up UV protection tents, sun cream, sun hats, pool toys and a full range of Aquashoe neoprene beach shoes. Just about the only beach essential they don't stock is designer sunglasses.

Praia da Mareta, Sagres

sand. On the cliffs above, hotels and apartment blocks loom, and in high summer this can be very crowded indeed.

**Meia Praia, Lagos** ★ Across the river from Lagos town centre, Meia Praia stretches apparently endlessly off to the east. It does eventually come to an end some 4 km away, so there is plenty of space for all, though in high summer it can be quite a hike before you come to a really deserted stretch of sand. Families will probably prefer to stay close to the west end, where there's at least one beach bar and a few kiosks selling crisps and cold drinks, and a watersports centre where you can hire windsurfers, pedaloes and canoes.

> **INSIDER TIP** 〉〉
> One of the phrases you'll hear a lot in the easy-going Algarve is 'Nao faz mal' – 'it doesn't matter' or 'it's no big deal'.

**Luz** Visit Luz in the off-season, and it looks like a ghost town (or a retirement home – most of the people who stay in this resort suburb west of Lagos town are elderly Brits, and it shows). In summer, it's a lot more lively, with an esplanade of beach-kit shops, ice-cream parlours, café bars and restaurants with open-air seating. The beach – which rates a Blue Flag – is magnificent but the waves can be rough, making it better for stronger swimmers, older children and surfers (who come here in numbers) than for babies.

**Praia de Martinhal** About 3 km east of Sagres, Martinhal is a 500-metre stretch of white sand backed by dunes and with clear, fairly shallow water that makes it good for smaller children except in the very windiest weather. Until recently it was almost completely untouched, but the first luxury villa and hotel-resort complex in the Sagres area opened here recently (see p. 140). For once, this is a sensitively designed property that blends in with the landscape instead of ruining it and the beach is truly superb.

## Ships' Graveyard

**The seabed offshore from Martinhal is a real ships' graveyard. Divers** have found the remains of many ships that have been wrecked while trying to sail round the Cape – including the cannon of the French warship *Ocean*, which was sunk by the Royal Navy in 1759.

## Water & Theme Parks

You won't find any big fun parks in this part of the Algarve, but Aqualand (see p. 97) and Slide and Splash (see p. 96) are both less than a 30-minute drive from Lagos and very easy to find, and Zoomarine (see p. 97) and Krazy World (see p. 98) are only around 45 minutes by car. Most of the fun parks offer complimentary or reduced price coach transfers from your hotel in the Lagos area.

## Zoos & Animal Parks

**Lagos Zoo** ★ ★ **ALL AGES FIND**
Lagos Zoo is about 12 km out of town, and it's tucked away in a maze of narrow back-country roads and not brilliantly

signposted. If you don't fancy driving there are shuttle buses from Lagos town centre and various hotel pick-up points. But it is well worth making the trip. On arrival, you are greeted by an ensemble of friendly macaws and cockatoos with which you can have your picture taken (they'll have a print for you by the time you leave). Then children will be lured onward by the noisy hooting of a family of gibbons who live in the trees on their own island. Next, there's a lake where Bolivian Squirrel Monkeys, lemurs and pelicans live – the squirrel monkeys have two islands connected by a tightrope, and it's fun to watch them as they cross from one to the other. The lemurs seem happy enough to

Lagos Zoo

share their island with pelicans, Mandarin Ducks and cormorants. Peacocks wander free along the paths, there are ponds full of sunbathing terrapins, and in the wallaby paddock there are usually a few 'joeys' poking their little heads out of their mums' pouches. When animal viewing palls, there's a play area with wooden climbing frames and climbing nets for children who feel inspired to emulate the gibbons, and in summer there are children's activities including face painting. There are also two snack bars (next to the play park) and a full-service restaurant – but be aware that the restaurant is usually packed out with coach parties in summer. If you didn't bring your own baby buggy and legs are getting tired, you can rent one at the zoo entrance for €2 per hour.

*Quinta Figueiras, Sitio de Medronhal, Barão de São João (📞 00 351 282 680 100; www.zoolagos.com).* **Open** *1st Oct–31st Mar 10am–5pm; 1st Apr–30th Sept 10am–7pm.* **Admission***: adults €10.00, children (4–11) €6.00.*

*From the A22 take the N120 exit in the direction of Aljezur, drive through Bensafrim village then turn right in the direction of Barão de São João. The zoo is approximately 2 km after Barão de São João.*

> **INSIDER TIP** »
>
> Feeding time for the gibbons, monkeys and other primates is 3pm. The pelicans and cormorants are fed at 11.30am and again (lucky blighters) at 3pm, so if you come in the afternoon you can watch both.

**Parque da Mina** ALL AGES For toddlers who are happy to see (and feed) geese, chicks, ornamental ducks, sheep, goats and miniature ponies, this oddball visitor attraction is quite fun. There are seven big aviaries full of various kinds of pigeon (and this is one of the few places that you will actually see a baby pigeon, if you visit in February when they're sat there on their nests). Be advised that the advertised 'lakes with birds' are small, muddy duck ponds. The price includes a guided tour of the former manor house, replete with photos and portraits of former owners and their families and walls hung with rusting firearms and fencing swords.

*Vale de Boi, Caldas de Monchique (📞 00 351 282 91 16 22; E: parque damina@mail.telepac.pt).* **Open** *1st Oct–31st Mar 10am–5pm; 1st Apr–30th Sept 10am–7pm.* **Admission***: adults €8, children (4–11) €5, under 4s free, family ticket €21.*

## Castles & Historic Buildings

### Fortaleza de Sagres ★★

ALL AGES You would think that the sheer 60-metre cliffs on all sides of this finger of land poking out into the Atlantic would have made it impossible to assault successfully. You would be wrong. Francis Drake seized the Fortaleza in 1587 and destroyed not only the fortifications but also the huge library of maps and records of the Portuguese voyages of discovery to Africa, Asia and the Americas that Henry the Navigator and his successors had assembled here. The only part of the fortress that they left intact was the little 14th-century chapel.

It's a fair old hike to the Fortaleza from the visitors' car park, and the road is annoyingly cobbled, making it a bit problematic for baby buggies. In any case, this isn't really a visit for toddlers. Older children with a taste for hidden histories – and awesome views – will like it, and will be impressed by the death-defying rows of local anglers who stand on the very edge of the cliffs to cast their lines into the deep water below (there are no guard rails of any kind, so keep bolder children on a tight leash – it's a long way down). Rusting iron cannons point out to sea at various spots around the fortress, as if to threaten Drake's ghost should he decide to return.

The fortress is really just one huge rampart stretching across the panhandle of the rocky peninsula, and dating from 1793 (by which time the Portuguese were on our side). Once you emerge from the tunnel that leads through it to the ticket office, you're on a vast, roughly circular promontory with, at its furthest point, a small stone lighthouse. A cobbled path leads to the lighthouse and around the rim of the promontory. Within the walls, the only buildings apart from the lighthouse are a buttressed, white-painted stone building that was the garrison's gunpowder store, the little church and a row of newer buildings that house a shop, café, toilets and an 'explanatory centre' (all of these suffered storm damage in late 2006 and when this book was written it was not certain when they would reopen). A few semi-abstract marble statues are dotted around the grounds. A family of half-wild cats basks in sunnier spots (and the kittens chase summer lizards, which can be entertaining to watch).

The rest of the promontory is rocky wasteland, covered with low bushes and splashed with colourful wild flowers in spring and early summer – it's a haven for wild birds and a great place too for spotting some of the Algarve's most colourful butterflies, as well as flocks of Gannets out to sea and maybe, if you're very lucky, the fins of a school of

**FUN FACT** **Wind Rose**

**Just inside the walls of the Fortaleza is the Rosa dos Ventos or 'wind** rose'. This circular paved area with its lines of cobles radiating from a central point lay buried and forgotten until it was rediscovered by accident in 1921. Nobody has yet figured out what it was for, but it appears to line up with a sundial, which is set into the fortress parapet above it, so it was probably some kind of medieval solar clock, perhaps used to help in the calculations of Henry the Navigator's map-makers.

dolphins. There's not a scrap of shade, so it can be scorching hot in summer, when the best time to visit is first thing in the morning or just before sunset.

Look north for a view of Cabo de São Vicente and its lighthouse – Europe stops here. In an odd sort of way, this is a very peaceful spot – the constant sound of the waves far below, and the non-stop chirping of thousands of grasshoppers in summer, is very soothing.

*Fortaleza de Sagres (✆ 00 351 282 620 140; E: fortaleza.sagres@ippar.pt). Tours in English daily 3pm, duration 30 minutes.* **Admission**: *adults €3, 15–25 years €1.50, under 14s free.*

### Forte de Ponte da Bandeira, Lagos ★ ALL AGES

This mini-fortress overlooks the river mouth, about a five-minute walk from the old part of Lagos, and is just a hop and a skip from sandy Praia de Batata. Built in the late 17th century, it was restored about 60 years ago and is now used for small exhibitions – some of them will interest some children, others won't, so check with the tourist office for what's on before you visit. Even if the exhibitions fail to fascinate, it's a fun little castle, with miniature turrets at each corner of its square, flat roof area from which you can gaze through arrow-slit windows out to sea or across the river to the great sweep of Meia Praia beach.

*Cais da Solaria, Lagos (✆ 00 351 282 761 410; www.cm-lagos.pt).* **Open** *Wed–Sun 9am–12.30pm and 2pm–5pm.* **Admission**: *€2.20.*

## Spectacular Views

### Cabo de São Vicente (Cape St Vincent)

The furthest tip of Portugal has drop-dead breathtaking views at any time of year – it's even quite spectacular after dark, when the blindingly powerful beam of its lighthouse stabs out into the darkness and can be seen 100 km out to sea. The cape is named after St Vincent, who was martyred in Zaragoza and whose body miraculously washed up here and was, it is claimed, buried in a tiny shrine on the cliffs. It was destroyed by the fiercely Muslim Almoravid rulers of the Algarve in the 12th century, so no one knows for sure where it stood.

It wasn't until the time of the 15th-century Portuguese and Spanish explorers that anyone knew for sure that there was anything out there on the other side of the Atlantic. As far as ancient Greek, Roman and Phoenician mariners were concerned, the Sagres peninsula really was the end of the world – hence its alternative name, Finisterra. Sagres was the last sheltered port where vessels from the Mediterranean could put in before setting out into the open Atlantic (on the way to Britain or south along the Moroccan coast). In Roman times it was known as the Promotorium Sacrum, and mariners would climb to the top to sacrifice to their gods and pray for a safe journey. Go early evening to admire the spectacular sunset over the Atlantic and the long

# Lighthouse Family

**The Cabo de São Vicente lighthouse is the second-most powerful** lighthouse in Europe. The Longstone lighthouse in the Farne Islands off the coast of Northumbria (where lighthouse-keeper's daughter Grace Darling became famous for her rescue of passengers from the shipwrecked *Forfarshire*) is claimed by some to be the most powerful European light. You can find out more about lighthouses around the world at **www.lighthousedepot.com**.

sweep of cliffs and sandy beaches either side of the Cape.

*Admission is free (no access to lighthouse). Buses leave three times daily (11.15am, 12.30pm and 6pm, €1.15 each way) Mon–Fri from Rua Comandante Matos near the tourist office in Sagres. You can also take a boat trip from Sagres harbour (€18) or rent bicycles (€6 for four hours or €9.50 per day) from Turinfo, Beco do Henrique, Sagres (☎ 00 351 282 620 083). The boat trip lasts two hours and is only recommended for good sailors – the ocean swell can make you quite queasy.*

**Monchique** The only real reason to stop in Monchique (unless you really need the loo) is for the view of the pretty, wooded hills and vineyards stretching away towards the sea from the ruined Convento da Nossa Senhora do Desterro.

**Ponta da Piedade** Steep sandstone cliffs, natural rock arches and sea caves where the water seems to glow with green or turquoise light make this stretch of coast a few kilometres west of Lagos the most visited of the Algarve coast's natural beauty spots. Take a boat trip from Lagos marina, or drive to the Ponta da Piedade lighthouse and walk down the steep stairs to the

waterline, where a flotilla of small boats waits to transport you around the rocks and grottoes.

Take a boat trip from Lagos Marina with Bom Dia Cruises (Marina de Lagos, Loja 10: ☎ 00 351 282 087 587; **www.bomdia. info**) which sail several times daily to Ponta da Piedade's famous grottoes. The trip takes two hours and costs €21 for adults and €10 for children. Bom Dia also runs four-hour barbecue cruises which also visit the caves of Ponta da Piedade.

Best visited first thing in the morning when the sun shines directly onto the water and the colours are most vivid.

## For Active Families

Lagos and the west Algarve are holiday heaven for families with older children who like excitement, and there are gentler family activities for smaller people too, such as river canoeing and cycling.

**Surfing** AGES 10 AND UP Tavira and Carrapateira are the surf capitals of the Algarve. This is an activity for older children who are already strong and confident swimmers,

Cape St Vincent

and there are several operations offering surfing tuition for teenage and adult novices, as well as surf camps that offer tuition and basic self-catering accommodation packages (see p. 141).

*Carrapateira Surfing Club (✆ 00 351 964 432 324; www.carrapateira-surfingclub.com).*

*Nomad Surfers (✆ 00 34 971 31 20 99; www.nomadsurfers.com) offers surfing and accommodation packages at Sagres and Carrapateira and surf courses from €45 per day, including three hours of tuition and all kit.*

### Deep Sea Fishing – Lagos

AGES 10 AND UP Go fishing for sharks, marlin, tuna and dorado with Joaquim 'Jacko' Rio and his crew and – with luck - come back with something to feed the family for the rest of the week. A trip on *Pescamar* also offers a good chance of seeing dolphins while out at sea. The twin-engined boat can take you up to 50 km out into the Atlantic (so it's definitely for people who already have their sea legs) and has onboard toilet facilities. Drinks and lunch also provided on request.

*Pescamar, Praia da Luz (✆ 00 351 966 193 431; www.pescamar.inf). Four-hour bottom-fishing trips from €45 for anglers, €35 for spectators, lunch €8.50 per person extra.*

FUN FACT ❯❯ **Another Battle**

**Commodore Horatio Nelson took his first step to naval glory at the Battle** of Cape St Vincent in 1797. Nelson's ship *HMS Captain* took on the biggest warship in the world, the *Santissima Trinidad*, and six others, capturing two. Nelson was knighted and promoted to Rear Admiral, and Admiral John Jervis, commanding the British squadron of only 15 ships, was made Earl St Vincent. Jervis's flagship was the same *HMS Victory* which Nelson commanded when he met a hero's death at Trafalgar (near Cádiz) and which is now a floating museum in Portsmouth.

Family rates on request. **Open** daily 3pm–7pm.

### Parasailing AGES 8 AND UP

Convince your children that you – and they - can fly like Superman or Peter Pan. Lagos parasailing says all ages are welcome, but in fact this isn't recommended for anybody much under eight years old, even when flying in tandem with mum or dad. For those who haven't sampled this thrill, parasailing involves being buckled into a parachute harness and towed behind a speedboat at heights of 40 to 100 metres above the water (depending on how brave you feel). You lift off and land from the boat. No experience is needed, and it's a great, safe adrenaline rush.

*Lagos Parasailing, Cais A, Marina de Lagos (☎ 00 351 963 427 788). Seven departures daily from 9am–6.30pm, June–Sept. €35 per person. Family discounts. All ages welcome.*

### Waterskiing AGES 8 AND UP

Waterskiing is easy at Praia da Luz – several waterski boats wait at the beach for punters. Just turn up and go. You can also waterski from Meia Praia, but it's less satisfactory for impatient young skiers as there is generally a queue at the water-sports shack (near the Lagos end of the beach) and you may have to wait for an hour or more for a boat to take you on a 15-minute ride.

*Praia da Luz, Luz; Meia Praia, Lagos. Prices start at €20 per person.*

### River Canoeing ALL AGES For a
gentle canoe experience, paddle around the lagoons and channels of the Ria de Alvor estuary with an English-speaking guide with Outdoor Tours. Canoe trips start from Alvor. There's a good chance of seeing storks and flamingos, and in summer the clear, shallow water is perfect for a dip. The trip starts with a short lesson on paddling and steering your canoe (it's dead easy), then you paddle upstream – passing under the N125 road bridge – to the biggest palm-tree oasis in Portugal (and Spain) for a half-hour guided tour and a snack in the onsite pizzeria. Then there's a stop on a desert island in the middle of the lagoon for swimming, sunbathing, shell collecting and (for the relentlessly energetic) a game of beach volleyball. The trips are led by English-speaking guides, and the hard-plastic Canadian canoes have room for two adults and one under-10 year old. There's room for a duffel bag with towels, beach mats, snacks and drinks. The canoe flotilla is accompanied by a support boat and is never more than a few hundred yards from civilisation – in the event of a childish sense of humour failure, you could just paddle to the shore and call for a taxi back to the beach! Bring swimsuits, sunblock and plenty of water.

*Outdoor Tours, Alvor (☎ 00 351 916 736 226; www.outdoor-tours.net). Departures mid-June to mid-Sept daily, 10am. Rest of year: Fri and Sun 10am. Trip lasts three hours. Adults €22.50, under 10s accompanied by two adults €5.00. Lifejackets (for adults, children and babies), guide and support boat included.*

## Bike Trips & Walking

`AGES 15 AND UP` The western Algarve is great for younger (or lazier) cyclists who are content to bumble along the mostly flat countryside around Sagres, but for keen off-road bikers the Serra de Monchique offers more challenging terrain. Sagres Natura runs guided cycle trips from Sagres along the coast to Cabo de São Vicente and beyond. Outdoor Tours has a choice of 10 routes of which the most family friendly is the downhill summer trip from Foia (900 metres above sea level) down to the coast – a 22-km ride, but 98% of it is downhill and the other 2% is on the flat. Not suitable for under 15s.

*Sagres Natura, Rua Mestre Antonio Galhardo, Sagres (📞 00 351 282 624 072; www.sagresnatura.com). €30 including bike, helmet, guide and transfers.* **Open** *daily 8am–5pm.*

*Outdoor Tours, Alvor (📞 00 351 916 736 226; www.outdoor-tours.net).* **Open** *daily 8.30am–midday and 2pm–6pm.*

## Scuba Diving `AGES 10 AND UP`

Sudeste Scuba offers 'discover scuba' lessons for those tempted to follow in the wake of Jacques Cousteau. Pre-teens can start to get the hang of the kit in a swimming pool, while older teenagers – and parents – can go off the deep end with a dive in the sea (close to shore). Both include a classroom lesson in the basics and a pool session, while the 'sea try a dive' option includes a boat trip and sea dive with a qualified dive leader as well.

*Sudeste Scuba, Porta da Baleeira Harbour, Sagres (📞 00 351 916 290 732; www.dive-centers.net).* **Open** *daily 8am–5pm. Pool discover scuba session (three hours) €25 with all equipment, sea discover scuba option (four hours including boat trip and dive) €70.*

## Tennis

Families with really dedicated tennis nuts can find hotels and apartments and villa complexes complete with floodlit courts and often with resident coaches too. Less fanatical players, or those staying at accommodation without onsite courts, can find court rental available at Break Point Tennis Club, which has two courts, racket and ball rental and tennis classes. Make reservations at the Break Point Coffee Shop, next door (which is also handy for a post-game rendezvous with non-playing family members).

*Break Point Tennis Club, Dona Ana Apartments, Lagos (📞 00 351 282 081 915).* **Open** *daily 8am–9pm. Court rental €4.99 per hour, racket €1.50, balls €1.25.*

---

`TIP` **Easy Walks**

**Julie Statham and Silvia Smetham lead easy walks in the gently rolling** hinterland of the western Algarve and the Parque Natural de Cabo de São Vicente. There are different routes most weekends, taking two to three hours. There's a small charge for each walk, which includes a donation to local charities.
📞 *00 351 282 697 298 or 00 351 965 753 033. Departure times vary.*

## Shopping

Lagos is the western Algarve's main shopping area, with supermarkets, a seemingly endless supply of look-alike souvenir shops selling look-alike pottery and leather accessories and an open-air produce market every Saturday. The main supermarkets are Modelo, part of a Portuguese chain, and Intermarché, both of which are strategically located on the outskirts of town, stock everything under the sun, and have large car parks. Both are good places for one huge shopping trip for essentials if you are catering for yourselves. The Saturday market is held on the waterfront esplanade, opposite the marina, and is crammed with stalls selling fresh local produce at prices way below the supermarkets. Like all Algarve produce markets, it's a great experience and for children it makes a welcome change from being dragged around supermarkets. For pottery, take a stroll along narrow Rua 25 de Abril, which has lots of little shops selling colourful ceramics.

# FAMILY-FRIENDLY ACCOMMODATION

## Sagres

**EXPENSIVE**

**Martinhal Resort** The western Algarve's newest five-star hotel and villa resort overlooks the beach at Martinhal, just east of Sagres (but not quite within walking distance). The hotel – designed by Sir Terence Conran – was due to open in summer 2007 and luxury townhouses, apartments and beach villas were already available for rental when this book was researched. The views are fabulous, the beach is splendid and for the big-budget family this will undoubtedly become the best place to stay in the western Algarve.

*Praia de Martinhal, Sagres (📞 00351 282 620 026; www.martinhal.com). **Rates**: two-bedroom townhouses from €960 per week. Contact reservations office via e-mail (E: info@ martinhal.com) for holiday rental prices as rates vary according to season and property type. **In room**: satellite TV, air conditioning, safe, minibar, Internet connection.*

**Pousada do Infante** The thunderous sound of the surf crashes against the cliffs below this low-rise, hacienda-like hotel. The pousada was built in the 1960s and shows its age just a bit – carpets on stairs are a bit worn and the corridors could do with a lick of paint, which they will no doubt get soon. It leans toward families, with a games room for children, a pool and extensive lawns but not much else for children, and it's a steep hike to the beach. It would be a very comfortable place for one or two nights on an exploring holiday – there is secure off-street parking, and there is lots to do nearby – but not perfect for a longer stay.

*Rua Infante Dom Henrique, Sagres (📞 00 351 282 620 240; www. pousadas.pt). 50 rooms. **Rates**:*

doubles from €120–230, extra bed free for children under 16 sharing parents' room, cots free. **Amenities**: pool, gardens, off-street parking, lounge with satellite TV and wireless Internet access, restaurant, bar. **In room**: TV, telephone, air conditioning, safe, minibar.

## Carrapateira

### Monte Velho Nature Resort

★★ On a verdant hilltop within sight of the rolling surf of the west coast, 3 km from Carrapateira, where there's not a sign of a high-rise hotel or apartment block, the Monte Velho Nature Resort is run by the friendly Balsemão family, who have young children themselves and so understand family needs. Accommodation is in single-storey, ranch-house style suites sleeping 3–4 people and decorated in bright pop colours. All of them open onto a pretty garden (with a toddlers' pool); this is definitely for people looking for a self-sufficient, quiet holiday, though, there is very little to Carrapateira apart from sand, surf and scenery. You can even take a donkey ride to the beach (which is 4 km away) with a pre-packed picnic lunch and surfing lessons at the Carrapateira surf club. There's a shared sitting room with rush mats, stereo and a library of books on surfing and adrenaline sports.

*Praia de Bordeira, Carrapateira (📞 00 351 282 973 207; www.iescape. com/montevelhonatureresort.ph).* **Rates**: two double bedrooms, seven non-smoking suites €90–100.

**Amenities**: garden, toddlers' pool, sitting room. **In room**: fridge.

### Nomadsurfers Surf Camps ★

These rustic surf camps aren't for everybody and certainly not for families with tots. You're paying for the surfing here, not for luxury accommodation, though the rooms are comfortable enough. If you have older children (12 years upwards) who like the open air and adrenaline sports and enjoy the company of a young and lively crowd of other surfers in their teens and 20s then this is for you, dudes. There are two camps – one just outside Carrapateira, where there are restaurants, bars and a super-market, and a second at Sagres. There's a surf school for beginners at Carrapateira, and packages including accommodation, return transfers from Faro airport, four hours' surfing every day, all equipment, breakfast and packed lunch daily and transfers to the west coast's top surf beaches.

Nomadsurfers also runs two special one-week surf training camps for boys and girls aged between 12 and 16 in Carrapateira each summer (though rolling both weeks together into a two-week holiday is recommended). There's a maximum of 30 children per week and courses are split into two levels – for total beginners and intermediate surfers, who can learn how to surf or improve their skills, and for advanced surfers. The coaches who speak several languages and

## Pousadas of Portugal

**Launched by the government in 1942 – not a great year for tourism –** Portugal's chain of luxury pousadas (inns) includes converted historic buildings (castles, palaces, monasteries and convents) and purpose-built hotels strategically located around the country. There are four in the Algarve – at Sagres (see p. 140), Tavira (see p. 167), São Bras de Alportel (see p. 47) and Santa Clara a Velha (see p. 222) – and one in Beja (see p. 221) They're grand, but family friendly, with great locations to choose from (mainly in historic towns, but also in the countryside) and family package deals including free accommodation for two children under 12 sharing with parents. For bookings and special offers, see *www. pousadas.pt.* Sunvil (📞 *020 8758 4747; www.sunvil.co.uk*) offers tailor-made pousada holidays from the UK including flights, car hire and accommodation.

all the elements are combined to provide children with professional, pleasurable training.

Accommodation is at **Carrapateira Surf House** in front of Bordeira beach, with lessons at nearby Praia do Amado. Facilities include a large lounge with a library of more than 200 DVDs, PlayStation, billiards, ping pong and large terrace where breakfast buffet is served. Children can even order a custom-made surfboard and watch it being shaped by resident big-wave rider Billy Boy. The instructors live in the house and children are supervised 24 hours a day.

For parents who want to spend holidays with their surf-crazed offspring, Nomadsurfers also rents apartments around Carrapateira and Sagres.

*Nomadsurfers (📞 00 34 971 312 099; www.nomadsurfers.com). Set weeks: June–July. **Rates**: one-week surf training camp €700 including seven nights' accommodation, full*

*board, surf classes and equipment, transfers from Faro airport.*
***Amenities**: surf school and club, lounge with games, buffet restaurant.*

## Lagos

**MODERATE**

**Tivoli Lagos** ★ The four-star Tivoli Lagos is part of a well-known Portuguese hotel chain and for families who are prepared to share a room it's surprisingly affordable. For the money you get the best of both worlds – a very comfortable full-service hotel in the heart of Lagos, handy for shops and old-town strolls, plus a well-equipped beach club 2 km away on Meia Praia beach, with a free shuttle service. Facilities at the hotel itself include outdoor pools for children and adults, plus a heated indoor pool and an indoor games room with table tennis, snooker, darts and board games. The Duna Beach Club, however, is the Tivoli's big selling point, with another outdoor freshwater pool, tennis courts, changing rooms and umbrellas and sun-loungers, as well as a children's club to keep them entertained. It's on a Blue Flag beach, supervised by lifeguards in summer. The Duna Restaurant has an à la carte lunch menu and from June to September there is a weekly barbecue party with live music and folk dancing.

*Rua António Crisógono Santos, Lagos ( 00 351 282 790 079; www.tivoli hotels.com). 324 rooms and suites.* **Rates***: family rooms from €85–115 (two adults and two children sharing), cots free.* **Amenities***: indoor and outdoor pools, games room, private beach club with children's club.* **In room***: satellite TV, safe, air condi-tioning, balcony or terrace.*

## Burgau

**INEXPENSIVE**

### Tempomar Apartments ★

Burgau, midway between Lagos and Sagres, is a small-scale resort that avoids the hurly-burly of Lagos (though its relatively small beach can be packed on summer weekends). The family-friendly Tempomar Apartments complex has pretty palm gardens, pools for grown-ups and children, an adventure playground and other facilities including bowls, tennis, table tennis and its own spa. It's a two-minute walk from the beach, and in summer there is a chil-dren's club with animators and child-minders to take the little darlings off your hands for a while and allow parents the

luxury of the occasional child-free lunch or outing. Accommodation is in one-bedroom apartments (which sleep four people) or two-bedroom apartments (up to six people). All the apartments have fully equipped kitchen and private balcony or terrace.

*Burgau ( 00 351 282 697 290; www. tempomar.com).* **Rates***: €1,240 per week for double apartment in high season, €650 low season, cots and highchairs free.* **Amenities***: adult and children's pools, tennis, snooker, table tennis, supervised children's club.* **In room***: fully equipped kitchen.*

# FAMILY-FRIENDLY DINING

## Attitudes to Children

Portuguese restaurants (with the exception of a few really expensive places) are designed to be an informal eating experience that is fun for all the family. Because Portuguese children get to go to restaurants relatively fre-quently and interact socially with their adult companions while they are there, they rapidly acquire a sense of how to behave properly. It's not just a question of parental control (although undoubtedly families are closer and more cohesive units in Portugal than they tend to be in Britain). It is also a question of letting children have a little responsibility for themselves, so learn how to use rather than abuse it – Portuguese adults tol-erate children in all situations, and are rewarded with general respect for adults from children.

## Aljezur

### Restaurante Pont a Pé ★

**VALUE** This is a very simple little café restaurant (with unusually smiley service) on a small riverside square shaded by trees where children can play and feed the sparrows and pigeons when they are fed up with sitting at the tables – which are outside in the sun or inside in the shade. There is free car parking just a minute's walk away, across the river. The place has at least one resident seven year old. They don't do child portions, but they do have lots of nibbles and starters that you can mix and match to junior appetites (ham, cheese, olives, sausage and so on), as well as sweet crêpes for dessert or on their own.

*Largo da Liberdade/Pont a Pé, Aljezur. Main course €10. No credit cards. Reservations not required.* **Open** *daily 10.30am–6pm.*

### Lagos Zoo Restaurante O Cangalho

The menu here is excellent and the surroundings are surprisingly formal, even elegant for the location – if you were expecting a cheap and cheerful zoo café, think again. There's a lot of starched white tablecloth about, and if your children are the kind who can't sit still, best have lunch somewhere else. It's not cheap – you'll be lucky to get out of here for less than €15 per head and the menu makes few concessions to non-Portuguese tastes, but if you like steak, grills or roasts you'll be in seventh heaven. There is no children's menu as such, but carnivorous children who spurn such offerings as steak diane can be fobbed off with the hamburger, and there's quite a good choice of salads and different kinds of omelette.

*Lagos Zoo (📞 00 351 282 687 218;* **www.cangalho.com**)*. Starters from €3, mains from around €12. Credit cards accepted. Reservations recommended.* **Open** *daily midday–4pm and 6pm–9pm.*

## Luz

**Paraiso** ★ Few of the string of restaurants along the little promenade at Luz are outstandingly family friendly, but the Paraiso, which is right on the sand close to the east end of the beach, makes an effort to please children with two sets of swings and a slide for toddlers beneath its beachside balcony. It serves English breakfast and child-sized meals and snacks as well as more substantial Portuguese dishes such as *cataplana,* a massive seafood stew cooked in a traditional copper casserole dish that looks a bit like a Chinese wok.

*Praia da Luz. English breakfast €8.50, hamburger and salad €2.50, sardine salad sandwich €2.80, grilled fish €15, cataplana for two €29. Credit cards accepted. Reservations*

*recommended for dinner in summer.*
***Open** daily midday–9pm (11pm mid-June to mid-Sept).*

## Sagres

**Restaurante Raposo** On the beach at Sagres's Praia de Mareta, this restaurant has a fishy menu but its main value for families is the big range of water sports that it offers in addition to food and drink – ranging from banana boats and rubber rings to para-sailing and boat trips.

*Praia de Mareta, Sagres (☎ 00 351 282 624 168). €10–30. Credit cards accepted. Reservations not required.* ***Open** Oct–May midday–4pm and 8pm–10pm, June–Sept midday–10pm. Closed Thurs.*

**Pousada do Infante ★** This is definitely the poshest place to eat in Sagres (which is not over-endowed with gracious dining experiences). It is perhaps too formal to be truly child friendly, but you can't beat the view across to the Fortaleza de Sagres but Cabo de São Vicente. The hotel offers babysitting services for guests if booked in advance,

so parents who are staying here and who have younger children who can be tucked up early could enjoy a rare, peaceful dinner à deux here. The specialities are maritime, and range from a wonderful fish soup to stuffed squid and tuna with onions.

*Pousada do Infante, Rua Infante Dom Henrique, Sagres (☎ 00 351 282 620 240; www.pousadas.pt). From €35. Credit cards accepted. Reservations essential.* ***Open** daily midday–3pm and 8pm—10pm.*

**Bistro Bar Dromedario**
Dromedario's core clientele especially in summer tends to be dreadlocked, tattooed, pierced and dressed in lurid surf fashions, which makes it entertaining for children who may never have seen dedicated surf freaks in the wild. This place rocks at night (until 3am in summer) but it opens early and its breakfasts are outstanding – no half-hearted attempts at the full English, but instead freshly squeezed exotic juices, muesli, fresh fruit, yoghurt and for lunch there's a great range of children-sized snacks, burgers and especially

---

**FUN FACT** ▶ **Punch Drunk** ◀

**The hills of the Serra de Monchique are covered in medronho (pronounced** 'medronyo') shrubs, which produce small, aromatic red berries that are picked in autumn, left to ferment through the winter, then distilled into a clear alcohol with a powerful punch. Don't drink it and drive – in fact, it's probably best not to try standing up. How does it taste? Drop the 'r' from medronho and you've got the answer – *medonho* (awful).

crêpes – mostly sweet and bad for their teeth, but at least it keeps their sugar levels up. It also has Internet access, so you can check your e-mail, reconfirm your flights or plunk young gamers down in front of the latest first-person shooter while you eat.

*Internet access available. Snacks and burgers from €3.50. Credit cards not accepted. Reservations not required.* **Open** *10am–3pm.*

## Carrapateira

**MODERATE**

**Sitio do Rio** The best (well, actually the only) option near Carrapateira beach, tucked away among the sand dunes with ample parking space. There are no special deals for children, but the menu ranges from vegetarian dishes (unusual, but driven by demand from greenie hippie-surfer types from the nearby surf camp) to meaty kebabs and excellent fresh seafood. Something for all the family then, and this is very much a shorts-and-teeshirts sort of place with plenty of room for children to play safely on the sand or splash

in the stream within sight of parents who want to sit still after lunch a bit longer than their offspring do.

*Praia de Carrapateira (📞 00 351 282 973 119). €10–15. Credit cards accepted. Reservations not required.* **Open** *midday–4pm and 8pm–10pm. Closed Tues.*

## Lagos

**INEXPENSIVE**

**São Roque** ★ Probably the best bet for families on Lagos's Meia Praia, which has surprisingly few recommendable places to eat (there are basic kiosks and snack bars in summer, but none are outstanding). This very pleasant beach restaurant has an excellent choice of seafood, and many locals come out here to eat at weekends – always a good recommendation. It has its own children's playground, with swings and seesaw, between the restaurant and the beach, so it's great for a relaxed family lunch.

*Meia Praia, Lagos (📞 00 351 282 792 101). €5–15. Credit cards accepted. Reservations not required.* **Open** *midday–10pm. Closed Mon and from Nov–May.*

# SOUTH EAST **ALGARVE**

**H**uge, uncrowded beaches, pretty old-fashioned towns that have not been turned into tourist honeypots, pretty villages and a smattering of history make the eastern end of the Algarve a perfect destination for families who want a quieter and more relaxing holiday.

The delightful riverside town of Tavira is the gateway to this eastern region, and from here as far as the Spanish border, which is formed by the wide River Guadiana, the coast stretches for almost 30 km in a long, unbroken sweep of soft white sand.

This part of the Algarve coastline is by no means undeveloped – there are apartment complexes and hotels dotted all along the coast – but there are no huge resort towns to compare with Albufeira, Portimão or Lagos. If you are looking for a more authentically Portuguese side of the Algarve, this is where to find it.

Tavira, straddling the River Gilao, is a charming old town with a riverside core of historic buildings and cobbled streets, surrounded by the usual outer sprawl of more modern suburbs, which are, happily, mostly invisible from the historic centre. The only other town of any size in the eastern Algarve is Vila Real de Santo António, formerly the main ferry port for crossings between Portugal and Spain, but now a rather sleepy backwater since the opening of a new international road bridge across the Guadiana, some kilometres upriver, made its ferries redundant.

Both towns are a few kilometres from the nearest beach, and families looking for a holiday in a full-scale beach resort along this stretch of coast have only one option: Monte Gordo, a purpose-built complex of hotels and apartments (with a casino) on a wide, white sand beach that is bounded at its eastern end by the mouth of the Guadiana. This is the eastern end of a seamless stretch of white sand that is dotted with smaller resorts, most of which are set well back from the shore so that the beach isn't marred by looming high-rise blocks.

# ESSENTIALS

## Getting There

Tavira is only 32 km west of Faro by the A22 motorway or the N125 coastal road – around 30 minutes by car. Vila Real de Santo António, the River Guadiana and the border with Spain lie around 24 km east of Tavira. The N125, running parallel to the coast, connects the two main towns with the chain of beaches in between, with a series of dead-end roads leading down to the sea (trying to get to the beach by car can be a frustrating experience, as sprawling suburbs of apartments and villas have sprung up all along the coast, creating a maze of dead-end streets). The best you can do is keep following the signs saying 'Praia'.

Tavira

Tavira's old centre, with its ruined castle and clutch of historic churches lies on the west bank of the Gilao, which is spanned by an iconic footbridge and two road bridges. The nearest beaches to town are on Ilha de Tavira, a long sand-bar that begins at the mouth of the Gilao and stretches for almost 16 km westward. A road bridge connects the island with the mainland at Santa Luzia, about 6 km west of Tavira.

## Orientation

The N125 highway and the A22 motorway connect Tavira with all points east and west along the coast, from Faro (about a 45-minute drive from Tavira) to Vila Real de Santo António, where a new road bridge carries traffic onward to Spain. Tavira is 36 km east of Faro airport, and Vila Real de Santo António is around 24 km east of Tavira. Dead-end side roads lead south off the N125 to the resorts along the coast.

## VISITOR INFORMATION

**Tavira Tourist Office** Rua da Galeria 9, just off Praça da República, Tavira (📞 *00 351 281 322 511; E: turismo.tavira@ rtalgarve.pt*). **Open** Mon–Fri 9.30am–1pm and 2pm–6pm.

**East Algarve Promotion Bureau** Rua D. Marcelino Franco, Tavira (📞 *00 351 281 381 963; www.eastalgarve.com*). It has

a useful English-language website with listings of hotels, restaurants, activities and events.

## Getting Around

EVA bus services and Portuguese Railways trains connect Tavira with Faro and all points east along the coast. Tavira and Vila Real de Santo António are compact and the central areas of both towns are largely pedestrianised and pushchair friendly. Metered parking is easy to find in all towns and resorts in the region, and by British standards is a bargain at 0.50 cents per hour. Tavira Taxis (📞 *00 351 960 170 789*) operates taxi transfers to Faro airport as well as shorter journeys around Tavira.

## WHAT TO SEE & DO

### Children's Top 10

❶ **Ilha de Tavira Beach** Miles of soft sand, seashells and dunes, with restaurants, cafés and lifeguards and a first-aid station in summer. This island beach is perfect for all ages (see p. 154).

❷ **Monte Gordo beach** The east Algarve's biggest beach resort offers water sports, shops, cafés and a dab or two of local colour, with a thriving fleet of little fishing boats owned by whiskery fishermen (see p. 157).

❸ **Praia Verde beach** For miles of uncrowded sand, you can't hope for much better than this. Praia Verde merges with Monte

Gordo to the east and Manta Rota to the west (see p. 156).

**4 Manta Rota beach** Local dads and sons line the beach here with their fishing rods at weekends, but even in summer there is space for all (see p. 156).

**5 Horse-drawn carriage tour of Tavira** The most stylish way to see Tavira's waterfront and old town centre is by hiring an old-fashioned open family carriage – its ambling pace is perfect for shooting holiday videos (see p. 158).

**6 Mini-train tour of Tavira** The toytown-sized road train trundles all the way around town, taking in the major historic sights, the Science Centre, and crossing the river twice. A cheap-as-chips alternative to a horse-drawn carriage (see p. 158).

**7 Ria Formosa Natural Reserve boat trip** Remember to pack binoculars for stork and flamingo spotting on the lagoons and creeks of the delta (see p. 159).

**8 Castro Marim fortress** There are views all the way to Spain from the battlements of this grim fortress which was once the headquarters of Templar knights, and inside it's a great place for sword and sorcery fantasies (see p. 162).

**9 Guadiana river cruise** This is a fun way to see the hinterland of the Algarve, aboard riverboats that sail all the way inland to Alcoutim, with Spain on one side

of the wide river and Portugal on the other (see p. 159).

**10 Tavira camera obscura** It looks like a 1950s flying saucer, it used to be the town's water tower – and now it's a miracle of old-fashioned technology that will amaze children with its magic panorama (see p. 159).

## Towns

**Tavira** ★ Tavira is, quite simply, the prettiest, calmest and most user-friendly town in the entire Algarve region for families with smaller children. That said, it lacks the purpose-built pizzazz of the central Algarve – you won't find any water parks, zoos or bowling alleys in this part of the world. Tavira's other downside is its lack of a sandy beach within walking distance of the historic centre – getting to the wonderful sandy expanses of Ilha de Tavira requires a 15-minute drive, followed by a boat trip. But this is authentic Portugal, with an admirable absence of tourist traps.

Tavira also peps itself up in summer with a calendar of funky open-air fairs and bazaars along the river front and live entertainment for youngsters in the shape of jugglers, bands and clowns.

The centre of historic Tavira is the Praça da República, a cobbled square on the right bank of the Gilao river, with a splashing modern fountain and pool in its centre and a palm-tree shaded expanse of public gardens and bandstand stretching off along the riverside. Most of Tavira's

# TAVIRA

SPAIN

PORTUGAL

Lisbon

Tavira

Rua dos Descobrimentos

Rua Feixinho de Vides

Rua de Dezembro

Rua Do Salto

Rua Poeta Emiliano da Costa

Rua José Joaquim Jara

Rua Comandante Henrique de Brito

Rua Eduarda Lapa

Rio Gilão

Rua Dr. Parreira

Rua da Silva

Rua das Salinas

Rua 4 de Outubro

Estrada das 4 Águas

Rua 1 de Maio

Rua Dom Marcelino Franco

Rua Guilherme Gomes Fernandes

Rua Montalvão

Rua Dr. Silvestre Falcão

Rua Almirante Cândido dos Reis

Rua das Oliveiras

Rua Dr. Cabreira

Rua Jaques Pessoa

Rua da Porta Nova

Rua 5 de Outbro

Rua do Cais

Rua Dr. José Pires Padinha

Carlos Palma

Rua da Liberdade

Rua Dr. Augusto

Rua Ten. Couto

Rua de Santana

Rua João Vaz Corte Real

Rua Borda d'Agua da Asseca

Travessa da Fonte

Calçada da Galeria

Calçada de Dona Anna

Rua dos Pelames

Rua Detrás dos Muros

Calçada de Santa Maria

Rua Dom Paio Peres Correia

Rua Dr. Miguel Bombarda

Rua dos Mouros

Rua dos Limpinhos

Rio Sequa

Rosado

Rua George

N

150 yards

150 meters

0

0

## Accommodation
Ilha da Tavira Camping **15**
Pousada Convento
   da Graca **12**
Quinta das Oliveiras **1**

## Dining
A Ver Tavira **6**
Ca D'Oro **9**
Mercado da Ribeira cafes **8**
Portas do Mar **11**
Praca da Republica cafes **4**
Quatro Aguas **10**

## Attractions
Camara Obscura **5**
Castle **14**
Ciencia Viva **2**
Igreja de Misericordia **7**
Igreja de Santa Maria
   do Castelo **13**
Ponte Romana **3**

main attractions are on the west side of the river. They include the remains of the medieval castle, the camera obscura, and a handful of churches, the most accessible of which are the Igreja de Santa Maria do Castelo and the Igreja da Misericórdia, and conveniently for families, they are all within a five-minute walk of the Praça da República and each other, clustered around the chunky tower that marks the site of the medieval castle. Exploring Tavira is easy even for children – though families with tots will prefer to use the miniature tourist train for their sightseeing.

The Ponte Romana footbridge spans the Gilão (with more modern bridges upriver and downriver carrying road and rail traffic). This bridge is an emblem of Portuguese independence, and a tiled plaque at the Praça da República end commemorates the local warriors who defended it against the Spanish during Portugal's war of independence in 1383–5. Most of the city's sights and attractions – which include the usual assortment of historic churches and the ruins of a small castle – are on the west side of the river. Downstream, fishing boats are moored along the Doca Pesca quayside next to the old fish market.

The nearest beaches are on Ilha de Tavira, the long sandy island that lies at the mouth of the Gilão and stretches almost all the way west to Olhão and the Ria Formosa. A regular passenger ferry goes to the island from Quatro Águas, a five-minute drive from the town centre.

**Santa Luzia** Santa Luzia is just down the road from Tavira (so close that it is now virtually a suburb of its bigger neighbour) but still feels like a community in its own right. It's proud to be the Algarve's 'octopus capital' (a sign announces this as you enter town) and is still a working fishing port. For visitors, it's only really of much interest as a jumping-off point for the Ilha de Tavira beaches (a long footbridge crosses the tidal mudflats of the Tavira channel to connect Santa Luzia with the island) and for boat trips on the lagoon.

*3 km west of Tavira*

### Vila Real de Santo António

The easternmost outpost of the Algarve, Vila Real deserves more attention than it gets from British tourists. In fact, most of its visitors come from Spain, just across the Guadiana river. The old part of town, stretching along the west bank of the Guadiana, is a neat grid of dignified buildings of grey stone and whitewashed plaster, built in the record time of just five months in 1775, on the orders of the Portuguese prime minister, the Marques de Pombal. Pombal was a dab hand at urban planning – 20 years earlier, he oversaw the reconstruction of Lisbon and other Portuguese cities after the Great Earthquake of 1755, seizing the opportunity to rebuild them as properly planned urban centres. He's commemorated in Vila Real by the

Praça de Pombal, a central square one block from the river front, surrounded by dignified buildings, lined with orange trees and paved with black and white cobbles.

Yachts, motor cruisers and fishing boats seem to compete for space along the river quays, but there is no longer a ferry to the Spanish side – it has been supplanted by a graceful suspension bridge, several kilometres upstream near Castro Marim. Admittedly, this isn't the most exciting sightseeing town in the Algarve, but it's a pleasant enough place for a family outing, with plenty of café-restaurants with outdoor tables. If you're thinking about staying here, however, don't: Monte Gordo, with its purpose-built resort facilities, fabulous beach and a much bigger choice of places to stay than Vila Real has to offer, is only 4 km downriver and for families is a much better choice.

*24 km east of Tavira*

**Castro Marim** A short distance inland from Vila Real de Santo António, Castro Marim sits on a hilltop overlooking the Guadiana river, the wetlands and salt pans of the **Reserva Natural do Sapal** and the impressive new international suspension bridge. It's a pretty little town, with a clutter of whitewashed houses spilling down the slopes of two hills, each crowned by the walls of a massive fortress. The more modern of these two strongholds, the grimly massive Fortaleza de São Sebastião, was built during the 17th century and is currently inaccessible as it is being restored, but the older of the two is a cracker of a castle (see p. 162). If children need to let off steam after too long in the back seat, there's a large and well-equipped public playground to the right of the road as you drive into Castro Marim, complete with wooden climbing frames, seesaws and other stuff.

*5 km north of Vila Real de Santo António on N12*

## Beaches & Resorts

From Tavira all the way east to Monte Gordo, the beaches of the eastern Algarve shore are all identically gorgeous, so much so that they are very hard to tell apart, merging into each other in one long strip, which is dotted with small villages and resorts. For white sand and clear blue water, however, Manta Rota, Praia Verde and Monte Gordo have the edge over lagoon beaches such as Cabanas and Cacela.

**Ilha de Tavira** ★★ FIND Just getting to Ilha de Tavira is a miniature adventure, involving a short boat trip across the channel that separates this long sandbar island from the mainland. The journey is well worth it – this is one of the best family beaches in the entire Algarve, uncrowded but with excellent facilities, including lifeguards and first-aid centre, campsite and picnic grounds under the pine trees, and half-a-dozen family-friendly restaurants and snack bars including **Restaurante Ilha Formosa,** with tables inside and out, which serves Portuguese and British food, and the cheap and cheerful self-service Dinoself cantina (see p. 173). The beach, on the southern, seaward side of the island, stretches for around 12 km from east to west, reaching almost as far as the estuary of the Ria Formosa, and finding an empty stretch of sand is never difficult (though in high summer you will have to hike a bit further down the beach to find glorious isolation). It's an enormous expanse of fine white sand, littered with shells and perfect for beachcombing, swimming and sandcastle building.

*Shuttle ferries leave from Praia de Quatro Águas, 3 km from central Tavira, hourly 9am–5pm, €1. Water taxis also leave from the Quatro Águas jetty on demand (☎ 00 351 964 515 073 or 00 351 917 035 207), €6 per boat (up to six passengers).*

**Cabanas** About 8 km east of town, Cabanas is a slightly scruffy, low-key fishing village of old-fashioned tiled houses that is more like a suburb of Tavira than a full-scale resort. There is plenty of accommodation here – mainly in cheap apartments along the waterfront – and no shortage of places to eat, but there are no big hotels or villa complexes, and you get the impression that it's favoured more by Portuguese weekend visitors from Tavira than package tourists. In short, the locals aren't outnumbered by visitors, and Cabanas is an amiable spot for families who want a bit more local colour than is offered by the Algarve's bigger, blander resorts. The downside of this is that Cabanas isn't a winner in the beach stakes – it stands on a tidal creek, sheltered from the open sea by a sand-bar island, and although it has its own patches of sand it can't compete with the mega-beaches further east.

*8 km east of Tavira*

Cabanas

**Beware of Woolly Caterpillars**

**One of the weirder little creatures children may encounter is the pine** processionary caterpillar. Brownish in colour, about 2 cm long and covered in white bristles, these 'woolly bears' are far from cuddly. The tiny hairs are toxic, causing painfully itchy red blotches.

The caterpillars infest pine trees, living in messy nests which they weave from a substance-like spider's web, and sometimes migrate from tree to tree in long nose-to-tail processions, which is how they get their name. Fascinating to watch – but don't touch!

**Cacela Velha** **FIND** Cacela Velha ('Old Cacela') is a charming and entirely unspoilt village of pretty old cottages on a headland, surrounding a miniature castle that is still in use by the Portuguese armed forces and therefore out of bounds to visitors – you can see an incongruous modern radar array spinning above the ancient stone ramparts. Below the village (a steep walk, and not very pushchair friendly) is a wide, tidal creek with a strip of narrow sandy beach backed by dunes covered with sweet-smelling lentisk bushes. Offshore, a sandy island shelters this stretch of water from the open Atlantic, making this a good spot for beachcombing, paddling and catching tiddlers but less than ideal for those in search of huge stretches of sand and open sea. There are no facilities for families (or indeed anyone) on the beach, but the village has a couple of small café-restaurants.

*12 km east of Tavira*

**Manta Rota** ★ Turn off the main coastal highway to Manta Rota to discover a stretch of

beach that is spectacular even by the demanding standards of the Algarve coast. The resort itself is a bland, ever-expanding settlement of low-rise apartment complexes and has few other amenities (it's distinctly short of cafés and restaurants, and clearly most visitors here are catering for themselves), but the beach is to die for. Manta Rota is set back a few hundred metres from its beach and separated from it by a wide stretch of dunes covered with lentisk bushes whose white and purple blossoms smell almost overwhelmingly sweet in spring, and a wooden boardwalk links the resort with the sands, and allows for easy walking or buggy-pushing along the beach, which has lifeguards, a first-aid centre and a few café-shacks in high season. In low season, especially at weekends, it is popular with local anglers, who populate the tideline with fishing rods and beach umbrellas.

*15 km east of Tavira*

**Praia Verde** ★ Praia Verde ('Green Beach') is an entirely artificial settlement – and none the worse for that. This stretch of coast above a superb stretch of sandy beach was uninhabited until the complex of villas, apartments and a four-star hotel were built here in the 1980s. The resort is much more sensitively designed than most, and its low-rise buildings are landscaped and concealed by pine woods. A short walk from the car park, the beach itself has lifeguards and water sports in summer, along with a couple of restaurants right on the sand (complemented by several more in the resort complex). Merging with Manta Rota to the west, the wide beach stretches for miles in either direction so there's plenty of space for all, and it shelves gently, making it a great safe spot for children.

*20 km east of Tavira*

**Monte Gordo ★★** Monte Gordo, the easternmost resort in the Algarve, stands close to the mouth of the Guadiana river and its looming high-rise hotels and pyramids of apartments can be seen as far off as Ilha de Tavira. It certainly isn't the most sensitively designed development in the Algarve, but if you seek a full-service resort with a huge beach, plenty of places to eat, water sports and lots of soft white sand, it's the no-brainer choice in the eastern Algarve. Its beach appears endless, stretching west to merge with Praia Verde and east all the way to the Guadiana, and has all the mod cons you could want, including shops selling beach kit, a buggy-friendly boardwalk, lots

of beach restaurants right on the sand, lifeguards and a first-aid centre in season. Although Monte Gordo has mushroomed far beyond its traditional roots, it is still a fishing village with a fleet of little wooden boats hauled up on the sand at the west end of town. Each of these has its array of brightly coloured pennants on poles, used to mark the location of nets and lobster pots when at sea, and giving the whole flotilla a rakishly colourful look, like an encampment of medieval lancers. Monte Gordo's beach shelves gently, making it friendly to toddlers as well as older children.

*24 km east of Tavira*

*Monte Gordo Tourist Office, Avenida Marginal (☎ 00 351 281 544 495; E: turismo.montegordo@ rtalgarve.pt)*

## Natural Reserves

### Reserva Natural do Sapal

AGES 11 AND UP Between Vila Real de Santo António and Castro Marim stretches a huge (2,089 hectare) expanse of salt marsh, wetlands, creeks and pools which shelters more than 150 kinds of bird – sometimes in huge flocks. Flamingos, storks and spoonbills are the most spectacular and most likely to impress children, but there are many more. That said, this isn't a spot that is likely to make instant converts of children raised on Discovery Channel documentaries – the scenery is flat and uninspiring, but there is a modern visitor centre (with washrooms and toilets) with walking trails, information panels and telescopes for young bird-spotters. Various tracks and trails enter and traverse the reserve, but unless you are in a four-wheel-drive vehicle they should be treated with caution – car hire companies take a dim view of clients who go off-road, and the reserve is decidedly pushchair-hostile so this isn't a great experience for toddlers. Finding your way into and around the reserve can be tricky, so visit the park headquarters in Castro Marim before setting out on your safari. The Sapal salt marshes are still extensively used for making salt – look out for giant greyish-white mountains of the stuff among the brackish pools and salt pans.

*Visitor Centre: off A122 northbound, take the exit for the Guadiana bridge and Spain, then follow signs for Reserva Natural.*

*Reserve headquarters: Sapal de Venta Moinhos, Apartment 7, Castro Marim (📞 00 351 281 510 680; E: rnscm @icn.pt; www.ccdr-alg.pt).* **Open** *Mon–Fri 9.30am–12.30pm and 2pm–5.30pm. Free admission.*

### Ria Formosa Natural Park ★★★ AGES 10 AND UP

The Ria Formosa Natural Park extends almost all the way to Tavira and can be explored by boat, canoe, bicycle, or on foot with boat tours in summer starting from Santa Luzia, 3 km west of Tavira (see p. 159).

*Centro de Educacao Ambiental (Environmental Education Centre), Visitor Centre, Quinta do Marim,*

*Olhão (Parque Natural da Ria Formosa) (📞 00 351 289 704 134). 2 km east of Olhão.* **Open** *daily 9am–12pm and 2pm–6pm. Free admission.*

## Children-friendly Tours

### Comboios Turisticos (Tourist Trains) ★★ ALL AGES

Miniature trains with three dinky carriages pulled by a mini-locomotive wind their way around Tavira, stopping at all the major sights and making sightseeing fairly effortless. They leave hourly from 9am until midnight, starting at Praça da República and calling at the castle, Convento da Graca, Igreja de Santa Maria, Ermida de São Roque, then crossing the Ponte Romana to the Convento do Carmo, Mercado do Ribeira, and all the way out to Quatro Águas (where you can hop on the shuttle ferry to Ilha de Tavira and its beaches).

*Daily, year round, on the hour from 10am–midnight, operated by Delgaturis (📞 00 351 289 389 067; www.deltrain.com). €4.*

### Horse-drawn carriages ★ ALL AGES

Tavira Tours has a choice of five trips round town in a horse-drawn open carriage. It's a great way for a family to explore in style – you can just take a 15-minute trot up and down the waterside or go all the way out to Quatro Águas, which takes around 75 minutes there and back. However, the longer tours, such as the 150-minute trip around the Salinas salt pans or the even longer four-hour trip out to the pretty Moinhos da

Horse-Drawn Carriage, Tavira

Rocha waterfalls, 10 km from Tavira, are likely to test the patience of younger travellers.

*Tavira Tours (☎ 00 351 963 126 597; www.tavira-tours.com). Prices start at €10 per carriage (up to five passengers) for the 15-minute tour.*

**Boat trips** ★ **ALL AGES** Boat trips up the Guadiana as far as Alcoutim and around the lagoons of the Ria Formosa Natural Park are offered by several boat companies. Most of these are based at Santa Luzia harbour, 4 km west of Tavira, but have pick-up points in Tavira town centre and in Vila Real de Santo António. Riosul (which also operates four-wheel-drive 'safaris' into the backwoods of the Algarve), runs day trips up the river with a stop for an open-air buffet lunch at its own riverside resort, Quinta do Rio, which has pools for children and grown-ups and a children's playground.

*Safari Boat (☎ 00 351 933 683 237; 00 351 977 286 382; E: safariboat @clix.pt; Cais da Santa Luzia). Several 'nature trips' including a*

*full-day outing for €15 per person; under 12s half price, under 5s free.*

*Riosul, Rua Tristão Vaz Teixeira, 15c based in Monte Gordo but with pick-ups in Tavira (☎ 00 351 281 510 201; www.riosultravel.com), offers cruises on the Guadiana.*

## Flying Saucers & Science

### Torre de Tavira camera obscura ★ **FIND** AGES 8 AND UP

Tavira's camera obscura is housed in the Torre de Tavira, a former water tower that looms over the town centre. Built during the 1930s, it is a landmark in its own right and was a futuristic building for its time (the tourist board describes it as 'charismatic and extraordinary'). Just look for the thing that looks like a concrete flying saucer. Inside, an arrangement of lenses and mirrors gives you an astonishing 360 degree view of the town.

*12 Calcada da Galeria (☎ 00 351 281 321 754; www.cdepa.pt). Open Mon–Sat 10am—5.30pm (1st May–30th Sept) and 9.30am–5pm (1st Oct–30th Apr). Admission: family*

# Wildlife Checklist

**Not so long ago (at least until the 1990s) you were more likely to see** larks, thrushes and other song birds hanging up in markets and restaurant windows than in the fields and woods of the Algarve. Portuguese hunters are still keen on blasting away at just about anything with fur or feathers, but the region's nature reserves give refuge to a wide range of birds and animals. Anorak dads will already be reaching for their binoculars as soon as they get off the plane, but for children less interested in distinguishing between lesser, greater and medium sized warblers there are some showier, easy-to-spot species out there. Here's a checklist of birds, butterflies, reptiles and amphibians to look out for:

BIRDS

- Flamingos – seek them out on the mud flats of the Ria Formosa and Sapal reserves in the eastern Algarve and the Pena reserve in the west.
- Storks – look up to find long-legged White Storks nesting and roosting on bell-towers, arches, old factory chimneys and even street lights, or wheeling overhead.
- Spoonbills – guess what? The spoonbill looks like a whitish heron, but has a dark beak shaped like a spoon. You'll see them dibbling around in muddy shallows at low tide.
- Egrets – look for these small, perky white relatives of our familiar British heron around lakes and ponds and in pastures, where they hunt insects stirred up by grazing cattle – or sometimes, perched on a dozy cow.
- Purple Gallinule – this water bird is a bigger, more brightly coloured relative of the coots and water-hens to be seen on most ponds at home. Look out for them in the inland stretches of the Ria Formosa reserve.

ticket €10, adults €3.50, schoolchildren €2.80.

## Ciencia Viva (Science Centre)

AGES 8-12   Housed, rather incongruously, in a former church building, Ciencia Viva aims to inform enquiring young minds about a range of aspects of the sciences as they impact on Tavira, its people and their environment – taking in everything from marine biology and sewage treatment to solar power and food science. The centre is really for local school children (and its grasp of English is patchy) but its interactive displays will amuse British children too.

*Convento do Carmo, Tavira ( 00 351 281 326 231; www.tavira.ciencia viva.pt). Admission: €5.*

- Hoopoe – the exotic-looking hoopoe, with its pale pink and black plumage and punk-rock style crest of feathers, is quite common in the Algarve – look for it hunting for insects on roadside verges and grassy stretches.

BUTTERFLIES

- Monarch butterfly – these tiger-striped butterflies were brought to the Algarve from America by accident – as eggs, on the leaves of their food plant, the milkweed, which was brought in to adorn shrubberies and golf courses and has since run wild. Look for the adults flying around in summer, and hunt for the huge stripy caterpillars on milkweed plants in parks and gardens.
- Scarce Swallowtail butterfly – The Algarve's other big and easy-to-see summer butterfly is pale yellow with zebra stripes and little tails on its hind wings.

REPTILES AND AMPHIBIANS

- European Chameleon – If you look very hard and patiently, you just might see one of these google-eyed miniature dragons in the low bushes of the Ria Formosa nature reserve. Chameleons are masters of camouflage, and this is among the only places in Europe where you might find one.
- Green Tree Frog – It's green, it's a frog, but it prefers reeds and bullrushes to trees. Only comes out at night, so heard more often than seen (and very noisy, for a critter that is less than 5 cm long) – but if you're staying in a country villa you may find him in your pool.
- Moorish Gecko – If you're staying in an old stone house, you may hear these little lizards scuttling around at night, or if you're lucky even see them clinging to walls and ceilings with their clever sticky feet. They eat spiders, mosquitoes, moths and other creepy-crawlies.

## Historic Buildings

**Tavira Castle** AGES 10 AND UP The view from what's left of the Tavira Castle ramparts is almost as impressive as the panorama from the nearby camera obscura. All that remains of this once formidable building is a few sections of wall and a square tower. The stone stairs lack a guard rail, so take children by the hand and carry toddlers if climbing to the top. The pretty walled gardens below the tower, with shady orange and mimosa trees, are a pleasant place for a breather on a walk around town.

*Largo Abu-Othmane.* **Open** *Mon–Sat 8am–5pm, weekends 9am–5pm. Free admission.*

### Castro Marim Castle ★ FIND

AGES 10 AND UP With its crumbling
battlements and eagle-eye views,
Castro Marim's medieval castle
appeals to anyone of any age
with a sense of historical drama
(especially dads who are fans of
Bernard Cornwell's ruffian fic-
tional hero of the Napoleonic
Wars, Richard Sharp). It's not
difficult to imagine it being
haunted by the ghosts of Moors,
fanatical crusaders, heroes of
Portugal's struggle for independence, or even bloody-minded
redcoat veterans of Wellington's
Peninsular War army.

The original fortress was built
in the early 14th century by King
Dinis of Portugal (on the site of
an even earlier Moorish castle)
and was the headquarters of the
knights of the Order of Christ. Its
defences were reinforced during
the Wars of Restoration
(1610–68) when Portugal strug-
gled to throw off the yoke of
Spain. It was badly knocked
about by the great quake of 1755.
What remains is suitably tumble-
down, and archaeologists are at
work tracing the foundations of
the soldiers' barracks, churches,
store-houses and other buildings
that stood inside the walls – this
was really a walled town, not just
a castle, and you can scramble
over its battered battlements to
your heart's content – but take
care, because with the usual cava-
lier Portuguese disregard for
heights and edges, the stone stairs
and parapets are without guard
rails, so you should hang on to
adventurous children (timid tots
are unlikely to want to climb the

vertiginous steps). On the hilltop
opposite the castle, about 1 km
away, the much more functional
fortress of São Sebastião was built
in 1641 to reinforce Portugal's
renewed independence from
Spain. Its massive, sloping stone
walls with their rows of gun-ports
were state-of-the-art military
technology at the time and pre-
sumably served their purpose
well, as they have never heard a
shot fired in anger.

*5 km north of Vila Real de Santo
António on N122.* **Open** *daily
9am–7pm (Apr–Oct), 9am–5pm
(Nov–Mar). Free admission.*

**Tavira Churches** Tavira's huge
collection of religious buildings
(more than two dozen churches,
convents, monasteries and her-
mitages) is unlikely to hold the
attention of young ones for long,
especially when the beach beck-
ons. However, the most impressive churches are packed close
together in the heart of the historic centre – literally a stone's
throw from the ruined castle –
which makes them easy to visit,
so they are worth mentioning
here.

### Igrej da Misericordia ALL AGES

Rated as one of the loveliest
16th-century buildings in the
Algarve, the Church of Mercy is
just a few steps from the tourist
office. Outside, images of the
Virgin, St Peter and St Paul
guard the Renaissance portico
and inside there are splendid
blue and white azulejo tiles
and an impressive gilt altar.

*Largo da Misericordia, Tavira
(☎ 00 351 281 320 500).* **Open**

**FUN FACT**  **The Order of Christ**

**Within Castro Marim's ramparts are the foundations of a smaller, older**
castle that was a keep of the Order of Christ – better known to fans of Dan
Brown's *Da Vinci Code* as the Knights Templar. These legendary warriors of
medieval Christendom fought and plundered from Jerusalem to Scotland, and
became wealthy, powerful and arrogant. In the 14th century, accused by some
of Europe's most powerful kings and princes of heresy and witchcraft, the
Templar order was banned by the Pope – only to reappear shortly afterwards in
Portugal under its new name, the Order of Christ.

*9am–12.30pm and 2pm–5.30pm.
Free admission.*

### Igreja de Santa Maria do Castelo `ALL AGES`
A story goes
with this gleaming white church
next to the old castle: within lie
the bodies of seven Portuguese
knights who were treacherously
ambushed and killed by the
Moorish occupiers of the city
when they came to discuss a
truce in 1239. This event, supposedly, inspired the townspeo-
ple to rise against the Moors and
retake Tavira. The truth is probably a lot more complicated, but
it's a good yarn and you can see
the seven crosses that mark the
burial places of Tavira's own
'magnificent seven'. The church
looks out over very pretty gardens, and is right next door to
the castle.
*Largo de Santa Maria, Tavira ( 00
351 281 320 500). Opening times are
erratic but normally 9am–12pm and
2pm–6.30pm Mon–Fri and 11am Sun
for Mass. Free admission.*

## Active Families

### Monte do Alamo `ALL AGES`
Just
outside Tavira (1 km from town

centre), Monte do Alamo is a
converted farmhouse that offers
accommodation (see p. 166) and
a range of activities that includes
boat trips on traditional wooden
boats and canoeing in the Ria
Formosa Natural Park, dinghy
sailing around the beaches of Ilha
de Tavira, and a choice of fairly
undemanding walks and hikes in
and around the Tavira area (you
don't have to stay with them to
take part in their activities). For
prices of walks and other activities contact the owners direct.
*Poco do Alamo, Tavira ( 00 351 281
324 449; E: montedoalamo@gmail.
com). www.freewebs.com/monte
doalamo.*

### Riding lessons `AGES 5 AND UP`
Riding and carriage-driving lessons, bridleway riding and riding
over jumps are offered at several
quintas (farms) in the eastern
Algarve. Transport from your
hotel is available on request and
there are varying levels of lessons
for all ages from five years
upwards, ranging from gentle
trots round the paddock to more
challenging sessions for older
children and those who already
have some riding experience.

**What to See & Do**

**163**

## TIP ›› Cats & Dogs ‹‹

**Stray cats and dogs are common in the Algarve – mostly because** Portuguese pet owners are reluctant to take full responsibility for their pets. Unwanted puppies, kittens and even donkeys are usually simply abandoned to die or fend for themselves. Sadly, this means that children should be discouraged from getting too friendly with any dog not wearing a collar. The Association of Friends of Abandoned Animals runs the Canil São Francisco in Loulé, which gives refuge to hundreds of such animals. You can find out more – and sponsor an animal in need of help – at *www.algarvepets.org*.

*Centro da Equitação Quinta das Oliveiras, Tavira ( 00 351 281 322 107, 00 351 963 126 597 or 00 351 966 177 428). Daily (winter) 9.30am– 6.30pm, (summer) 8.30am–8pm.*

*Centro Equestre Quinta do Cavalo, Monte Francisco, Castro Marim ( 00 351 281 531 385). Daily 9am–1pm and 3pm–7pm.*

## Shopping

### Tavira

**Tavira's Mercado da Ribeira,** on the riverside west of the Praça da República gardens, is no longer the town market (which is now housed in a big modern building on the western edge of town, about 1 km away). Instead, its atrium now houses a handful of cafés and restaurants as well as a selection of gift shops. Most of them aren't very inspiring, but **A Farrobinha,** sells locally made sweets, jams and honey, small decorative bottles of the fruit and herb liquors for which the Algarve is famous (lemon, almond and vanilla are some of the more familiar flavours), as well as kitsch china dolls. The (nameless) bookshop in the south west corner of the market has a

very limited range of paperback thrillers in English, mostly by the usual holiday-reading suspects.

**A Doca** is a cut above most tourist tat shops, with chunky woollen knits, goatskins, sea shells, model ships, sheepskin slippers for children and adults, rag dolls and colourful marionettes.
*88 Rua Dr José Pires Pedinha, Tavira*

**Bead shop** three doors along from A Doca has no name above the door but is easy to spot – it's covered in blue and white tiles – and sells colourful necklaces and bracelets of big, bold, chunky ceramic beads.
*100 Rua Dr José Pires Pedinha, Tavira*

**Casa do Artesanas** is the base of the Association of Arts and Tastes of Tavira and sells the products of local craftsmen and women, including colourful woven rag rugs, leather belts and bags, textiles and ceramics, pretty little brightly coloured knitted booties for babies (€8.60), rag dolls in traditional costumes (€16.50) and perfect scale-model painted wooden carts made by local craftsman Jose Mestre (€40).
*11 Calcada da Galeria, Tavira*

**Top Chocs**

**Look out for Frank Vermorgen's Quinta do Xocolatl stall at Luz de Tavira** every Saturday. Belgian-born Frank makes the best choccies in the Algarve, using natural flavourings and melt-in-your-mouth 100% cocoa. A revelation to children who have only ever tasted cheap British chocolates.

*Quinta do Xocolatl, Sitio de Pinheiro, Luz de Tavira (☎ 00 351 968 327 812; www. quinta-xoc.com).*

Tavira also holds a series of fairs in summer, when local artisans, artists and farmers sell their products from white tented pavilions along both banks of the river, below the Roman bridge. Depending on the event, look out everything from handmade riding boots, rag dolls, brightly coloured kites, hats, leather goods, pretty ceramics, olive oil, cheese, herbs, wines and locally made liqueurs. To keep children amused, there's usually a band and other street entertainers at these events. To find out if there's a fair in Tavira

Tavira Bead Shop

during your visit, contact the tourist office.

### Vila Real de Santo António

Vila Real de Santo António does a thriving trade with Spanish shoppers who come across by the coachload at weekends. For some reason, they mainly seem to want to buy cotton towels and other household cottons and linens, so if you are in the market for a matching set of **brightly coloured beach towels,** look no further than the shopping streets that run inland from its main esplanade. Vila Real's main square, the Praça de Pombal, is the venue for occasional open-air bazaars which mainly sell mass-produced factory outlet products including toys, designer jeans and even miniature motor bikes and other high-tech kit for sub-teens.

## FAMILY-FRIENDLY ACCOMMODATION

Neither of the eastern Algarve's main towns is right on the beach. If you're looking for the kind of family holiday that involves heading straight for the sand after breakfast with the minimum of planning, Tavira and Vila Real de Santo António are probably not for you. That said, there are great beaches within about a 20-minute drive of each town, and Tavira has a fairly good assortment of hotels with pools in and around the town centre. The only full-on resort along this stretch of coast, however, is Monte Gordo, with the biggest selection of resort hotels and apartment complexes and the widest choice of places to eat and shop, right on top of a huge beach with room for all.

## Tavira

### Monte do Alamo ★ ★ ★ VALUE

With only four double, en-suite bedrooms in cottages recently rebuilt on the site of a farmhouse only 1 km from the centre of Tavira, this has to be one of the most user-friendly options for families in the region. There's a choice of bed and breakfast, half-board or full board and an

excellent range of amenities, including a shared living room with a fireplace, video and DVD library, and a paperback library revealing a good deal about the holiday-reading tastes of previous guests. It is set in a small but pretty (300 square metre) garden and the beach is around 2 km away – accessible by bike for active families. In fact, this is one of very few places in the area where you could manage quite well without a hired car – the owners arrange airport transfers on request. Tavira town centre and its sights, shops and restaurants are within walking distance, and you can cycle to Quatro Águas for the shuttle-boat to Ilha de Tavira and its beach in about 20 minutes – it's dead flat all the way. Boat trips on the river and the Ria Formosa lagoons can also be arranged. The English-speaking owners are passionate about cooking (they run 'Summer Flavours' cookery workshops in July) and the food is much, much better than in most Algarve

Monte do Alamo

hotels, with freshly squeezed juices for breakfast, fresh-baked bread and the best local produce, all beautifully presented.

*Poco do Alamo, Tavira (📞 00 351 281 324 449; www1.iha.com).* **Rates**: *from €50–70 for two, extra bed €15.* **Amenities**: *baby-sitting, cots, child beds and high chairs on request, WiFi and broadband internet access.* **In room**: *all rooms have en-suite shower/bath and WC.*

**MODERATE**

### Aldeamento Quinta das Oliveiras ★★★ FIND

Quinta das Oliveiras (which means 'The Olive Farm') is a semi-rural sub-urb around 1 km north of the centre of Tavira, on the north side of the N125 highway, so it's both accessible and fairly peaceful. Activities nearby include horse riding. Aldeamento Quinta das Oliveiras is a three-star complex of studios, two- and three-bed-room apartments and villas. Facilities include baby-sitting and a children's play area, outdoor pool, tennis court, snooker and table tennis, restaurant and snack bar. It's a fair way from the beaches, and therefore not ideal for a longer stay, but perfectly adequate for a short break. Baby cots and high chairs are available by prior arrangement.

*Quinta das Oliveiras, Almargem, Tavira (📞 00 351 213 300 541; www.maisturismo.pt).* **Rates**: *two-bed-room apartments start at €120.* **Amenities**: *baby-sitting, children's play area, outdoor pool, tennis court, snooker and table tennis, restaurant, bar, high chairs.* **In room**: *air condi-tioning, TV, fridge, kitchenette or (in vil-las) full kitchen.*

**EXPENSIVE**

### Pousada Convento da Graca ★★★ VALUE

This beauti-ful building, with its mellow yellow stucco walls and bell-tower, looks intimidatingly grand at first sight – and it is indeed the grandest address in the eastern Algarve. Don't be put off. Dignified and serene, yes; but family friendly too – and, if you can pick your dates, surpris-ingly affordable for what you get, with a range of family pack-ages. Set among gardens in the heart of the old town – Tavira's ruined castle is just a minute's walk away, across a pretty square shaded by palm trees and full of tweeting sparrows – the hotel has a long history. It was founded by King Dom Sebastião in 1569, when it was a convent for nuns of the Augustinian order. Within, its arched clois-ters surround a calm courtyard with a fountain and a mermaid statue, which might have shocked the convent's original guests, and a wide marble stair-case leads to the bedrooms on the upper floor. Small girls with a fondness for making a grand party entrance to dinner when dressed in their holiday best will enjoy this feature. The serv-ice is Portuguese at its best – extremely professional and help-ful without being effusive – and with fewer than 40 rooms and suites it never feels crowded.

Outside are grassy lawns sur-rounding a toddlers' pool and,

ADA

Pousada Convento da Graca

next to it, a full-sized pool with umbrellas and sun loungers. The best of the five suites has its own terrace and garden. Breakfast is included in the room rates and is served buffet-style, which is handy for picky and impatient children, with a choice of cheeses, cold cuts, yoghurt and fruit, fresh juices, cereal and hot dishes including sausage, bacon and scrambled eggs. Parents in need of a discreet hair of the dog can start the day by helping themselves to a complimentary glass (or two) of sparkling wine. The hotel also has off-street parking, and is only a minute's walk from the Praça da República, the Ponte Romana and the river front. Baby-sitting and cots are available by prior arrangement.

*Rua D. Paio Peres Correia (☎ 00 351 281 329 040 or ☎ 00 351 213 000 541; www.pousadas.pt). **Rates**: 40 rooms. Standard doubles from €150–230,*

*extra bed from €45–69, suites from €203–311. All rates include buffet breakfast. **Amenities**: gardens, courtyard, secure parking, pool, toddlers' pool, restaurant, cots, baby-sitting by arrangement. **In room**: air conditioning, TV, safe, minibar.*

## Ilha de Tavira

**INEXPENSIVE**

### Ilha de Tavira Camping ★

**VALUE** With space for more than 1,500 people, this island campsite in high season (which is mid-July to the end of August) is a bit like one of those jam-packed penguin colonies in Antarctica – it's a wonder everyone manages to keep track of their offspring. But it's good fun, it's cheap as chips, it's well serviced (security and CCTV cameras, as well as lock-ups for your valuables and an onsite ATM in case you run out of cash), and it's on a completely car-free sand island – perfect for beachcombing as well as swimming, sandcastles and sunbathing. Just a toddler's sprint away is one of the Algarve's great beaches, complete with half a dozen places to eat (see p. 154), lifeguards and first-aid centre, water sports, umbrellas and loungers and – best of all – 11 km or more of dazzling white sand. It opens in April, and if you can dodge the peak periods, you can stay here without the crowds in May and in the autumn. Pine trees give plenty of sweet-smelling shade and in spring the jasmine-like perfume of the lentisk bushes all around the island is almost overwhelming.

*Ilha de Tavira (📞 00 351 281 321 709; www.campingtavira.com). Capacity for 1,550 people. **Rates**: six-person (three-room) tent €52, refundable deposit €50, optional sleeping kit including air mattress, sheet, sleeping bag, pillow and cushion €7. Various seasonal promotions available – see website. **Amenities**: secure storage, 24-hour security, ATM.*

## Monte Gordo

**MODERATE**

### Iberotel Praia de Monte Gordo ★★ Love it or hate it,

you can't ignore this massive four-star hotel that squats on the beach at Monte Gordo like a futuristic pyramid. It's a landmark in its own right – so vast that you can see it from as far away as Ilha de Tavira. Architecturally sensitive, it ain't.

If you're on the inside looking out, however, there's a lot to be said for it. It does, for starters, have truly world-class views along the coast and out to sea. It's an all-suite hotel – with eight family suites that sleep up to six, assuming two of you are willing to use the sofa-bed in the living area. It has two restaurants – one of them a self-service, all you can eat buffet, the other a slightly unimpressive à la carte spot – three bars, and indoor and outdoor swimming pools, including an outdoor pool for children with a maximum depth of 50 cm. All the rooms are air conditioned, and have Internet connection and satellite TV with pay per view movies. The hotel also has a Children's Club with child-minders, aimed mainly at people between five and eight years old. And the enormous Monte Gordo beach is more or less on the doorstep.

If this hotel has a problem, it is that it tries a little too hard to appeal to everybody – it is occasionally swamped by people in suits attending business conferences, but ultimately, if you want a full-service hotel on the beach in the eastern Algarve's only fully developed beach resort, this is the one to choose.

*Av Infante Henrique, Monte Gordo (📞 00 351 281 008 900; www.iberotel. pt). **Rates**: 368 suites (eight family suites). From €700 for a family suite. **Amenities**: bars, buffet and à la carte restaurants, indoor and outdoor pools, children's club. **In room**: internet, satellite and PPV TV, fridge, safe, air conditioning.*

## Praia Verde

**MODERATE**

### Hotel Praia Verde ★★★ This

recently built four-star hotel-apartment complex, set back from a glorious sweep of beach at Praia Verde, is a cut above the bland, lookalike resort complexes that predominate along this stretch of coast. It stands on its own, which means that those staying here get first pick of space along the beach of a summer morning, and its architects have made a reasonable effort to make it, as well as the surrounding low-rise apartments, much more visually appealing than most, with a nod to typical Algarvean architecture. The low-rise, two-storey main building looks out over the pool terrace to pine woods that cloak the surrounding villas and the line of sand dunes that leads to the sea.

The hotel doesn't, admittedly, fall over itself to cater for children (though it does offer sensible family rates) and its own bars and restaurant are a bit on the sterile side. But to balance that, there's a cheap and cheerful seasonal complex of restaurants and cafés on site – between the hotel and the beach – along with the usual summer array of beach cafés and one stand-out fish restaurant on the beach, the **Pezinhos N'Areia** (see p. 174) that stays open all year. The rooms are described as 'junior suites'. Each has twin beds and a double sofa-bed, plus a basic kitchenette with a fridge – not big enough for full-on self-catering, but certainly adequate for making a cup of tea or even boiling an egg, and you can stuff the fridge with favourite cold drinks. They all have terraces or balconies, air conditioning and flat-screen satellite TV, as well as a daily linen service, so it's a really good balance between a hotel and a self-catering holiday.

*Praia Verde, Altura (📞 00 351 281 950 700; www.hotelpraiaverde.com).* **Rates**: *doubles from €98 (Nov–Jan)–€227 (Aug), 40 junior suite apartments sleeping up to four, extra child beds €13–32, free baby cots.* **Amenities**: *pool, bar, restaurant.* **In room**: *mini-kitchen, fridge, satellite TV, safe.*

# FAMILY-FRIENDLY DINING

Away from the beaches (which is to say in the town centres of Tavira and Via Real de Santo António, the eastern Algarve arguably panders a bit less to British families with children than do the big resort centres west of Faro. That's not to say the area is child-hostile. It isn't, but it hasn't been built from the ground up in quite the same way that Quarteira, Vilamoura, Portimão or Albufeira have. British-style pubs and fish and chips are definitely thinner on the ground around here – but in Tavira and Monte Gordo, at least, you'll find plenty of places with menus in English and even a few advertising Sky Sports if you *must*.

Most places welcome children without going very far out of their way to do so (one restaurant we checked out at Vila Real Santo António advertised an 'English children's menu': the only dish was beans on toast), but Tavira is a notable hot spot for friendly, open-air restaurants offering children's menus and child-sized portions, and located well away from busy traffic. As everywhere along the coast, most restaurants offer appetisers and snacks that are suitable for child-sized appetites, and there is no objection to ordering these smaller dishes without a main course. Most restaurant owners have a stab at an English translation of their menu, though the translation can be a bit erratic, and English isn't as widely spoken in restaurants here as it is further west. The town centres of Tavira and Vila Real de Santo António are mainly pedestrianised, however, so pavement cafés and ice-cream parlours – of which there are plenty – are fairly toddler friendly.

Down on the beach, in summer, it's a whole different story, with a string of amiably relaxed café-restaurants along the boardwalks of every beach. These are decidedly temporary affairs – they generally open around Easter as the main holiday season kicks off, and pack up around mid to late September. Often, they flourish for just one season, never to be seen again, so only a few stalwarts arc listed here. Generally, though, on every beach strip you will find several places that can be relied upon to keep families happy with a supply of fruit juices, soft drinks, sweet and savoury pancakes, ice-cream and basic burger-style snacks, and several more serving high-quality Portuguese seafood – often fresh from the sea – with tables on the sand and well away from traffic.

For drinks, coffee, cake or ice-cream, look no further than the **Praça da República in Tavira,** on the banks of the Gilao and at one end of the famous Roman bridge, where you will find a small parade of cafés and ice-cream parlours on a cobbled square beside a modern fountain and reflecting pool. For a leisurely lunch or alfresco dinner, stroll to the far end of Rua Dr

José Pires Pedinha, where next to the fishing boat quay stands a row of cheerful fish restaurants, where the menus and prices – displayed on blackboards outside – are all very similar and where your best bet is just to grab the first available table.

What you spend at any of these is very much a matter of choice – stick to cheaper dishes such as sardines, chicken or squid and you can eat for as little as €5–10 each, but opt for the lobster or the *cataplana* and the bill leaps to around €30 each or even more.

## Tavira

**MODERATE**

### Restaurante Ca' Doro ★★

One of the half-dozen restaurants by the fishing quay, Ca'Doro has a children's menu that offers sausage, egg and chips, spaghetti Bolognese, pork steak with fried egg, hamburger or fish fingers for €3.90. For more sophisticated tastes, grilled chicken for €4.80 or a plate of fresh grilled sardines for €4 are still affordable. Push-ing the boat out for a final night splurge, you could go for the lobster at €58 per kilo, or if the children have been persuaded to try Portuguese specialities the hearty *cataplana* stew (chicken or seafood) at €26.50 is big enough to feed a couple of smaller appetites as well as the two adults it is intended for – portions are huge.

*Doca Pesca, Rua Dr José Pires Pedinha. €8–60. Credit cards*

accepted. **Open** *midday–10pm daily
Apr–Oct, midday–4pm and 8pm–
10pm daily. Closed Sun.*

**A Ver Tavira** ★★★ This is a
good spot for a family lunch
while exploring the old part of
Tavira. The location couldn't be
better – it's on a quiet cobbled
square, right next to the arched
entrance to the pretty castle gardens. Across the square is the
Igreja de Santa Maria do Castelo,
where the tourist train makes a
regular stop (which is handy) and
just around the corner is the camera obscura. It's quite posh, but
children are welcome (and if they
get fidgety they can run off excess
energy in the castle gardens) and
the food is excellent, with dishes
such as roasted shrimp with sweet
basil sauce, octopus with cabbage
(their speciality), pork leg with
chestnuts and duck rice. Older
children with more adventurous
palates might be tempted by the
lunchtime 'tasting menu' – a set
of starters, two or three miniature
main dishes and a set of desserts.
*Calcada da Galeria 13 Tavira (📞 00
351 281 381 363). Tasting menu €15.
Credit cards accepted. Reservations
recommended for dinner.* **Open**
*11am–2am weekdays and 6pm–2am
weekends.*

### Ilha de Tavira/Quatro Águas

Two smart seafood restaurants
lurk on the waterside at Quatro
Águas, which is where Tavira
folk go for the best seafood.
Either would be a good (but not
cheap) choice if you arrive with
hungry people in tow and have
just missed the hourly shuttle

ferry across to Ilha de Tavira.
The cheap and cheerful alternative this side of the water is
Quiosque Florencio, beside the
ferry pier, which serves soft
drinks, beer, wine, coffee and
basic snacks (bread, cheese and
sausage, €1.50). If you're lucky,
you might grab one of half a
dozen plastic tables under its
awning; if not, you'll just have to
sit under the shade on the ferry
dock while you eat your sandwich and wait for your boat.

When you get to Ilha de
Tavira, there's a choice of at least
half a dozen restaurants and café
bars strung along the boardwalk
on the beach side of the island.
As everywhere along the coast,
these come and go with the seasons, but stalwarts include
Restaurante Ilha Formosa.

### Restaurante Marisqueira Quatro Águas ★★★ FIND This
restaurant is highly recom-
mended by locals. It looks a bit
posh from the outside, with its
pure white linen and serried
ranks of wine glasses on each
table, and is probably not ideal
for tots, even in summer when it
has tables outside. It's also the
pricier of the two – you'll be
lucky to get away with paying
less than €25 each, and it makes
no compromises with tourist
menus (though the excellent
Portuguese menu is translated
into English). They also offer
cut-price deals on boat trips on
the lagoon for diners, starting at
€10 per person and with pick-
ups at Quatro Águas, Tavira and
Santa Luzia – a morning on the

water followed by an extended seafood lunch.

*Sitio de Quatro Águas (☎ 00 351 281 325 329). €25–50. Credit cards accepted. Reservations recommended. **Open** noon–3.30pm and 7pm–10.30 pm. Closed Mon and 10th Dec–31st Dec.*

### Restaurante Portas do Mar ★★★
The competition for a sit-down meal at Quatro Águas comes from the **Portas do Mar** restaurant, just the other side of the car park, which has a children's menu (*ementa enfantil*) and serves snacks and salads from as little as €3–6. Grown-ups could eat here for as little as €15 per head, and the seafood menu is complemented by grilled meat dishes, duck and chicken.

*Sitio das Quatro Águas (☎ 00 351 281 321 255). €15–35. Credit cards accepted. **Open** 12.30pm–4pm and 7pm–10.30pm. Closed Mon.*

### Restaurante Ilha Formosa ★★
This restaurant (with tables inside and out and where service is brisk and friendly) has a mainly fishy, Portuguese menu (sardines and potatoes cost €7) but it also serves its own slightly eccentric take on English-style breakfast, advertising 'mix egg and bacon and drink' for €7.50, and a variety of toasted sandwiches. We're not sure what vegetable soup is doing on the breakfast menu, but it only costs €1.25.

*Ilha da Tavira (☎ 00 351 281 324 056). Credit cards not accepted. No reservations required. **Open** daily 10am–10pm June–Sept, 11am–4pm Oct–Feb.*

**Dinoself** ★ No reservations are required to eat at the cheapest spot on Ilha da Tavira's boardwalk. Also not required (at least in summer): shoes or shirt. Dinoself caters mainly to people staying on the campsite next door, so it is always full of families and does a mix of self-service plated meals, salads, pizzas to order, sandwiches – you name it. You could feed a family of four here for as little as €25.

*Ilha da Tavira. No credit cards. No reservations required. **Open** daily 10am–10pm June–Sept, 12am–3pm Oct–Feb.*

## Vila Real de Santo António

**O Coração da Ciudade** ★ Give these guys credit – they're really trying to appeal to the wandering British family with their 'Special UK Menu – Beans on Toast' (€1.50). They also do other typical British dishes – fish and chips (€3.90), spaghetti Bolognese (€4.50) and an array of snacks and sandwiches, as well as more authentically Portuguese treats including grilled sardines (€5.00) and chicken piri piri (€6.00), which are not too weird for most non-picky Brit-kids.

*Rua Dr Teofilo Braga, opposite the Centro Cultural António Aleixo on the town's main shopping street. €10–12. No credit cards. No reservations required.*

## Monte Gordo

As in all the Algarve's boom-town resorts, restaurants in

Monte Gordo come and go with the seasons and none stand out from the crowd. Along the beach boardwalk, however, there are informal and reliable options.

### Restaurante do Jaime ★★

**VALUE** This is a cheap and cheerful seafood shack, favoured by locals, and standing on the sand next to the row of boathouses (each bearing the name of the owner's fishing boat) at the west end of the esplanade where the fish is fresh off the boat.

*Praia Monte Gordo. €10–12. No credit cards. No reservations required.* **Open** *Mon–Sat midday–4pm and 8pm–10pm.*

### Restaurante Bar Esplanada Jopel ★★

Just opposite the tourist office on the beach, this restaurant is slightly more upscale and has tables outside on the sand or indoors for slightly more formal eating.

*Praia Monte Gordo. €10–20. Credit cards accepted. No reservations required.* **Open** *Mon–Sat midday–4pm and 8pm–10pm.*

## Praia Verde

### Pezinhos N'Areia ★★★

Praia Verde beach in summer has a full-service concession zone with lifeguards, first-aid centre, water sports and a choice of seasonal bars and snack-bars. These come and go with the seasons, but Pezinhos N'Areia is an all-year-round operation that attracts people from all over the Algarve with its superb fresh fish and seafood menu served right on the water's edge. Perfect for parents who want to enjoy a sit-down meal while letting children run wild, still within sight, on the beach. This is a restaurant that caters mainly to locals, so most fish – which is served simply grilled with accompanying vegetables – is priced by the kilogram, which can confuse British diners. Pick your victim from the ice table, have it weighed, and they will show you how much you'll pay. Don't be fooled by the simple surroundings – expect to pay at least €30 each here for a full meal, but they also have a snack menu that is served all day in summer and will keep children happy.

*Praia Verde (📞 00 351 281 513 195; www.pezinhosnareia.com). €30. Credit cards accepted. Reservations recommended at weekends.* **Open** *daily midday–4pm and 7pm–10.30pm June–Sept, midday–4pm Oct–May. Closed Mon.*

# 7 Onwards to Spain

**T**he eastern Algarve adjoins Spain's 'sherry triangle', the three points of which are **Huelva** (about 60 km east of Vila Real de Santo António, Seville (a further 100 km further east and inland) and the famous seaport of Cádiz. Portugal's IP1 (E1) motorway becomes the Spanish A49 (E1) after crossing the Guadiana road bridge just north of Castro Marim. The frontier crossing is seamless and there is rarely any need to stop (or even slow down) for border checks, but you should carry all the family passports just in case. The Spanish AP4 (E05) motorway connects Seville and Cádiz, and Jerez de la Frontera, home of sherry, is 55 km east of Cádiz on the same route. Within the triangle bounded by these highways lies one of Spain's last bits of wilderness, the Marismas del Guadalquivir, surrounding the **Parque Nacional de Doñana**, while the whole long sweep of coast from Huelva to Cádiz is known as the **Costa de la Luz**. It's this great expanse of pint-sized white villages, pine-scented woodlands and sparkling coves that holds the most allure for British families – all 260 km of it, of which more than half is sandy beach. It's hardly virgin territory, but many of the villages remain reassuringly Spanish and the coastline is pleasantly uncommercial compared with the more built-up stretches of the Algarve to the west.

Picture-postcard Vejer is the trendiest, most upscale spot on this stretch of coast, while Tarifa's long beaches and rolling surf make it a favourite for surfers, windsurfers and kite-surfers – if you have active teenagers, this is definitely the place to be. Los Caños de Meca and El Palmar, near Conil, are more laid back, and Barbate is a working fishing port, with all that implies: trawlers, oil-stained docks and a pervasive reek of fish and diesel fuel. To the north west, the cheery resorts of Zahara de los Atunes and Chiclana are bordered by beaches that – high summer aside – are never crowded so are ideal for playful little ones. Prettiest of all is Bolonia, with its magnificent Roman ruins beside a beach backed by high sand dunes.

## ESSENTIALS

### Getting There

Since both Portugal and Spain are full EU members, border formalities are non-existent – you just drive straight through, across the new Guadiana international road bridge. However, as the UK is not part of the Schengen group of passport-free EU countries, you should take all your family passports, and the rental papers for your hire car, just in case you are stopped at a random police checkpoint anywhere in Spain.

With a car, it's dead easy to tack a tour around this part of Spain onto a stay in the eastern Algarve. Huelva is around an hour's drive from Tavira, Seville around 90 minutes and Cádiz around three hours. Without a car, it's still doable – there are cross-border buses to Huelva and

## Mind How You Go!

**If the Spanish cops catch you speeding (or committing a parking** offence) you will be escorted to the nearest ATM and required to pay a spot fine in cash. Until now, it's been harder for them to chase up drivers of rental cars caught on unmanned speed cameras – but since March 2007, Spanish (and Portuguese) authorities can ask the UK DVLA to chase you up back home and fine you or add penalty points to your licence. So watch it. That goes double around Tarifa – where the local authority uses British debt collection agencies to pursue delinquent drivers in the UK.

a high-speed rail link between Seville and Cádiz – but not highly recommended for travel with children, or even all that much cheaper than renting a car.

See *www.raileurope.com* or the Renfe (Spanish Railways) website *www.renfe.es* to plan a rail journey in Spain.

A standard one-way rail ticket between Seville and Cádiz costs €9.40 adult, €4.70 under 14, free under two years.

Most car hire companies in the Algarve have no problem with taking cars across the border, but double check to make sure that your insurance and other terms and conditions are not affected.

There are also flights from several UK airports to Seville and to Jerez de la Frontera (next to Cádiz). If you want to combine a trip to the Algarve with a foray into this part of Spain, consider flying into Faro and home from Seville or Jerez (or the other way round). The only snag is that you will almost certainly have to pay a hefty surcharge to pick up a rental car in Portugal and drop it off in Spain (or vice versa).

# VISITOR INFORMATION

### Provincial Tourist Office
Alameda Apodaca, Cádiz (00 34 956 807 061; *www.cadizturismo.com*).

### Regional Tourist Office
C/Calderon de la Barca, Cádiz (00 34 956 211 313).

## Getting Around

The easiest way to explore the interesting old quarters of Cádiz, Seville and Jerez is on foot. These are compact areas, walkable even for smaller children, and with quite extensive pedestrianised (or at least semi-pedestrianised) areas. There are extensive and inexpensive (metered) public car parks on the fringes of all the old city areas, as well as underground parking garages (which are more expensive than open-air car parks but are also more secure, so are a better bet if you have luggage in the car). Most of the hotels listed in the Family-Friendly Accommodation section below also have their own car parks.

# WHAT TO SEE & DO

## Top Family Attractions

**❶ Dancing horses of Jerez**
Young and old alike can delight in 90 minutes of spectacular showmanship from this troop of beautiful, highly trained horses and their riders (see p. 192).

**❷ Whale and dolphin spotting in Tarifa** Dolphins can be seen offshore at any time of year and killer whales (orcas) may be spotted in July and August (see p. 197).

**❸ Cádiz Museum** Home of the Tia Norica puppet theatre with colourful props and characters that have delighted children for many years (see p. 195).

**❹ Cota Doñana National Park** Take a trip round this wilderness area on horseback or by boat. Plenty of bird life and stunning views are guaranteed (see p. 193).

**❺ Zoologico de Jerez** Zoo with lions, white tigers, lots of other animals (see p. 192).

**❻ Flamenco Show, Jerez** Little girls especially will love the spirit of flamenco dancing – and the costumes (see p. 185).

**❼ Bolonia Beach, Tarifa** The region's most spectacular beach has huge sand dunes and Roman ruins. One for the teenage surf dudes (see p. 190).

**❽ Aqualand** Cracking water park with lots of thrilling rides (see p. 192).

## Spanish Festival Calendar

Spain is just unbeatable when it comes to colourful festivals – and Andalusia seems to have more of them than most parts of Spain.

They're not all ideal for children (they tend to go on all night, and most children will be more puzzled than amused by the solemn religious parades) but some of the more entertaining events include:

**January** (one day, last week in January, 11am–2.30pm)
Jerez
Fiesta de San Antón Abad
Dedicated to pets and children (see p. 203)

**February** (week starting 14th February)
Cádiz, Jerez and Seville
Carnival
Week-long parades, dancing and fireworks

**February–March** (starts last week in February for three weeks)
Jerez
Flamenco Festival
Guitars and frilly frocks. Great for girls

**April** (Palm Sunday–Good Friday)
Jerez Holy Week
Costumed religious parades

**May** (second week in May)
Jerez
Feria del Caballo (Horse Fair)
Horses and horse-lovers from all over the world meet in the home of the Andalusian thoroughbred

Flamenco Dresses

**July/August**

Huelva

Columbus Festival

Celebration of Columbus's voyage of discovery to the Americas, with musicians and dancers from a different South American country each year.

For up-to-date information on fiestas in the region visit *www.spanish-fiestas.com* or *www. spain.info*.

## Towns & Cities

It's a big step from the tranquil small towns and purpose-built resorts of the Algarve to the cities of Andalusia. While spots like Faro, Albufeira and Portimão have gone from sleepy fishing village status to full-blown resort areas in just one recent generation, Seville, Jerez and Cádiz have been cosmopolitan cities for many centuries.

There is plenty to see and do in these historic places, but tourism comes second to everyday life – and that is part of their charm.

### Huelva

Huelva, on the Rio Odiel, is the first city you come to after crossing the border from Portugal. Heavily damaged by the Great Earthquake of 1755, it is now a rather dull industrial city. Christopher Columbus (or Cristobal Colón, as he is known in Spain) set sail from Palos de la Frontera, just across the river from Huelva, on his voyage of discovery to the Caribbean and the Americas in 1492. The **Monumento a Colón** (Columbus Monument) at Punta del Sebo, overlooking the mouth of the Rio Odiel, commemorates the event and there are Columbus exhibits in the **Museo Provincial** (Alameda Sundheim 13, ☎ 00 34 959 259 300, open Tue: 3pm–8pm; Wed to Sat: 9am–8pm, Sun: 9am–3pm, free admission) along with a variety of finds from ancient and medieval times, including a collection of ancient Roman mining equipment from the Rio Tinto region and a unique water wheel. Huelva's main shopping streets – Concepción, Palacio, Pérez Carasa and Berdigón form one long, pushchair-friendly pedestrian precinct and if you like traditional markets you'll enjoy the town's Mercado El Carmen, with its great seafood section where clams, prawns, lobsters and sea and river fish are piled on trays of ice and where you can buy delicious ham from the hill farms of the Sierra de Aracena north of the city. Great for picnics.

All in all Huelva is not somewhere that you will want to linger long, especially with the treasures of Seville only half an hour down the road, but not far away is the main departure point for tours of the huge **Parque Nacional de Doñana**, with its shifting sand dunes, lagoons, wild deer, eagles and flocks of pink flamingos.

*Tourist office: Avda Alemania, 12 (☎ 00 34 959 257 403).*

## Seville

It's impossible not to be charmed by southern Spain's largest city. Seville is the provincial capital of Andalusia, and in the Middle Ages was an important Moorish city. It still has several photogenic relics of that time, along with the opulent cathedrals and palaces built after the Christian reconquest in the 15th century, and an array of fine architecture harking back to its heyday as Spain's gateway to the wealth of South America.

### Orientation

Seville stands on the east bank of the Rio Guadalquivir. Right on the river, the Arenal district was the city's docklands until the Guadalquivir began to silt up during the 17th century, big ships could no longer make their way up river and Cádiz took over Seville's sea trade. Today, it's a quiet maze of small streets, which suddenly gets very busy during the summer bull-fighting season, when aficionados

**FUN FACT** >> ## Sour Seville Oranges

**It wasn't until the 18th century that an enterprising Dundee grocer,** James Keiller, had the idea of making marmalade from Seville oranges (he had bought a shipload but discovered he couldn't sell them because they were too sour). Keiller's marmalade made his family's fortune – and to this day, you can't buy Seville oranges in Seville, because they are all sent to British marmalade factories. You can pick them straight off the tree – but if you do, you'll soon see why nobody bothers, as they really do taste bitter.

## Bullfights

**You have to be Spanish to really appreciate bullfighting – and most**
British families will be repelled by the spectacle of an animal being tormented, then killed, for amusement. Nevertheless, *toreo* remains very popular in Spain, and Seville is one of its capitals. The Plaza de Toros de la Maestranza, in the Arenal district, is one of the country's top bullrings and draws huge crowds in the summer season.

(bullfight fans) flock to the 18th-century Plaza de Toros, a prominent landmark with its yellow and white baroque façade.

Along the Guadalquivir runs a long, tree-shaded pedestrian esplanade, the Paseo Alcalde Marqués de Contadero. Boats leave from the jetties here for cruises along the river, and at the south end the Torre del Oro (Golden Tower) is a memento of the Moorish era. This multisided stone tower, with its battlements and spire, was built during the 13th century to defend the city from the Spanish.

Inland from El Arenal is Seville's real treasury of superb historic buildings, the old quarter of Santa Cruz. The heart of this old part of Seville is Plaza del Triunfo, a square lined with orange trees (they are impossible to get away from in Seville). Over the square looms the huge cathedral, and facing it across the plaza is the ancient, graceful Alcazar, one of the most beautiful Moorish buildings in Spain. Barrio Santa Cruz was the city's Jewish quarter under the rule of the tolerant Moors, until the reconquering Spaniards turned the Inquisition loose on anyone who was even suspected of

Alcazar, Seville

# SEVILLE

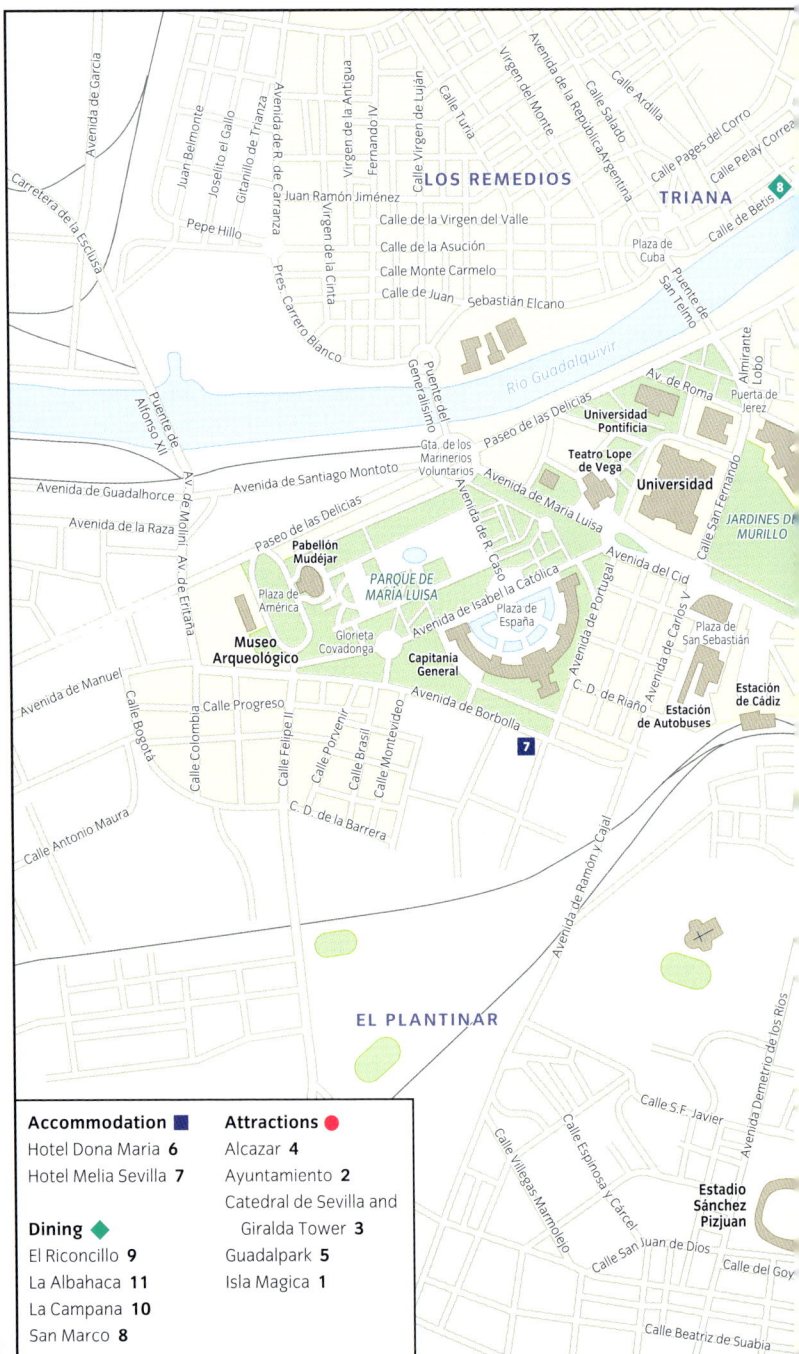

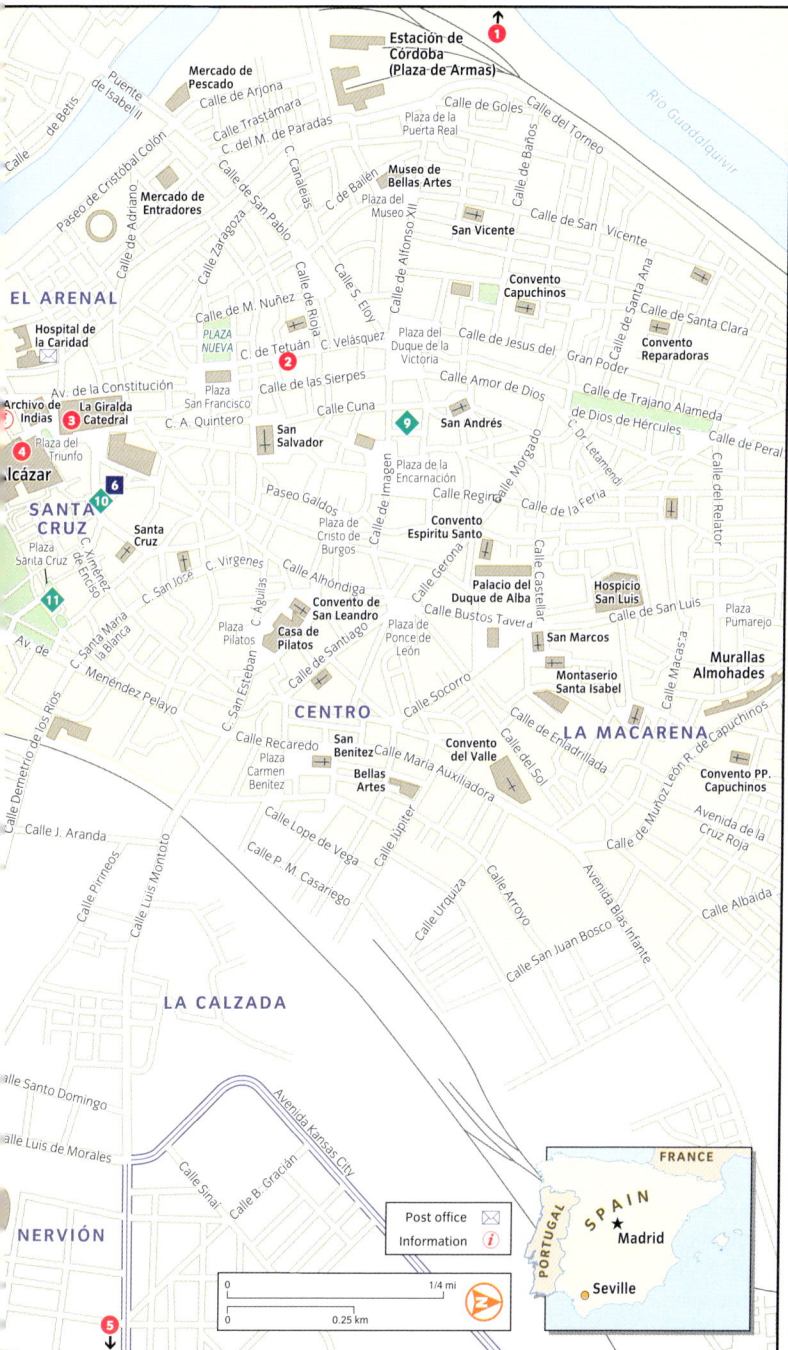

Estación de
Córdoba
(Plaza de Armas)

Mercado de
Pescado
Calle de Arjona
Calle Trastámara
C. del M. de Paradas
Plaza de la
Puerta Real
Calle de Goles
Calle del Torneo
Río Guadalquivir

Museo de
Bellas Artes
Plaza del
Museo XII
San Vicente
Calle de San Vicente

EL ARENAL

Mercado de
Entradores

Convento
Capuchinos

Hospital de
la Caridad
PLAZA
NUEVA
Calle de M. Nuñez
C. de Tetuán
C. Velásquez
Plaza del
Duque de la
Victoria
Calle de Jesus del
Gran Poder
Convento
Reparadoras
Calle de Santa Clara

Archivo de
Indias
La Giralda
Catedral
C. A. Quintero
Calle de las Sierpes
Calle Cuna
Calle Amor de Dios
Calle de Trajano Alameda
de Dios de Hércules
Calle del Peral

Plaza
San Francisco
San
Salvador
San Andrés

Plaza del
Triunfo
lcázar

SANTA
CRUZ
Santa
Cruz
Paseo Galdos
Plaza de
la Encarnación
Calle Regina
Convento
Espiritu Santo
Calle de la Feria
Calle del Relator

Plaza
Santa Cruz
C. San José
Plaza de
Cristo de
Burgos
Palacio del
Duque de Alba
Hospicio
San Luis
Plaza
Pumarejo

C. Virgenes
Calle Alhóndiga
Calle Bustos Tavera
Calle de San Luis

Convento de
San Leandro
Casa de
Pilatos
San Marcos
Murallas
Almohades

Plaza
Pilatos
Plaza de
Ponce de
León
Montaserio
Santa Isabel

CENTRO
Calle Socorro

San
Benitez
Convento
del Valle
LA MACARENA

Plaza
Carmen
Benitez
Bellas
Artes
Calle María Auxiliadora
Calle del Sol
Calle de Enladrillada
Convento PP.
Capuchinos

Calle J. Aranda
Calle Lope de Vega
Calle P. M. Casariego
Avenida de la
Cruz Roja

LA CALZADA
Avenida Kansas City
Calle San Juan Bosco Infante
Calle Albaida

alle Santo Domingo
alle Luis de Morales
NERVIÓN

Post office
Information

SPAIN
FRANCE
PORTUGAL
Madrid
Seville

0   1/4 mi
0   0.25 km

183

being less than wholeheartedly Catholic. Here, there are still more orange trees that flower late in the year and bring forth delicious looking but sour fruit in January and February – bite into one of these bad boys in expectation of a rush of sweet juice, and you will be bitterly disappointed. The Man from Del Monte would not say 'si' to these. Just north of the cathedral, the Ayuntamiento (Governor's Palace) is a lavish relic of Seville's wealthy 16th-century heyday, covered in every kind of architectural frippery.

Calle de las Sierpes, which runs north from Plaza del Triunfo, is the old quarter's most attractive shopping street, with small market plazas to either side, and north of the cathedral. The Alcazar is a whitewashed labyrinth of narrow streets where pots of geraniums grow on balconies and caged canaries tweet in upstairs windows.

*Tourist office: Edificio Laredo, Plaza San Francisco 19, 4th floor (☎ 00 34 954 592 915; www.turismo.sevilla.org).*

### Jerez

There's a whole lot of dancing in Jerez. Maybe it's all that sherry. The city is famous for its flamenco dancers. In fact, it's almost impossible to get away from them as almost every restaurant seems to have a flamenco show at some point in the evening. These are usually more of a hit with girls than with boys (it's a bright pink petticoat thing), but they certainly make a change from Strictly Come Dancing. There's dancing in the streets during **Jerez's Carnival** ★ (14th–18th February), which is much more child friendly and less frenzied than most carnivals – it even features seven 'damas infantiles' and seven 'damas juveniles' to make the parades more appealing to younger participants. And there are even dancing horses. **The Royal Andalucian School of Equestrian Art** on Avenida Duque de Abrantes is renowned for its thoroughbred white stallions, which are trained in a repertoire of 'dance steps' which they perform to music. In May every year there is the annual **Horse Fair** (*Feria del Caballo*) with still more horses going through their paces. It's a one-week event with free displays of horsemanship in the streets and public areas.

#### Orientation

Founded by the Moors, the old part of Jerez, known as the *Casco Antiguo*, has pretty palm-fringed plazas and wide streets lined with purple-flowering jacaranda trees. Its heart is an 11th-century Moorish fortress, the Alcazaba. It shows its age, but has been partly restored. From the family point of view, the Casco Antiguo is more a place for a gentle wander or a snack in a pavement café than a big sightseeing destination – it's a place for being, not seeing.

# TIP ⟫ Jerez Flamenco Festival ⟪

**Jerez is famous for its stamping, twirling flamenco dancers, accompanied** by thrilling gypsy guitars. The Flamenco Festival of Jerez (usually the last week in February and the first week in March) attracts flamenco dancers and musicians not just from Andalusia but from all over Spain and South America.

The Barrio de Santiago, facing the cathedral, is the heart of Jerez's 'flamenco quarter', where you can watch the dancers and guitarists do their stuff in long-established traditional flamenco venues such as Bar Arco de Santiago (*Calle Barreras 3*) or La Taberna Flamenca (*Angostillo de Santiago)*. The Andalucian Flamenco Foundation is housed in an aristocratic 18th-century townhouse, the Palacio de Permartín, on Plaza de San Juan, which has exhibitions of glamorous flamenco costumes. Little girls who – after seeing a flamenco performance – fancy themselves as Carmen can find versions to suit all sizes and most budgets in shops all over Jerez (and also in Seville and Cádiz).

*Jerez Tourist Information Office: Edificio Los Claustros, Alameda Cristina (📞 00 34 956 324 47; www. turismojerez.com).*

**KID'S QUOTE ⟫**
"I thought the flamenco dancers were the best part, but the Spanish dancing horses were really cool too." *Jane, age 9*

## Cádiz

Cádiz is steeped in history – founded by seafaring Phoenicians around 1100 BC, it claims to be one of the oldest cities in western Europe – but don't make the mistake of thinking that this bustling cosmopolitan seaport city is a resort tailor-made with families in mind, as it is nothing of the kind. Cádiz has always been one of Spain's most important ports – which is why it attracted the attention of earlier English visitors including Sir Francis Drake and the Earl of Essex, each of whom trashed the place during England's wars with Spain in the late 16th century. The city really came into its own during the 18th century, when it became the official port for trade between Spain and its colonies in South America, and grew hugely wealthy from its share of the Atlantic trade in silver, slaves, sugar, spices and tobacco. Most of the grand Gothic and Neoclassical buildings which still dominate its streets date from that era.

When Napoleon's armies conquered the rest of Spain in 1808, Cádiz – with the help of the British Royal Navy – held out as the last outpost of Spanish freedom, and the headquarters of a liberal Parliament that was years ahead of its time in granting votes and rights to ordinary people. The restoration

# CADIZ

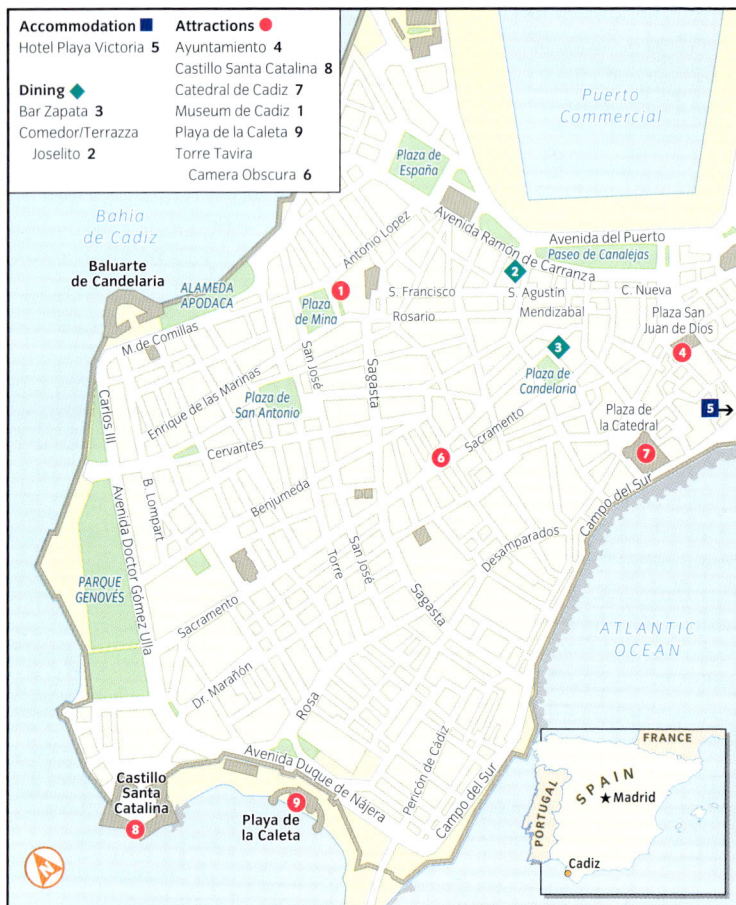

**Accommodation** ■
Hotel Playa Victoria **5**

**Dining** ◆
Bar Zapata **3**
Comedor/Terrazza
  Joselito **2**

**Attractions** ●
Ayuntamiento **4**
Castillo Santa Catalina **8**
Catedral de Cadiz **7**
Museum de Cadiz **1**
Playa de la Caleta **9**
Torre Tavira
  Camera Obscura **6**

of the Bourbon monarchy after Napoleon's defeat set the clock back, with the aristocracy and the Catholic clergy reasserting their power in Spain, but Cádiz continued to be a bastion of liberal thought. Unlike many Spanish cities, however, it was spared much of the destruction of the Civil War of 1936–9, as it fell to General Francisco Franco's fascist rebel troops after only one day.

## Cádiz – the Old Town ★★★

The old town isn't entirely pedestrianised but it is largely traffic free, which makes it fairly family friendly, with numerous open squares lined with benches, shaded by orange, lemon and palm trees, and surrounded by cafés and ice-cream parlours where you can take a breather. However, bag-snatching is not unknown, so keep a close eye on

Swimming in Cádiz

handbags, purses and cameras at all times.

Old Cádiz is very nearly an island, which is why Napoleon's troops were unable to take it even after they had conquered the rest of Spain. It's stuck out at the end of a long, narrow peninsula that juts out into the Bahía de Cádiz (Bay of Cádiz) and

## Towering Above

**Look up, and old Cádiz bristles with towers that were built as lookout** platforms by city merchants when Cádiz was one of the wealthiest seaports in the world. Spain's conquering fleets first set sail for the Americas from Seville, further up the River Guadalquivir, but as the gold and silver flooded in from Peru and Mexico, bigger and bigger galleons were built and it became impossible to sail them up the river. Cádiz, with its superb natural anchorage, took over from Seville. The lookout towers were built so that merchants could spot incoming convoys and be the first to meet them and bid for their cargoes – a fleet of sailing ships, tacking into the wind, might be sighted days before it finally reached Cádiz harbour, so enterprising traders would send their own fast boats out to meet incoming ships and start negotiating a deal even before the fleet dropped anchor. Of course, from the 16th through to the 17th century, the fleet on the horizon might turn out to be English – in which case it would be time for the folk of Cádiz to hide their valuables, lock up their daughters or head for the hills.

shelters one of Europe's finest natural harbours. It's easy to see why, in the centuries before steamships, this became such an important seaport.

### Orientation

A wide green park, the **Paseo de Canalejas,** faces the **Avenida del Puerto** and the busy and somewhat grimy commercial harbour on the Bay of Cádiz, on the north side of the old town.

South of here, the old town is a patchwork of plazas, connected by 18th- and 19th-century streets laid out on a grid plan – it's surprisingly easy to find your way around. If you do get lost, just keep walking in a straight line until you hit the sea, which surrounds the old town on three sides, then walk clockwise or anticlockwise to get back to Avenida del Puerto.

**Plaza San Juan de Dios,** just south of Avenida del Puerto, is a busy square lined with pavement cafés that serve fresh-squeezed orange juice in the shadow of the impressive 19th-century **Ayuntamiento (Governor's Palace).**

A few hundred metres further south, the **Catedral de Cádiz** is the last of the great cathedrals built with the proceeds of Spanish Christian imperialism, slavery and genocide in South America.

Inside are gold and silver crucifixes, altars and icons made with gold melted down from the temples of the Aztec, Inca and Mayan empires of Mexico and Peru, and encrusted with precious stones mined by native South American slaves. Work started on the cathedral in 1720 and went on until almost a century later – by which time Spain had lost all of its South American colonies. Across the square, the **Iglesia de Santa Cruz** was one of the buildings burned down when Essex's English freebooters sacked Cádiz in 1595, but it was quickly rebuilt. Behind it a sign points to the scanty remains of the Teatro Romano (Roman Amphitheatre) but unless your children are really obsessed with the Roman Empire, it's a big disappointment as there is very little to see. Much more entertaining is the **Plaza de Topete,** which locals call Plaza de los Flores (Plaza of the Flowers) – and with good reason. This is the site of

---

**TIP  Carnival Time**

**Cádiz's Carnival, in mid-February, is an extravaganza of colourful** costumes and parades of elaborately decorated floats. It's the sort of thing that looks great on a TV travel programme, with singing, dancing in the streets, and the music of mandolins, tambourines, guitars and whistles. For smaller children, though, the sheer numbers of people can be intimidating at street level, and the noise tends to go on all night, with the last party-goers staggering off home at dawn. To enjoy it the easy way, find a hotel room with a balcony from which you can watch the parades passing – and well-soundproofed double glazing!

TIP **Pickpockets**

**The old town is generally safe, but bag-snatchers and pickpockets do** work the streets around Plaza de Mina in summer, when unwary visitors may be paying more attention to the bands and buskers than to wallets and purses. Pay that little bit of extra attention, especially when the streets are busier at sunset. Playa de la Caleta and la Vina are other spots where it makes sense to be rather more vigilant than usual.

Cádiz's **Mercado Central** (central market) and is surrounded by stalls selling huge bouquets of flowers, budgies, parrots and other caged birds (as well as an array of weirder pets ranging from chameleons and iguanas to tarantulas and scorpions).

Two blocks north of Plaza de Topete, **Torre Tavira** is the tallest of the forest of towers that cluster around the old town centre, and is surmounted by a camera obscura that gives a 360-degree view of the city.

The old quarter's beach is **Playa de la Caleta** – a surprisingly attractive south-facing stretch of sand that is popular with local children in summer. It's OK for a paddle but it is after all a town beach, so it can sometimes be a bit littered and does not bear comparison with the great sweeps of sand over in the Algarve or east of town on the Costa de la Luz. It does have a rather splendid pier with a dome at the end, and the usual collection of brightly painted fishing boats pulled up on the sand. At the north-west end of the beach is the **Castillo Santa Catalina,** a grimly functional fortress (see p. 196).

*Cádiz Tourist Office: Plaza San Juan de Dios, 11 Edif. Amaya (☎ 00 34 956 241 001; www.Cadizayto.es/turismo)*

## Beaches & Resorts

You may think that it makes no sense to abandon the magnificent strands of the Algarve, only to drive to not-so-different beaches some three hours away. You might be right, but try telling the back-seat drivers that. If you've decided to build in a trip that includes Huelva, Seville, Jerez and Cádiz, allowing for a couple of days at one of the beach resorts is recommended. Travelling with older children and teenagers, a trip to surf-mad Tarifa will give them something to brag about back at school.

**Playa Victoria** ★ This is Cádiz's beach resort suburb – a mini-Miami Beach with a skyline of hotels and apartment blocks on the outskirts of town. It's almost completely artificial (the sand is dredged up offshore and dumped on the beach several times a year to keep it looking pristine), but it's also very well managed, with lifeguards and a first-aid station in the summer season and dozens of tapas bars,

## Drake

**We remember Francis Drake as the English hero who defeated the**
Spanish Armada that tried to invade England in 1588. To the Spanish, Drake
was just a pirate. When he sacked Cádiz in 1587, he gave the King of Spain
the perfect excuse for a counter-attack, which was commanded by an
Andalusian noble, the Duke of Medina-Sidonia, who took Drake's raid on Cádiz
a bit personally. Sadly, the Duke had never commanded a fleet before, and
Spain lost to England away as well as at home. Result!

*chiringuitos* (summer beach bars)
and restaurants. It's (in summer)
very lively, very Spanish, and as
far as British families with
younger children are concerned
it can't hold a candle to the
UK-colonised Algarve, but it
has plenty of family-friendly
places to stay (see p. 199), and
as a place to stay for a few nights
on a whistle-stop tour it's a
good bet.

**El Puerto de Santa Maria** Part
of the 'Sherry Triangle', this old,
dilapidated port is most easily
reached from Cádiz but is also
within easy reach of Jerez de la
Frontera. An historic port, it
opens onto the northern shores
of the Bay of Cádiz. Everyone
comes here in the summer when
it's a lively town to sample the
fish and tapas along the beaches.
It also has two water parks
nearby.

**Tarifa** With active teenage dudes
on board, Tarifa is the one to
head for. In surfing, boardsailing
and kite-surfing circles, this huge
stretch of Atlantic sand is legendary. Tarifa's relentless wind
lets windsurfers built up huge
speeds while kite-surfers take to
the air for long flights, but the

beach can sometimes be a little
too windswept for sunbathing
comfort. Tarifa is still small, and
the buildings of its old town
are painted in pretty ice-cream
colours instead of the usual
Andalusian blinding white.
Inside the old town walls are
smart boutiques, posh jewellers,
ecru homeware shops, child
toggles from Polartec fleece
material and posh nosh.
Outside, it's all bit less picturesque and a bit more blandly
high rise. From Tarifa town
heading west is a long strip of
beach that eventually curves
around at a right angle and
becomes the aptly-named Las
Dunas (the dunes). When the
conditions are right more than
400 kites will be out on the
water jostling for space along
the best stretches.

**Bolonia** ★ Bolonia beach lies
between two craggy hilltops,
(20 km from both Zahara and
Tarifa) and unlike its neighbours
to either side, its wide bowl of a
bay is sheltered from the perpet-
ual breezes and so, although it's
less popular with the sailboard
and kite fraternity, it's good for
less active beach fans. It's at the

Kite Surfing in Tarifa

end of a dead-end road, so, considering how idyllic it is, gets relatively little footfall. Lifeguard towers and Red Cross facilities make the central patch of beach popular with families. Beautiful hippies with dreadlocks make a little business beside the restaurants by the Roman ruins. The south end of the beach has mineral seams which you can grind to a powder then add seawater to make your own all-body mud mask.

## Water Parks

**Isla Magica** ALL AGES This exciting theme park claims to be inspired by the voyages and conquests of the Spanish explorers of the 16th century so it will appeal to *Pirates of the Caribbean* fans. It stands on an island in the Guadalquivir, not far from the centre of Seville (it was the site of the Expo 92 showground) so it's well located for a fun break after seeing the sights. New

attractions include the Captain Balas ride, on which you do battle with laser guns; and an evening lake show with multicoloured laser and firework effects projected onto walls of water. There's also an indoor, air-conditioned dining area, The Fort, with live entertainment.

*Isla de la Cartuja, Seville ℘ 00 34 902 161 716. **Open** Apr–mid-June 11am–10pm daily; mid-June–20th Sept 11am–11pm daily; Oct–Nov 11am–9pm weekends only). **Admission**: adults €21, children €14.50.*

**Guadalpark** ALL AGES Seville is a scorcher in summer and it is a long way to the beach, so this smallish water park (with only 10 rides and slides) is doubly welcome. Even if it is not really worth going a long way out of your way to visit, its location means you can make it a stop en route.

*Poligono Aeropuerto, Sevilla Este, Seville ℘ 00 34 954 406 513). **Open***

*25th May–15th Sept, 11am–7pm (May, June, Sept) and 11am–8pm (July and Aug).* **Admission:** *adults €11.15, children €7.85 (all day); adults €9, children €6 (half-day).*

### Aqualand Bahía de Cádiz ★

**ALL AGES** This water park at El Puerto de Santa Maria – midway between Cádiz and Jerez de la Frontera – is a sister to Aqualand in the Algarve and is a great place for children to unwind and let off steam after a long drive. The rides include the terrifying Kamikaze, the Black Hole – a 100-metre tunnel ride on a double-seater raft – the winding Super Slalom and plenty more. For more timid and smaller children, there is also a mini park with gentler slides, mazes, fountains, a ship and a submarine to play on.

*Carretera del Puerto-Jerez Km. 647. 11500 Puerto de Santa María, Cádiz ( 00 34 956 870 900, reservations  00 34 956 332 534; www. aqualand.es).* **Open** *13th June–2nd Sept, 11am–6pm (June) and 11am–7pm (July—Sept).* **Admission:** *adults €17.50, children (4–12 years) €12.50.*

## Family-Friendly Animal Parks, Zoos & Nature Reserves

### Zoobotanico de Jerez ★

**ALL AGES** Jerez's child-friendly zoo has lions, white tigers (with cubs), camels, bison and giraffes among its 200 species and 1,300 animals and birds in all. You can download and print out the free Juego del Zoobotanico board game from the zoo's website – players answer 64 questions about animals to move round the board. Unfortunately, there doesn't seem to be an English translation, but if your children are learning Spanish they can have fun puzzling them out. (Alternatively, you could run them through a downloadable translation programme such as Babelfish before leaving home.)

The zoo has a funny history – in 1952 a shipment of wild animals was delivered to Cádiz harbour. Nobody turned up to claim them, so they were kept in the municipal gardens until Alberto Duran, the Jerez town councillor in charge of parks and gardens, proposed creating a zoo, which opened in February 1953 and is now named after Sr. Duran.

*C/ Taxdirt, Jerez ( 00 34 956 153 164; www.zoobotanicojerez.com).* **Open** *1st Oct–31st May 10am–6pm, 1st June–30th Sept 10am–8pm.* **Admission:** *children under 3 free, 4–14 years €4.90, over 14 €7.50.*

### Real Escuela Andaluza de Arte Ecuestre ★★

**AGES 9 AND UP** Horse-mad children will delight in this combination museum and riding stables where there are weekly displays of dressage from Andalusia's beautiful white horses and their riders, lessons in bridle-making and saddlery, a museum with audio-visual displays – including a marvellous one that teaches you how to understand the language of horses – as well as a collection of grand old horse-drawn

Zoobotanico de Jerez

carriages that belonged to local aristocrats and dignitaries. The horses go through their full dance routine twice a week, but on their days off you can watch them in training.

*Av. De Abrantes* 📞 *00 34 956 311 111;* www.realesculea.org). **Open** *Mon and Wed 11am–2pm, Fri (except in Aug) 11am–2pm. Ticket office open 11am–12.30pm.* **Admission**: *adults €9.00, children (4–12) €6.00. Performances Tues and Thurs, midday.* **Admission**: *adults €18, children (4–12) €12.*

## Parque Nacional de Doñana ★

ALL AGES Near Huelva, this vast area of lagoons, marsh, heath and sand dunes between the Guadiana and Guadalquivir rivers has been a national park since 1969. Before that, it was the private hunting ground of the Dukes of Medina Sidonia, who conserved and hunted its deer and wild boar. Covering some 1,300 square km, it is almost the size of London. This is good news for the animals that it shelters, but not so good for visitors with impatient children, as there is plenty of room for wildlife to avoid human contact. However, in winter and spring the flocks of Greater Flamingos feeding on the brackish lagoons are hard to miss, in late summer there is a good chance of seeing Red Deer stags clashing antlers in contests of strength before the autumn mating season, and some of the landscapes are truly stunning. Self-guided walks along waymarked park trails start from the park information centres at La Rocina, Palacio del Acebron (which was once the ducal hunting lodge) and El Acebuche, on the outskirts of the protected area. The best of these for families is the 45-minute walk from El Acebuche, close to the beautifully unspoilt sandy shoreline and a wilderness of huge coastal sand dunes, some of which are up to 30 metres high. To explore the interior and with luck spot some of its denizens (see Checklist below), you must take a four-wheel drive, 21-seater bus from El Acebuche.

*Information Centres: La Rocina (☎ 00 34 959 442 340). Exhibition 'Man and Doñana' at Palacio del Acebron. Facilities: Park reception, café, shop and audio-visual exhibition. El Acebuche (☎ 00 34 959 44 87; www.parquenacional Doñana.com).*

*Walking trails free, open daily.*

*Guided tours daily except Mon, May–Sept Mon–Sat and Oct–Apr Tue–Sun, 8.30am and 5pm (☎ 00 34 959 430 432). Book in advance. Guides speak some English. Tours last four hours.*

> **INSIDER TIP** ⟩⟩
>
> Bring a picnic, spend the afternoon on the beach near Acebuche, then take the evening tour at 5pm for the best chance of seeing Roe Deer, Red Deer and with luck even Wild Boar, which are more likely to be spotted at twilight than during the day.

Doñana National Park

# Historic Buildings

## Reales Alcazares, Seville

**ALL AGES** You'd have to be a very blasé child to find this wonderful medieval palace anything but awesome. Sometimes just known as the Alcazar, this was the seat of the Moorish *emirs* (kings) of Seville before the city was reconquered by the Spaniards. In 1364, King Pedro I of Castile commissioned a royal palace to be built within the walls. It was completed in just two years (Pedro was not a nice man – he was known as Pedro the Cruel, which probably encouraged the architects and builders to work fast) and is a fairy-tale place of tiled patios decorated with elaborate plasterwork, arched halls hung with fabulous tapestries, lush gardens and fountains. The upper floors are still used by Spain's royal family when they are in town. You could easily spend half a day wandering around this opulent labyrinth.

## Doñana Wildlife Checklist

- Red Deer – the biggest animal in the park – look out for males clashing antlers in mating season
- Fallow Deer – small, pretty deer with a spotted coat. Watch for them on the fringes of woodland
- Greater Flamingo – hard to miss on shallow lagoons
- Wild cattle – seen on grassland and drinking at marshy ponds
- Spanish Lynx– if you're very, very lucky you might see one of these shy, nocturnal cats at twilight. The lynx is very rare (there are only around 100 left in Doñana) and several are killed by cars on roads near the park each year
- Spanish Imperial Eagle – also very rare, but may be seen soaring above marshes or roosting on treetops
- Purple Gallinule – common, larger and more brightly coloured relative of the British coot.

*Patio de Banderas* ( 00 34 954 502 323). **Open** *Tues–Sat 9.30am–8pm and Sun 9.30am–6pm.*

**Cádiz Cathedral** ALL AGES It's called the Catedral Nueva (new cathedral) – not because it's all that new (its dome was finally completed in 1838) but because it was built on the site of another, much older cathedral. It's not likely to entertain children for long, nor is it meant to, but the puppet collection in the **Museo de Cádiz** ★ next door, where the cathedral's glittering relics and works of art are also on display, will amuse them more. The miniature characters of the Tia Norica puppet theatre have delighted young and old for years.

*Calle Santa Inés 9* ( 00 34 956 221 788). **Open** *June–Sept Tues–Fri 9am–1pm and 5–7pm, Sat–Sun 9am–1pm; Oct–May Tues–Sun 9am–1pm and 4–7pm. Bus: L1 or L7. Free admission.*

**Museo de Cádiz** *Plaza de Mina s/n.* ( 00 34 956 212 281). **Open** *Tues 2.30pm–8pm; Wed–Sat 9am–8pm; Sun 9.30am–2.30pm.* **Admission:** *€1.50.*

**Seville Cathedral** ALL AGES The largest cathedral in Europe, begun in 1401, stands on the site of a 12th-century Moorish mosque. It's a massive, gloomy, awe-inspiring Gothic pile, clearly built to celebrate Castile's triumph over the Moors of Seville and Andalusia. The gilded chapels and altars may hold the attention for a moment, but for some children the most interesting bit is the Tomb of Columbus – even though it dates from the 1890s, not from the explorer's own era. The tomb depicts Columbus's coffin being borne by figures representing the four Spanish kingdoms of Castile, Leon, Aragon and Navarra. This would no doubt please Columbus, who

Seville Cathedral

never felt he got the rewards he deserved from his royal patrons during his lifetime. The best bit, though, is the giddy climb to the top of La Giralda, the cathedral bell-tower, for a (literally) breathtaking view of old and new Seville and the Guadalquivir.

*Avda. Constitución (📞 00 34 954 214 971; www.catedralsevilla.org).* **Open** *Sept–June Mon–Sat 11am– 5pm, Sun 2.30pm–6pm; Jul–Aug Mon–Sat 9.30am–1.30pm, Sun 2.30pm–6pm.* **Admission:** *€7.00 (free on Sun); no shorts or T-shirts.*

## Castillo Santa Catalina

`AGES 7 AND UP` After the English turned up and sacked Cádiz for the third time in 10 years, King Philip II got fed up and ordered a massive fortress to be built to protect the town. The Castillo Santa Catalina was begun in 1597 and took almost 25 years to build. It seems to have done the job – the English didn't come back in force until the Napoleonic Wars, this time as allies of the free Spanish govern- ment based in Cádiz. It was a

**FUN FACT** ▶ **Christopher Columbus** ◀

**Christopher Columbus wasn't Spanish. He came from the seaport city** of Genoa, in Italy. He didn't set out to discover America (he was looking for a new sea route to China). And on his famous first voyage in 1492 he only got as far as the Caribbean islands – it wasn't until he had found the Bahamas, Jamaica and Cuba that he finally hit South America. He died and was buried in Cuba and his body was brought back to Seville in 1902. It's not even certain that the body in the tomb is actually his – DNA tests are being made to try and find out if it is.

military prison from 1769 until 1991. It's still owned by the Ministry of Defence, but is open to the public so you can wander over its imposing battlements and pretend you're gallant Spaniards bravely defying the dastardly English – or, if you prefer, the dastardly French.

*Playa de la Caleta, Cádiz (℡ 00 34 956 226 333; www.castillosnet.org). Open Mon–Fri 10am–6.30pm and weekends and public holidays 10am–1pm. Free admission.*

### Baelo Claudia Roman Ruins

AGES 10 AND UP The Roman ruins at Baelo Claudia date from a settlement here from the 2nd century BC. The hamlet grew rich from a relish known as *garum*, the fermented fish sauce that was the Roman Empire's favourite food flavouring. Most of what you see today is from the 1st century AD when Emperor Claudius granted the town self-government. Archaeologists found the ruins of its forum, three temples (Jupiter, Juno and Minerva), and the remains of a basilica. The ruins of a theatre

have been restored and you can cross the old high street. There are even the remnants of the fish factory where the highly valued *garum* was produced – and what a smelly business that must have been.

*(℡ 00 34 956 688 530) Open July–mid-Sept Tues–Sat 10am–6pm, Sun 10am–2pm. In other months, hours are Tues–Sat 10am–5pm, Sun 10am–2pm. Free admission.*

## Boat Trips

### Real Fernando Doñana Cruises The dinky riverboat *Real Fernando* chugs up the Guadalquivir slowly from Sanlúcar, at the mouth of the river about 32 km north of Cádiz. The noisy commentary (in Spanish and English) is a bit uninspiring, but there is an onboard documentary about the park and its protected wildlife. You are unlikely to see anything more than the occasional flock of flamingos or other water birds, but it is certainly a painless way of seeing the scenery.

## Whale Spotting

**The narrow Strait of Gibraltar between Tarifa and North Africa is a** marine highway for whales, dolphins and porpoises migrating between the Mediterranean and the Atlantic. The Tarifa-based Foundation for Information and Research on Marine Mammals runs whale-spotting trips on which with a bit of luck you may see Pilot Whales, Bottlenose Dolphins, Common and Striped Dolphins and in July and August you may even see Killer Whales (orcas). They promise that if you don't see at least one whale or dolphin you can have another trip free (*Pedro Cortés 4, Tarifa, ℡ 00 34 956 627 008; www.firmm.org. Price: adults €30, under 14 €20, under 6 €10).*

*00 34 956 363 813; www.visitas Donana.com). Ave Bajo de Guia, Sanlucar daily 9am– 7pm, leaving 10am all year round, spring and autumn 4pm, summer 5pm; €15. Tickets can be booked online or bought at the Visitors' Centre in what used to be the Ice Factory, which also has a sweet exhibition on the bird and aquatic life of the park (Bajo de Guia, 00 34 956 381 635. Open 9am–7.50pm. Free admission).*

## Shopping

### Seville

Shopping in Seville centres on Calle Serpes and Calle Tetuan, which run parallel to each other, leading off Plaza San Francisco in the city centre and lined with international-brand fashion stores, shoe shops and souvenir shops.

For department store shopping, El Corte Ingles (Spain's biggest department store chain) has its main city-centre branches on **Plaza del Duque** and is an excellent one-stop location for all family needs, including clothes, baby supplies, souvenirs, books (including an English-language section), beach kit, food and drink, and it also has an in-house pharmacy. For any minor emergency, El Corte Ingles is a godsend as it sells everything and is open until 10pm Mon–Sat.

Seville is also infested most of the year with street vendors selling an array of fake designer accessories, sunglasses and handbags, bootleg CDs and gaudy Latin American clothes and jewellery. The city also has a collection of bustling open-air markets,

some of which are great fun for children even if you don't want (or need) to buy anything. The website **www.exploreseville. com** is an unbeatably compendious and useful, regularly updated, guide to what to buy where.

> **INSIDER TIP**
> Keep a tight grip and a close eye on bags, wallets, cameras and other valued possessions when visiting Seville's markets – violent crime against tourists is happily rare, but pickpocketing and bag-snatching are common.

**Torneo Pet and Animal Market** FIND Held on the outskirts of the city every Sunday morning at Torneo, along the bank of the Guadalquivir river, this is a great family outing. It's really like a free zoo – there are vendors selling ducks, chickens, geese and rabbits, puppies and kittens, and more exotic creatures such as geckoes, chameleons, iguanas, gerbils, chinchillas, salamanders, snakes and Siamese fighting fish

*Torneo. Open Sun all year 8am–1pm.*

**Plaza del Cabildo Antiques Market** FIND Like the Torneo market this Sunday morning affair is fun to watch and walk through even if you're not a collector – and your children may be surprised at what Spaniards find collectable – not just stamps, medals, coins, and antique watches but 50s-style retro sunglasses, dozens of old-fashioned badges and lapel pins and yes,

## FUN FACT ❯ Sherry ❮

**Jerez is where sherry wine comes from – 90 million litres of it every year.**
The English have always had trouble pronouncing the city's name properly. Say
it 'Herreth', with a really hard 'H' sound like the Scottish 'ch' in 'loch' and you'll
be pretty close. There is almost twice as much alcohol in some sherries (up to
22%) as in ordinary table wines, which is why it was traditionally popular in
Britain – the high alcohol content stopped the wine from going sour on long
sea voyages.

even bottle tops and phone
cards.

*Plaza del Cabildo.* **Open** *Sun all year
9am–2pm.*

### Plaza del Duque Crafts
**Market** It may be over charita-
ble to call this a 'crafts market'
and indeed most locals call it
the 'hippy market' – vendors sell
the familiar array of brightly
coloured ethnic clothing, cheap
jewellery, belts and bangles, all
of which may be worryingly
alluring to would-be groovers
who want to look like grannie or
granddad in that photo from the
1970s.

*Plaza del Duque.* **Open** *Thurs, Fri and
Sat all day.*

## FAMILY-FRIENDLY ACCOMMODATION

### Cádiz

**MODERATE**

#### Hotel Playa Victoria ★★
Although it rates four stars, this
rather glamorous modern hotel
is surprisingly affordable and is
one of the better family options
if you want to stay in Cádiz
itself. It's on the town's Playa

Victoria seafront, and it wouldn't
look out of place in Miami
Beach. Make sure you get a
room with a sea-view balcony
to make the most of the view.
Hotel facilities include swimming pool, parking with lift
straight to reception, and 24-
hour security and baby cribs are
available if booked in advance.

*Plaza Ingeniero La Cierva 4 (📞 00 34
956 205 100; www.palafoxhoteles.
com). Rates: €90–150. Amenities:
pool, restaurants, bar, secure parking. In room: air conditioning, satellite TV, safe, minibar, cots available by
prior arrangement.*

### Puerto de Santa Maria

**EXPENSIVE**

#### Hotel Duques de Medinaceli
★★★ Your family may feel
like minor royalty in this 17th-
century palace, formerly the
residence of the Dukes of
Medinaceli. There are 19 suites
(including several family suites)
and, if your budget will stretch
to it, a two-bedroom royal suite.
The hotel is spread over two
buildings, connected by a glassed-
in patio, and also features one of
Cádiz's best restaurants. It's in
the centre of Puerto de Santa

Maria, a 10-minute drive from the beach, but it has its own small pool – actually better for children than grown-ups – which in summer is a more peaceful place to be than on the crowded beaches. The hotel is surrounded by gorgeous botanical gardens with palms, oranges and jacarandas and has private parking. Breakfast, which is served buffet-style, costs extra – it's lavish, but only worth it if you're going to take full advantage, otherwise take picky children to the nearest open-air café for a Spanish-style breakfast of juice, milky coffee and cakes.

*Plaza de los Jasmines 2, Puerto de Santa Maria (☎ 0034 956 860 777). **Rates**: €160–250 double, €50 extra bed, €400–500 Royal Suite; €18 breakfast; 50% discount (low season) and 25% discount (high season) for children between 3 and 12 sharing parents' room, under 3s: free. **Amenities**: gardens, pool, restaurant, bar. **In room**: satellite TV, minibar, room service, air conditioning, cots available by prior arrangement.*

**INSIDER TIP**

Don't even think about going to Jerez during big events including Holy Week, the Flamenco Festival, or the Fiera del Caballo unless you have booked accommodation several months in advance. The place will be heaving.

## Jerez

**INEXPENSIVE**

**La Casa de Vecinos Rosaleda** ★★★ **FIND** This beautiful old (and very recently restored) town house in the heart of the old part of Jerez

really is a home from home. It has just six self-contained apartments (most of which have basic 'breakfast kitchens' which are great for making snacks but aren't really up to the task of cooking a full meal) as well as a huge roofed patio and a smaller, flower-filled inner courtyard in which toddlers can play safely. The favourite for families is probably El Caracol, which has a bedroom with a full-sized double bed plus a single bed, a sofa bed in the separate living room, a proper bathroom (with a bathtub) and two balconies overlooking the street. Children under six go free (and cots for them are also provided free of charge) and the very reasonable weekly rates include bed linen and twice a week room cleaning (if you want the place to be really spic-and-span, they offer a 'fairy godmother' daily cleaning and bed-making service for an extra €10 daily). The owners speak good English, and are a mine of useful information about where to go and what to do in and around Jerez.

*Calle Palma (☎ 00 34 956 328 777; www.casarobaleda.com). **Rates**: €275–350 per apartment per week plus €150 deposit (against breakages – returnable) and €30 end-of-stay cleaning (understandable). **Amenities**: patio and courtyard. **In room**: kitchenette.*

## Tarifa

**INEXPENSIVE**

**Camping Torre de la Peña** ★ This is a brilliant place to

park with the children if you like camping and it carries a slightly lower price tag than the others. You'll be in good, outdoor-enthusiast, company. The facilities are good, you'll get hot showers kept spotlessly clean, baby changing, a small store for essentials, an on-site beach-bar for food and drink, washing machines, Wi-Fi access and electricity. What you won't get is music, or horns, and midnight to 8am is noise curfew. The campsite is cut in two by the national road N-340 but a tunnel links the two halves, so traffic isn't an issue. The swimming pool is on the inland side. Some are sworn fans of the spaces at the top of the hill on this side, under trees, with more privacy and great views, but to live more sociably, plump for the pine-needle beach side of the site.

*Carretera Cadiz-Malaga (Cadiz Malaga highway km 78 (℡ 00 34 956 684 903; fax 00 34 956 681 473; www.campingtp.com). Rates: €5, €3.30 tents, €5.40 adults, €4 children (2–12). Discounts for stays longer than three days. Amenities: pay phone, shop 9am–10pm; bar, snacks and tapas 9am–midnight; restaurant 2pm–4pm and 7pm–11pm; swimming pool 11am–9pm; 24-hour hot showers; 24-hour washing machine; baby changing.*

MODERATE

**Punta Sur** ★★ The perfect family location, with a large pool, lush green gardens, a bubbling stream with ducks bobbing in the water and peacocks strutting alongside, a tennis court, pool table, bar and one of the best restaurants in Tarifa. Parents with babies can plug in the monitor and enjoy a quiet dinner à deux in the dreamy, illuminated garden in the evenings (see restaurants). Bedrooms are quirky and modern but extremely elegant and comfortable. Mosaic floors, mirrors, eclectic ceramic work and vast photo prints on the walls, jazz up the interiors. Ten of the rooms sleep four (or more) in great style.

*Motorway N340, km 76, 11380, Tarifa (℡ 00 34 956 684 326; fax 00 34 956 680 472; www.hotelpuntasur.com). Rates: €83–155 double, €153–220 family room, €163–230 suite, €25 extra bed; breakfast is included (prices do not include tax). Amenities: restaurant, bar, pool table, swimming pool, tennis court (€5 an hour) In room: fans, TV, air conditioning, DVD player, bath.*

EXPENSIVE

**Hotel Dos Mares** ★★★ Dos Mares, which is built a bit like a castle with a moat, has a swimming pool, tennis court, volleyball court, stables on site, windsurf, kite-surf, catamaran school, massage, garden, pool with slides into the shallow end, and pool bar for the parents, ping-pong tables and even an aviary with ostriches and peacocks rattling about. The formal sit-down restaurant is downstairs, and there's simpler food served in a converted military bunker. The four suites sleep four, and lots of the standard double bungalows, which mostly

Hotel Dos Mares

feature Arabic touches, are spacious enough to fit an extra one, but there are also bungalow specials, with extras like double showers, and sofa beds. Bungalow 23 sleeps three; 26 has an annex for children; 44, 45, 36 have gardens overlooking the stables, but the best is number 14, which has its own salon, a big double and four sofas.

*Ctra Cádiz – Málaga km 79.5 (℡ 0034 956 684 035; www.dosmareshotel. com). Rates: €200–284 4 suites, €95–189 8 rooms, 34 bungalows, €86–126 standard, €102–147 special, €26–37 extra bed. Amenities: swimming pools, tennis, volleyball, riding, water sports, massage, garden. In room: flat-screen TV, phone, air conditioning.*

## Seville

**MODERATE**

**Hotel Doña María** Located behind the cathedral and the Giralda, this four-star hotel is one of the most gracious hotels in the old quarter of Seville, with a hidden history. In the 14th century, this was the palatial home of Samuel Levi, one of the closest advisors of King Pedro 'the Cruel', and legend has it that a secret tunnel connected it with the Alcazar palace. The garden courtyard and the rooftop pool delight adults and children alike. Rooms contain wide beds and bathrooms with dual sinks, and some rooms are large enough for the entire family. The central location makes it a good base for exploring Seville's historic sights.

*Don Remondo 19, Seville (℡ 00 34 954 224 990; www.hdmaria.com). Rates: 64 rooms from €150, cots free, extra bed on request €35 per night for children under 11. Amenities: bar, restaurant, rooftop pool, garden courtyard, spa. In room: TV, radio, air conditioning, telephone.*

**Hotel Meliá Sevilla** Part of Spain's largest mid-range hotel chain, this 11-storey hotel on the outskirts of town is easy to find (unlike some hotels in the older parts of town) and has secure

## TIP ▶▶ Bless My Dog ◀

**If you're in Jerez on Saint Anthony's Day you'll see thousands of people** heading for the Parque Gonzalez Hontoria – and leading dogs, carrying cats and even riding horses. They're heading for the blessing of the animals, for St Anthony is the patron saint of pet-lovers. It's big fun, and free, with lots of fun-fair-type activities, animal shows and the inevitable blast of flamenco. There's a special toddlers' festival with games, races and prizes too (for details of the next event, see *www.turismojerez.com*).

off-street parking, making it a good choice for car-touring families. It also has many of the facilities you would expect to find in a resort hotel, so you and your children can kick back beside the rooftop pool during the heat of the afternoon. Other facilities appreciated by families include a fitness centre and squash court, an alfresco restaurant terrace and a garden snack bar.

*Hotel Melia Sevilla, Dr Pedro Castro 1 (☎ 954 422 611 www.solmelia.com). Rates: doubles from €140, room only, cots free, extra bed from €30. 364 rooms, all outward-facing, including 127 double rooms, 168 twin rooms, 10 superior doubles, 54 singles and 5 junior suites. Amenities: wireless, Internet access, secure parking, rooftop pool and sun terrace, spa and fitness centre, disabled access, buffet and à la carte restaurants (high chairs available on request), poolside snack bar, lounge bar with live music on Fridays and Saturdays (open 11am–3am). In room: satellite TV, minibar, phone, radio, 24-hour room service, air conditioning.*

## FAMILY-FRIENDLY DINING

This part of Spain isn't like the Costas, so don't expect English pubs, fish and chips, and bacon and eggs. Seville and Cádiz make few culinary concessions, but Spain does have a massive bonus for families – the tapas bar. Going on a *tapeo* – a tapas crawl – is part of the local way of life. Seville has hundreds of tapas bars – there are plenty in the Santa Cruz area – and they are great when children need feeding pronto. What you see is what you get, you order at the bar and your tapas are ready in minutes. You don't even need a word of Spanish – just point at what you want. You can take your tapas with you to eat on the move or on a park bench, or sit at an outdoor table. Some posher tapas bars do have table service, but you will pay extra to be served by a waiter. And you have total control of how much you spend – order a few at a time and if anyone is still peckish, just order a few more. Expect to pay €1.50–2.50 per tapa. There are also plenty of full-service restaurants. In general, they make few special concessions to children, but as in Portugal younger diners are made just as welcome as adults. Almost all restaurants accept credit cards but tapas bars generally prefer cash.

Eat early to avoid the rush. Most Spanish restaurants open from around midday until 4pm, and from 8pm to midnight. Locals eat lunch and dinner late by British standards, sitting down to lunch at around 2pm and starting dinner no earlier than 10pm.

## Seville

**INEXPENSIVE**

**La Campana** ★ The best things for children in this long-established city-centre café are the coloured *Nazareno* marzipan images of Semana Santa penitents in their long-hooded robes – you can bite their heads and eat them, or keep them as souvenirs. There are lots of other sweet cakes and biscuits too, including egg *yema* and almond biscuits called *lenguas de almendra*. Good for energy levels, if not for teeth.

*Calle Sierpes 1, Seville. From €4 for coffee or soft drink and cake. No credit cards. No reservations. **Open** 9am–11pm.*

**El Rinconcillo** ★ This city centre tapas joint is claimed to be the oldest one in Seville, and apart from the addition of electricity it certainly doesn't seem to have changed much since the 17th century, when it opened. Some of the clientele look like they have been here ever since, and there are equally ancient bottles of wine and sherry racked along the walls. Bags of atmosphere, and very popular, so not great for younger children when the local lunch and dinner crowd arrives – go in the morning or early evening.

*Calle Gerona 40, Plaza Encarnacion, Seville. From around €8 for a tapas meal and drinks. No credit cards. No reservations. **Open** 9am–11pm.*

**MODERATE**

**San Marco** ★★★ FIND This is a small chain of Italian-style restaurants dotted around the city, and a good choice when you need to feed them something familiar – like pizza, which is excellent here, along with pasta and other good, trustworthy Italian main dishes, salads and appetizers. The Italian desserts are head and shoulders above most local rivals, too.

*Mesón de Moro 6; Calle Cuna 6; Calle Betis 68; and other branches (📞 00 34 954 280 310, 00 34 954 212 440). €10–15. Credit cards accepted. Reservations not required. **Open** 9am–11pm.*

**FUN FACT** ❯ **Sticky Sweets**

**Turron de Cádiz is a sticky and very sweet marzipan, supposedly dating** from the two-year long French siege of the city during the Napoleonic Wars, when the locals ran out of flour to make bread and took to using ground almonds instead. This seems a bit unlikely, but today's turron – usually shaped and coloured into imitation oranges, lemons, apples and other fruit – is delicious and is sold in all the local cake shops.

**Farewell to Meat**

**Our word 'carnival' comes from the medieval Latin 'carne vale' which** means 'farewell to meat'. Carnival was traditionally a splurge of conspicuous eating, drinking and misbehaviour before the Lenten fast, when meat, rich food and drink were forbidden. These days, most people don't take Lent quite so seriously, but it's still a good excuse for a party.

**EXPENSIVE**

**La Albahaca** The menu here is a bit too sophisticated for younger British diners, with dishes such as oysters au gratin with dill and cava, roast pork with pear and vanilla sauce, even millefeuille of bull's tail (eh?). In summer, when you can sit outside on the lovely Plaza de Santa Cruz, the location is okay for families, but really this is one for grown-ups on a rare child-free evening and a special occasion, because it is among the more expensive places to eat in Seville. Worth it, though, for adventurous foodies – and great value compared with British restaurants of similar calibre.

*Plaza Santa Cruz 12 ( 00 34 954 220 714) €30. Credit cards accepted. Reservations recommended.* **Open** *12pm–4pm and 8pm–12am. Closed Mondays.*

## Cádiz

**Bar Zapata** ★★ **VALUE** Let the children take their pick from the glass-fronted refrigerated cases on the bar (you may have to lift little ones up to let them look inside). From the bar, you can watch the busy cooks slamming together dishes such as roast loin of Iberian pork, anchovies in olive oil, and fried or scrambled eggs served with fresh asparagus, filets of pork, or cured Iberian ham. There is nowhere to sit here, so adjourn with your tapas to Plaza Candelaria, outside, which in the evening is full of Andalusian mums, grannies and children and even the occasional father. Just don't forget to bring the plates back when you're done.

*Plaza de Candelaria, Cádiz. Individual tapas from €1.50, platters from €10. No credit cards. No reservations.* **Open** *9am–midnight.*

**INEXPENSIVE**

**Comedor Joselito and Terrazzo Joselito** ★★★ These twin eating places are cheap, cheerful and authentically colourful – and the food is both fabulous and approachable. Children who can be persuaded to try new things may be inveigled to try the anchovies vinaigrette or the fried baby cuttlefish. Those with stubbornly conservative tastes can go for fried fish, meatballs, prawns or other less challenging dishes. The main restaurant is a stone-fronted building open on two sides to the narrow streets outside. There's a basic *comedor*

## Semana Santa

**Semana Santa (Holy Week) is marked by parades by members of Jerez's**
32 'brotherhoods' who march through the old town centre carrying effigies
which represent scenes from the Passion of Christ and silver-embroidered ban-
ners. In their hooded robes, they look weird and a bit scary to anyone who isn't
used to such rituals.

(dining room) with sit-down tables in the back room, and this is one place where you don't need to worry about spilling things. It's not grand, but the plastic breadbaskets, paper table-cloths, and a gruff but in most cases, friendly staff are all pretty much child-proof. Round the corner is the even cheaper and more basic Terrazo Joselito, with plastic chairs and tables on the pavement and pretty much the same menu served from a hole-in-the-wall kitchen.

*San Francisco s/n (Comedor) and Paseo Canalejas s/n (Terrazo) ( 00 34 956 255 551). Main courses €4.50–7.70. No credit cards. No reservations. Open 11am–midnight. Closed Sundays.*

### Jerez

**EXPENSIVE**

### La Taberna Flamenca ★★★
This restaurant in Jerez with its full-on flamenco shows may be a little too noisy and intense for smaller children but anyone over about seven years old will enjoy the flamboyant dancers and guitarists. No children's menus, but plenty of small tapas-style dishes to pick and choose from, and you can look at the menu in advance on their website

*www.latabernaflamenca.com*.
Summer flamenco 'spectacles' are in mid-afternoon, which is handy for families unused to staying up until midnight as Andalusians do.

*Angostillo de Santiago 3, Jerez. ( 00 34 956 323 693). Main courses €15–35. Credit cards accepted. Reservations essential for shows. Open Tues–Sat midday–4pm and 8pm–midnight. Shows May–Oct Tues, Wed, Thur and Sat 2.30pm and Nov–Mar Tues–Sat 10pm.*

### Huelva

**INEXPENSIVE**

**Taberna El Condado** Just off one of Huelva's main shopping streets, the Calle Berdigon, this small tapas bar is good for a snacky family lunch with lots of tasty tapas dishes that children won't find too frighteningly unfamiliar: ham, chorizo sausage, and the local version of scrambled eggs and mushrooms, *revueltos de gurumelos*. Freshly squeezed fruit juices, and for (non-driving) parents there's a good selection of local wines and sherries.

*Calle Sor Ángela de la Cruz 3, Huelva ( 00 34 959 261 123). Tapas from €2.00. No credit cards. No reserva-tions required. Open Mon–Sat 11am–4pm and 8pm–midnight.*

# 8  The Alentejo

# NORTH ALGARVE

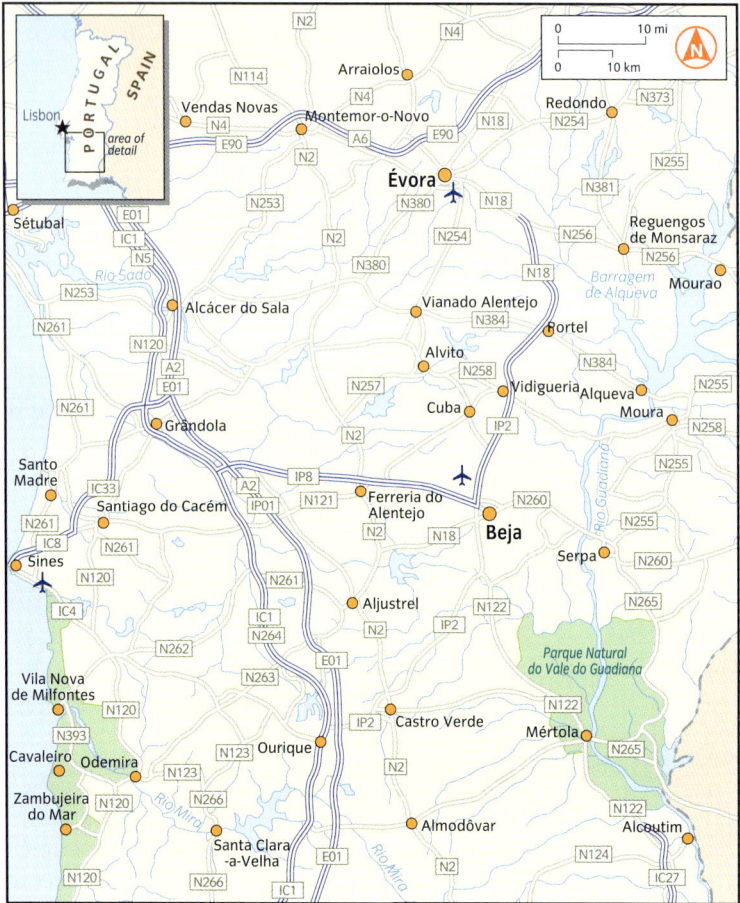

**T**his wide rural region north of the Algarve is great for families who aren't beach-obsessed and prefer the peace and quiet of a house with a private pool in beautiful countryside to the bustle of a beach resort. If you do want some time on the beach, the Alentejo has its own long stretches of sandy Atlantic coastline, but there are no full-scale resorts to compare with those along the Algarve coast, and this is a part of Portugal that is more frequented by weekend visitors from Lisbon rather than by foreign holidaymakers.

Beautiful and wild as it is, the west Atlantic coast of Lower Alentejo is not ideal for all but the most adventurous family for much of its windswept length. The waves can be intimidatingly strong for littler children, accommodation is basic to spartan, and there is very little to occupy older children of the Gameboy and MTV generation. The only real exception is Vila Nova de Milfontes, at the mouth of the Rio Mira, with an attractively unspoilt old town, good fish restaurants (people drive down from Lisbon at weekends just to eat here), and an assortment of simple small hotels and other places to stay.

Inland, though, the terrain could hardly be more family friendly. The Alentejo has none of the purpose-built attractions of the Algarve. As yet, golf courses and waterparks are conspicuous by their absence (though that may change if plans for a new airport to be built at Beja, the regional capital, bear fruit). But parents and children who love open-air activities such as riding, fishing and canoeing on lakes and rivers, cycling (on terrain that is generally pancake-flat and so ideal for less energetic bikers) will be very pleased indeed with the Alentejo. And the Portuguese national passion for dam-building has given the region plenty of artificial lakes that are perfect picnic spots – some of them even have toddler-friendly patches of sand, snack bars and water sports.

It's also one of the most beautiful places in Europe. The region around Beja is known as the Planície Dourada ('Golden Plain') for its endless fields of grain, interspersed with cork-oak plantations where sheep, goats and cattle graze under the shady trees. In spring, autumn, and even for most of the (very short) winter, every patch of pasture, roadside verge and wasteland is splashed with wildflower colours – red poppies, yellow buttercups, white daisies and purple vetch. In high summer, under a blazing sun, the plains remind some people of Africa. Dotted around this pastoral landscape are timeless white-washed villages and pretty market towns, along with a handful of impressive castles, cathedrals and churches.

The region is also rich in wildlife. Storks seem to be everywhere in spring – making their messy nests on rooftops, trees, chimneys and telephone poles. Flocks of Cattle Egrets patrol alongside grazing white heifers, snapping up grasshoppers and other insects. Exotic-looking Hoopoes and Bee-eaters are often seen, and buzzards, eagles and the silver-winged Montagu's Harrier with its distinctive black wingtips are quite common too.

To sum up: the Alentejo is the perfect antidote to the bustle of the Algarve in summer. If your family includes toddlers and active older children, it's great, and if you have bicycle-addicted teens or sub-teens they can roam for miles. Accommodation-wise, this is really for families who are happy with full-scale self-catering, with the occasional evening out at a typical local restaurant. Ideally, seek out a converted farmhouse with its own pool, within walking distance of a village with shops and restaurants – not difficult to find, and there are quite a few that offer the services of a cook and housekeeper.

# ESSENTIALS

## Getting There/Getting Around

All but the most dedicated gree-nies will yield to the need for a rented car in the Alentejo. In the-ory, you could fly to Faro, then take the train or bus along a route that runs north to Beja (four trains daily from Faro, journey time 3½ hours; four express buses daily from Faro, also 3½ hours) and on to Évora, then use a local taxi to get to your accom-modation, but for convenience, shopping and exploration you really need wheels.

The fast drive into the Alentejo from Faro follows the A22 motorway west from the airport, then hooks north on the A2-IP1 motorway (the main road to Lisbon) from Boliqueime. The IP2 highway to Beja leads northwest of the A2-IP1 at Ourique. The slightly slower, but more scenic, N2, goes straight up the middle of the Alentejo from Faro, passing through São Brás de Alportel, Almôdovar and Castro Verde (where it connects with the IP2).

## Orientation

The Alentejo (which means 'beyond the Tejo (Tagus)') stretches all the way from its border with the Algarve to a line drawn roughly between Lisbon, Portugal's capital at the mouth of the Rio Tejo, the city of Évora and the Spanish border, and is divided into two sections, the Alto Alentejo (Upper Alentejo)

with its capital at the medieval town of Évora, and the Baixo Alentejo (Lower Alentejo), sur-rounding the regional capital of Beja, 90 minutes drive north of Faro.

# WHAT TO SEE & DO

## Top Family Attractions

❶ **Castelo de Beja** This 400-year-old castle keep rises above the town and the surrounding planes and the view is tremen-dous – but the climb up the nar-row stone stairs needs a good head for heights (see p. 218).

❷ **Barragem de Alqueva** In summer you can swim, fish and take boat rides on Europe's largest artificial lake – its wiggly shore-line is said to be more than 1,000 km long, so there are plenty of peaceful picnic spots (see p. 217).

❸ **Herdade de Badoca** Lions, tigers and more familiar (and less scary) farmyard animals live in this wildlife attraction close to the Atlantic coast (see p. 218).

❹ **Baronigg Ostrich Farm** See ostriches roaming the fields of the Alentejo, shop for painted eggs and ostrich leather bags and purses, and even ride a specially trained ostrich (see p. 218).

## Towns & Villages

**Beja** ★ `OVERRATED` The capital of the Lower Alentejo rises like an island above a sea of wheat fields that glimmer in the summer sun so that it is easy to see why the

Beja Castle

Portuguese call the surrounding area the 'Golden Plain'. Beja was founded by Julius Caesar after the Roman conquest of Portugal (which the Romans called 'Lusitania') and went on being an important place long after the Romans left – its castle stands on the foundations of the Roman fortress that Caesar built. Today, it's a sleepy, peaceful market town with some pleasant restaurants and an outstanding pousada to stay in – but there is sadly little to keep families with children of any age occupied for more than an overnight stay.

**Orientation**

Beja's obvious landmark is the Castelo, which stands on a low hill smack in the centre, with the older part of town – several tiers of narrow cobbled streets and whitewashed houses – spreading downhill. The further you go from the castle, the more modern the buildings become, with modern residential suburbs, shopping centres and factories forming the outer ring. Praça da República, a cobbled square lined with shops and cafés and planted with orange trees, is at the foot of the hill, about 500 metres east of the Castelo. Rua Capitão João Francisco de Sousa is the main shopping street in the town centre.

*Alentejo Regional Tourist Office: Rua Capitão João Francisco de Sousa 25, Beja (☎ 00 351 284 319 913; www.rt-planiciedourada.com).* **Open** *daily 9am–6pm (7pm June–Aug).*

**Évora** FIND Évora comes as a pleasant surprise after the somnolence of other Alentejo towns such as Beja and Altino, where life moves at a snail's pace most of the year. Évora is a university town, which lends it a bit more youthful pep and sophistication than towns like Beja. A UNESCO World Heritage Site, it's on the tourist trail from Lisbon – meaning it's busy with sightseers in summer, but also meaning today's English newspapers are on sale, and there are plenty of excellent restaurants and cafés and places to stay.

**Orientation**

Évora is the largest town in the Algarve, with streets winding up to and around a series of squares arrayed on a hilltop. Praça do Giraldo, in the heart of the old town, is cobbled in black and white stones and packed with café tables – a good place to stop and take stock before pushing on to the ruined but

# BEJA

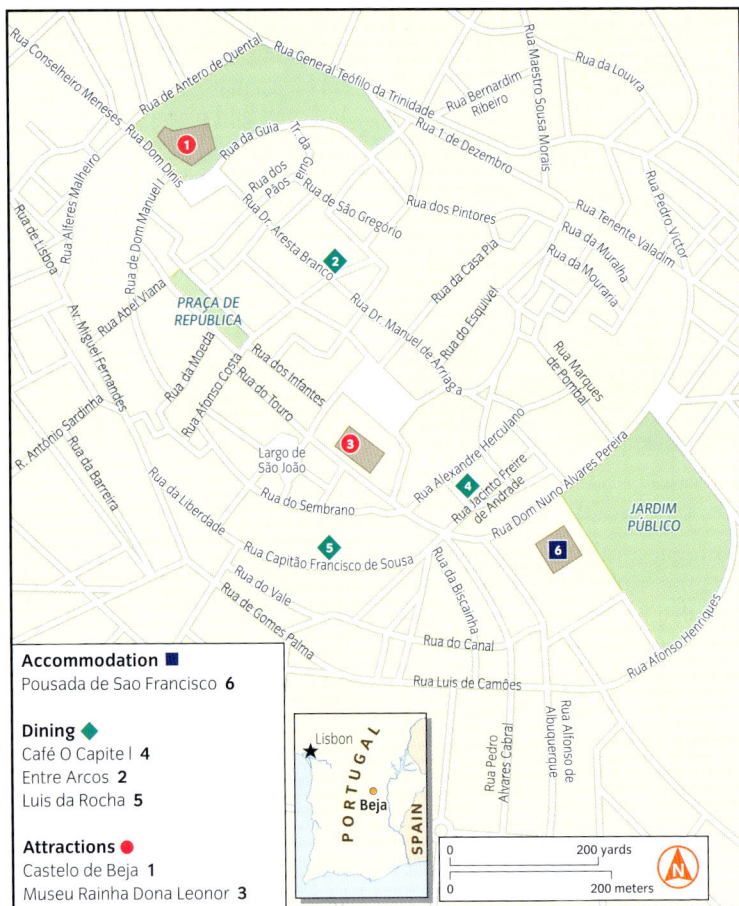

**Accommodation** ■
Pousada de Sao Francisco **6**

**Dining** ◆
Café O Capite l **4**
Entre Arcos **2**
Luis da Rocha **5**

**Attractions** ●
Castelo de Beja **1**
Museu Rainha Dona Leonor **3**

still elegant Templo de Diana, on Largo do Conde de Vila Flor, which is the highest point of the city.

*Tourist office: Praça do Giraldo 71 (📞 00 351 266 730 030; **www.rtÉvora.pt**). **Open** daily 9am–6pm (7pm June–Aug).*

**Alvito** If you thought Beja was peaceful, wait until you see Alvito, around 30 minutes' drive further north on the way to

Évora. The most exciting thing that happened on our most recent stay in this trim little settlement of blue, yellow and white cottages was when two of the peacocks that live in the walled gardens of the **Pousada Castelo de Alvito** hopped over the wall and made a break for freedom, much to the surprise of the row of locals who spend all day snoozing in the shade next to the municipal fountains.

# EVORA

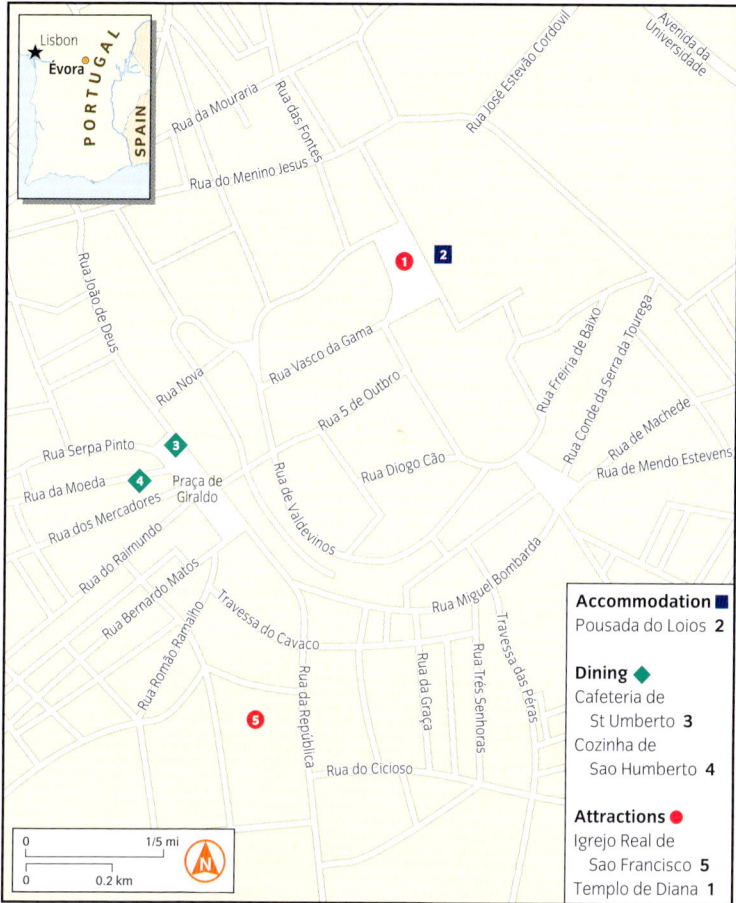

**Accommodation** ■
Pousada do Loios **2**

**Dining** ◆
Cafeteria de
  St Umberto **3**
Cozinha de
  Sao Humberto **4**

**Attractions** ●
Igrejo Real de
  Sao Francisco **5**
Templo de Diana **1**

There is very little to see or do here, but for families on a tour of the Alentejo, it's almost worth making an overnight stop here just to stay in a real medieval castle (see p. 212).

**Serpa** Serpa huddles below an impressive castle, surrounded by crumbling medieval walls. Within the gates, it's a maze of largely traffic-free cobbled streets. Climb to the castle and up onto its battlements (as usual, keeping a tight grip on toddlers) – there's a huge view of the surrounding countryside with its green fields and olive groves, but more entertainingly you can spy down on the well-kept little courtyard gardens of the houses below, full of dozing cats, ducks and chickens and lemon and orange trees that fill the air with sweet perfume when in blossom (which is most of the year). The other aroma that you'll quickly detect in this village is the pungent and appetizing smell of the local cheese, made from the milk of the huge flocks of sheep that graze the Alentejo plains. You can sample a slice or two in one of the pleasant café-restaurants on Praça da República, below the castle. The local tourist office, also on Praça da República, has its own small shop selling local honey, wine, cheese and handicrafts including little pottery doll-houses, earthenware figures and rag dolls.

**Mértola** FIND Mértola is as far as you can travel up the Guadiana River by boat, and this made it an important spot in ancient times. Phoenician and Carthaginian traders from North Africa brought their galleys up the Guadiana to trade, and were followed by the Romans, who named the town Mirtillis. They all wanted the wheat and olive oil that the Alentejo still produces in great quantities. After them came the Moors, who built the very impressive **Castelo** that to this day looms over the red roofs and whitewashed walls of this little town from its hilltop. Its towers and battlements were rebuilt and made even more impressive after the Christian reconquest of southern Portugal in the late 13th century.

Next to the castle is the **Mesquita,** one of only two Moorish mosques to have survived the Christian reconquest and the expulsion of the Muslim people who called the Algarve

their home for more than 500 years. After all that history, Mértola seems to have been happy to have a bit of a snooze. Nothing much goes on here, but it is a pretty enough little town to wander around, and if you're renting a self-catering house near by it has enough stores and an open-air market to keep you stocked up with everything you need. It's also the gateway town for one of Portugal's newer nature reserves, the Parque Natural do Vale do Guadiana.

**Monsaraz** FIND There are plenty of things for active families to do in the rolling countryside that surrounds this pretty little town, including riding, cycling and canoeing or boating on the Rio Guadiana or on the waters of the nearby Barragem de Alqueva.

Narrow cobbled streets lined with old cottages and a castle which like Beja's was built in the

Mértola

14th century by King Dinis to guard Portugal's frontier with Spain make Monsaraz one of the most charming little towns in the Alentejo. Not a lot seems to have changed here over the centuries – until the building of the **Barragem de Alqueva** flooded a vast stretch of the Guadiana river valley and altered the landscape near Monsaraz for-ever. Like most of the Alentejo's towns, Monsaraz stands on a low hill surrounded by rolling plains, with the shores of the lake not far away. Lusitanians, Romans, Visigoths and Moors all built forts and castles here, and after the Moors were driven out in 1167 the town was given to the crusading knights of the Templar order. Apart from the castle and a 13th-century parish church, there is nothing to see here, but Monsaraz is a pleasant, peaceful little town surrounded by beau-tiful scenery.

**Odemira** Around 20 km inland from the Atlantic coast, Odemira is a riverside town on the banks of the Rio Mira. It is renowned for its pottery workshops, and on a hill on the outskirts of town stands one of the few Alentejo windmills that is still in working

order. Families staying in or around Odemira have the best of both worlds – the little town is on the edge of the **Parque Natural de Costa Vicentina,** a vast expanse of wild coastal heathlands, dunes, beaches and cliffs that stretches all the way south to Cabo de São Vicente. Downriver is the delightful little beach resort and fishing town of **Vila Nova de Milfontes** – the best spot for families on the Alentejo coast (see p. 216).

Heading upriver from Odemira, the Barragem de Santa Clara is yet another of the Alentejo's artificial lakes, with beaches and water sports.

## Beaches & Resorts

The Atlantic coast is rich in undeveloped, windswept beaches, but many are rugged, surf-pounded and without facili-ties of any kind. Nor are they likely to be developed any time soon, as much of the coast is protected within the **Parque Natural de Costa Vicentina,** which stretches most of the way from Cabo de São Vicente to Cabo de Sines. There are only a few spots on the Alentejo coast

**FUN FACT** **Stones & Tunnels**

**Long, long before the Romans arrived, the people who lived in the** Alentejo set up tall standing stones and constructed tunnel-like buildings roofed with big stone slabs. They did this between 4000 BC and 2000 BC – around the same time that people in Britain erected Stonehenge. Around Monsaraz, look out for signposts saying 'Anta' – the Portuguese name for these incredibly ancient monuments. The biggest, at Outeiro, is almost 6 metres tall, and there are more than 100 scattered around this part of the Alentejo.

that can really be recommended for families.

### Vila Nova de Milfontes FIND

The little beach town of Vila Nova de Milfontes, on the north shore of the wide Rio Mira estuary, is the place to go if you want family seaside fun in the Lower Alentejo. Only 186 km south of Lisbon, it attracts more Portuguese weekenders than foreigners, and there is absolutely nothing to do except hang out at the beach all day and eat in one of several good fish restaurants at night. If you are looking for somewhere that's still largely untainted by package tourism, Vila Nova is a good bet. That said, it has none of the frills you will find in the full-on resorts of the Algarve, nor does it have any large resort hotels (though you can stay in an expensively converted, 17th-century castle, the **Castelo de Milfontes.**

There are uncrowded, white-sand beaches right next to town (on either side of the river) and a little further north there are rocky foreshores where low tide reveals rock pools that are miniature aquaria, full of tiny fish, sea anemones, crabs, shrimps and even, if you are lucky, an octopus or two. Probably not ideal for a longer holiday, but worth visiting if your holiday base is inland and the children are demanding a spell at the seaside.

**Zambujeira do Mar** This little village perched above the sea within the Parque Natural do Sudoeste Alentejano e Costa Vicentina (Southeast Alentejo and Vincentina Coast Natural Park) is the other beach magnet for families on the Alentejo coast. The views are fantastic and the beach equally so though when the tide is high the waves and currents can be quite strong, so keep a close eye on toddlers and indeed more adventurous older children.

Vila Nova de Milfontes

## Lakes & Rivers

The Rio Guadiana flows down the eastern edge of the Alentejo – where for most of the way it is the historic border between Portugal and Spain – to reach the sea at Vila Real de Santo António, in the eastern Algarve. It's a wide, impressive stream that lends itself to fishing and boating. West of Beja, the Guadiana is dammed at the Barragem de Alqueva, creating a huge, many-armed artificial lake. About 40 km south of Beja, the small market town of Mértola is the jumping-off point for trips into the Parque Natural do Vale do Guadiana.

**Barragem de Alqueva** ★ This many-limbed artificial lake is a pretty awesome piece of engineering – and it is still growing. The Alentejo is Portugal's hottest, driest region and has always faced chronic water shortages in summer. The first plans for the dam were made in the 1950s, when Portugal was ruled by the dictator António Salazar (nobody knows why dictators love dams, but they do). Work finally began in 1974 after the 'carnation revolution' that overthrew the dictatorship (and good riddance) but ground to a halt four years later after arguments over compensation for the peasant farmers who owned the land that was to be flooded (Salazar would just have sent the army to clear them out.) After things had settled down a bit – and after Portugal joined the EU and got access to lots of lovely regional development funds – the project was restarted. The dam was completed in 2002 and has been slowly filling up ever since. The lake is dotted with islands that were formerly hilltops, and along the shoreline, the small villages of Alqueva, Amieira and Estrela have been turned into mini-resorts (though without any big hotels) offering canoeing, sailing and fishing trips and riding in the surrounding countryside.

**INSIDER TIP ▶**

For a panoramic view of this inland sea, head for the castle at Monsaraz, on a hilltop overlooking the lake.

### River Guadiana (Parque Natural do Vale do Guadiana)

**GREEN** The Parque Natural do Vale do Guadiana protects a swathe of the Guadiana valley next to the Spanish border, providing a refuge for a handful of Iberian Lynx, numerous storks, bustards and the rare Bonelli's Eagle. It can be explored on foot, by car or by bike, and you can rent canoes in Mértola (which is just within the park boundaries) for a day on the river.

*Parque Natural do Vale do Guadiana, Rua Dom Sancho II, 15B, Mértola (☎ 00 351 286 610 090; www.icn.pt).*

### Barragem de Santa Clara

Formed by damming the Rio Mira about 20 km upstream from Odemira, this lake with its wiggly shoreline is great for canoeing, boating, fishing and swimming.

# Animal Parks & Farms

## Herdade da Badoca ★

**ALL AGES** The Alentejo's most high-profile, purpose-built visitor attraction brings a touch of Africa and Asia to the Atlantic coast, with tigers, giraffes, zebras, buffalo, ostriches, chimps and lots more animals and birds from all over the world, as well as a petting zoo with goats, donkeys and sheep. There are 60-minute 'safaris' on a mini train, a huge aviary full of tropical birds, and the park has its own restaurant.

*Herdade da Badoca, Apartado 170, Vila Nova de St André ( 00 351 269 708 850; www.badoca.com). **Open** 1st—28th Feb 10am–5pm; 1st—31st Mar 10am–5pm weekdays, 9.30am—7pm weekends; 1st Apr—31st May and 15th Sept–31st Oct 9.30am–7pm; 1st June–14 Sept 9am–8pm. Safaris leave hourly; last safari one hour before closing time. **Admission**: adults €14, children (4–10) €10.50, two adults and two children €43.*

## Baronigg Ostrich Farm ★

**FIND** **ALL AGES** Explore Portugal's first and biggest ostrich ranch with an English-speaking guide, enjoy an ostrich steak or an ostrich burger, and buy ostrich products (feathers and painted egg shells as well as ostrich leather goods) – and even ride specially trained ostriches. When the children discover that you can buy live ostriches for only around €600 each you may come under some pressure to take one home...

*Baronigg Criação de Avestruzes, Alqueva ( 00 351 266 63 00 01; www.baronigg.com).*

# Historical Sites

## Beja

## Castelo de Beja/Museu Rainha Dona Leonor ★

**ALL AGES** Beja has plenty of typically Alentejan restaurants and shops, but few irresistible visitor attractions. The only one that may entertain children for a while is the **Castelo de Beja,** built by King Dinis more than 400 years ago. It has been knocked about a bit – only a few of its original 40 towers remain – but it is still impressive. Climb (carefully) to the top of its 40-metre inner keep and look for the holes through which the defenders could pour boiling oil on attacking Moors, Spaniards, or anybody else. Like you should. The other noteworthy sight is the **Museu Rainha Dona Leonor,** which is housed in a beautiful building with arched cloisters, whitewashed walls and elaborate carved stonework that was founded as a convent in 1459. It has been a museum since 1927, and its main attraction is its collection of *azulejo* Portuguese and Spanish tiles, along with a handful of archaeological finds from the Alentejo region.

*Castelo de Beja, Largo Dr Lima Faleiro ( 00 351 284 311 800). **Open** June–Sept Tues–Sun 10am–1pm and 2pm–6pm; Oct–May Tues–Sun 9am–midday and 1pm–4pm. **Admission**: adults €1.25, under 18s €0.65.*

*Museu Rainha Dona Leonor, Largo de Conceicao ( 00 351 284 323 351; www.museuregionaldebeja. net). **Admission**: adults €2, over 15s and students €1, under 15s free.*

## Évora

**Templo do Diana** ALL AGES Built by the Romans almost 2,000 years ago, the grey stone columns of the Templo do Diana overlook a garden shaded with palm trees that has a kiosk-café selling cold drinks and is scattered with modern sculptures that some children will find more entertaining than the ancient temple. Right next to the temple is the arched gateway that leads into the Alentejo's grandest hotel, the **Pousada dos Loios** (see p. 224) – even if you can't afford to stay here, its white and gold salon decorated with antiques, tapestries and crystal chandeliers is worth a peek. Also worth seeing in Évora is one of the spookier spots in the region, the Capela dos Ossos (Chapel of Bones) within the Igreja Real de São Francisco, on Praça 1 de Maio. Translated into English, the sign above the door says: 'Our bones that lie here are waiting for yours'. Nobody has ever said the Portuguese were a cheerful nation.

*Largo do Conde de Vila Flor.* **Open** *daily 24 hours. Free admission.*

## For Active Families

### Lake Alqueva Boat Trips
ALL AGES

**Capitão Tiago** Capitão Tiago small boat cruises sail from Monsaraz to Mourão, Aldeia da Luz and Alqueva. Out on the water, it is easy to see just how vast the lake is and imagine what its effect on the environment has been – but it's also a pleasant outing (900 metres from the hotel – reservations needed).

*Monte dos Poços Novos, Telheiro, Monsaraz ((mobile)* 📞 *00 351 962 653 711; (landline)* 📞 *00 351 266 557 180). Cruises cost from €10 to €31.*

**Gestalqueva** Gestalqueva, the company which manages the dam and the lake, also explores the lake under its own power.

*Gestalqueva, Barragem de Alqueva, Apartado 124 Mourão (*📞 *00 351 285 250 730;* www.gestalqueva.pt*).*

### Bike rental AGES 10 AND UP
Families can explore in and around Beja by bike. Rent bicycles (including electric bikes for those who don't feel up to dealing with hills by pedal power alone) from Petras, in the centre of Beja at the Camara Municipal de Beja (Beja Town Hall), Praça da República, the Beja Tourist Office, Rua Capitão João Francisco de Sousa, or on the outskirts of Beja at the Casa de Cultura (cultural centre), Rua Afonso de Albuquerque. Bike rental is also available in Évora from Scootbik, on Praça do Sertório. Rentals start at €3.50 for one hour.

### Canoe Rental
**Clube Nautico de Mértola**
AGES 10 AND UP The Mértola Boating Club (Clube Nautico de Mértola) rents canoes, lifejackets and paddles for trips on the Rio Guadiana. Mértola is well off the beaten tourist track, and the club's services are mainly for local people and Portuguese visitors. Several of the Clube

Nautico's staff speak English, but fluent communication isn't guaranteed so this isn't an experience that can be recommended as ideal for absolute novices.

*Clube Nautico de Mértola, Rua Dr Serrao Martins ( 00 351 286 612 044).*

### Horse Riding AGES 8 AND UP

**Tiago Kalisvaart Riding School** Riding lessons for beginners and experienced and advanced riders and guided countryside trail rides are offered by this riding centre near Monsaraz. Although beginners are welcome, children (and parents) who are already fairly experienced riders will enjoy this more than beginners will.

*Reguengos de Monsaraz, Monsaraz ( 00 351 962 653 711; E: TKsebastian@hotmail.com).*

## Shopping

There's not a lot to buy in the Lower Alentejo, but Beja is renowned for handicrafts including hammered-copper pots, pans and serving dishes, which are easy enough to take home if you have a few spare kilograms in your baggage allowance – apart from anything else, they are unbreakable, which the pretty pottery also sold around the region sadly isn't. You'll find handicrafts and all manner of other things to buy along **Rua Capitão João Francisco de Sousa,** the main thoroughfare in the town centre. Also surprisingly unbreakable are the painted and unpainted

ostrich eggs sold at the Baronigg Ostrich Ranch near Alqueva, which also sells wallets, belts, purses and handbags made of ostrich leather. At **São Pedro do Corval,** 12 km from Monsaraz, you'll find the biggest pottery centre in Portugal, with numerous workshops and a huge selection of decorative and practical ceramics, large and small. Smaller pieces such as bowls, jugs, mugs and candlesticks make pretty souvenirs, but if you are tempted to buy in bulk – a complete dinner service, for example – the makers can ship your purchases to the UK for you. There are also pottery painting classes, which creative children will enjoy, and these must be booked at least five days before your visit (book through the **Hotel Rural Horta da Mourão in Monsaraz,** see below).

## FAMILY-FRIENDLY ACCOMMODATION

### Beja

**MODERATE**

#### Vila Galé Clube de Campo

★★★ This four-star 'country-club hotel' is part of a chain which also operates several Algarve resort hotels, and it is the nearest thing the Alentejo has to a full-scale resort. About 19 km southwest of Beja, it stands beside yet another artificial lake, the Barragem de Roxo, on its own 1,620 hectare estate, so although it is also one of the largest hotels in the region there is plenty of space to breathe. The hotel is big on activities, with outdoor pools for children and adults, mini-golf, a children's club with childminders and a playground, riding, clay shooting, mountain bikes and quad bikes, and fishing. Children under four stay free and there is a 50% reduction on the cost of an extra bed (one only per suite) for children between 4 and 11 years old. It's very popular with well-off Portuguese families from Lisbon, especially at weekends.

*Herdade da Figueirinha, Albernoa, Beja (☎ 00 351 800 204 224; www.vilagale.pt). 78 rooms. **Rates**: doubles/twins €70 Sun–Fri, €120 Sat; junior suites €91 Sun–Fri, €156 Sat; extra beds €21 Mon–Fri, €36 Sat. **Amenities**: adult and children's pools, supervised children's club, riding, cycling, fishing, shooting. **In room**: TV, fridge, air conditioning*

**EXPENSIVE**

### Pousada de São Francisco

★★★ Like most pousadas, this hotel exudes historic charm. First built in the 13th century, it was a Franciscan monastery, then an army barracks until it was attractively converted into a pousada in the 1950s. It's slap in the middle of Beja, but because it has large, palm-shaded gardens it doesn't feel at all urban and there is plenty of room for tots to romp in the gardens and walled courtyard.

*Largo D. Nuno Alvares Pereira, Beja (☎ 00 351 284 313 580; www.pousadas.pt). 35 rooms. **Rates**: €125–180; children (0–2) baby cot free; children (3–12) staying in an extra bed pay 15% of the double room rate; children over 13 staying in an extra bed pay 30% of the double room rate. **Amenities**: Large garden, off-street parking, children's (unsupervised) play area, children's pool, full-size pool, à la carte restaurant, bar. **In room**: TV, air conditioning, safe, mini bar, room service.*

## Monsaraz

**INEXPENSIVE**

### Hotel Rural Horta da Mourão

★★ This little hotel only 900 metres from the lake side is great for active families. The rooms are spacious, modern and fitted with all mod cons, including satellite and cable TV (though there's the usual limited choice of English channels), air conditioning and mini bar. There's an outdoor pool, tennis court, pool, snooker and ping pong tables, a children's play zone and babysitting is available by arrangement. But it's the activities that can be arranged around the hotel that really give it an edge – everything from open horse-drawn carriage rides to boat trips on the lake, guided quad-bike adventures, riding lessons and lake and river fishing. The hotel's own restaurant is one of the best in the area and prides itself on its use of fresh, locally grown seasonal ingredients collected from local farms and businesses.

*Horta da Mourão, Monsaraz (☎ 00 351 266 550 100; www.horta damoura.pt). 26 rooms. **Rates**: €70; children sharing parents' room free (one child per room maximum). **Amenities**: pool, tennis court, play area, babysitting. **In room**: TV, air conditioning, fridge, safe.*

## Santa Clara-a-Velha

**EXPENSIVE**

**Pousada de Santa Clara-a-Velha** ★★★ Overlooking a wide stretch of blue water that in summer looks more like an arm of the Mediterranean than the artificial lake that actually it is, the Pousada de Santa Clara-a-Velha is a swish rural retreat with a dreamy location, room for children to play (and a children's pool as well as a full-sized swimming pool), gorgeous views and heaps to do in the surrounding countryside, where you can go four-wheel driving off-road on forestry trails, horse riding, cruising on the lake or canoeing on the Rio Mira, which flows through the nearby Barragem de Santa Clara to meet the sea at Vila Nova de Milfontes. All of these activities can be arranged at the front desk, and you can also borrow bikes to pedal around the shores of the lake or into the countryside. Activities and facilities within the hotel include two pools, family games and a children's play area to keep them amused during the day and in the evening.

*Barragem de Santa Clara, Santa Clara-a-Velha (☎ 00 351 283 882 250/ 83 882 404).* **Amenities**: *restaurants, bar-terrace, swimming pool, cycling, family games, play area.* **In room**: *TV, air conditioning, safe, minibar.*

## Cavaleiro

**INEXPENSIVE**

**Monte da Moita Nova** ★★★ **GREEN** Fully equipped kitchens, a children's paddling pool, an assortment of games and toys for the beach make this collection of four family apartments one of the most child-friendly spots in the Alentejo. There's no swimming pool, but as the beach is only 300 metres away that is not a great hardship – it is close enough that families can commute back and forth during the day, which is handy if you forget your bucket and spade, run out of cold drinks or have to change a nappy. Nor do you have to cross any roads to get to the sands – you just stroll through the green fields where the owners, Walter and Ute, keep their herd of gentle, well-trained riding horses. The only minor snag is that getting a baby buggy across the sandy expanse between the field and the beach is nigh-on impossible. You could happily spend a week or a fortnight here (it's cosy even in winter, when you have an excuse to fire up the wood-burning fireplace with which each apartment is equipped) but it is also a good exploring base for the Costa Vicentina, midway between Vila Nova de Milfontes and Zambujeira do Mar.

All the apartments are roomy and sleep four (two on trundle beds in the living/dining room). In summer, of course, you'll be spending most of your time out of doors, on the terraces front and back of each apartment. The kitchens are fully equipped and bed linen and bath (but not beach) towels are provided. This is a good holiday spot for the eco-conscious as well – most of the hot water and electricity is provided by wind and solar power.

*Moita Nova, Cavaleiro* (📞 *00 351 283 647 357; www.moitanova.com).* **Rates**: *four apartments €55–80.* **Amenities**: *riding stables.* **In room**: *kitchen, fireplace, bed linen, bath towels.*

## Zambujeira do Mar

**MODERATE**

### Herdade de Touril de Baixo

★★ FIND VALUE This is a very comfortable, charming little hotel beside the sea – but it is also a working farm, spread across 365 hectares of land, with a herd of 150 cattle. If you were in any doubt, the quirky collection of toy animals – made from wood, tin, pottery and fabric – that are scattered around the rooms and terraces would be a clue. The whitewashed walls tinged with blue, tiled roofs and ceramic floors definitely say 'rural Portugal' but the level of comfort is far from being rustic. The rooms are simple but tastefully decorated with comfortable beds and each room has its own private terrace. For active families, leisure pursuits nearby include rambling, horse riding, fishing and diving and Zambujeira do Mar with its fishing boats and fish restaurants is within easy reach.

*Zambujeira do Mar* (📞 *00 351 214 647 430; www.touril.pt).* *10 rooms.* **Rates**: *€65–124.* **Amenities**: *garden.* **In room**: *private terrace.*

### Monte do Papa-Leguas ★★★

FIND VALUE This little place just 2 km from Zambujeira and its beach, shops and places to eat and drink is a real find for families with active older children as off-road bikes, water bottles, helmets, maps and trail guides come included in the price, as does a lavish breakfast which is served until 1pm – so in fact you can treat it as brunch. It's an excellent spread, too, with fresh local bread, ham, cheese, home-laid eggs, fresh-squeezed orange juice and home-made cake. There's a salt-water pool, a little courtyard shaded by palm trees, and the rooms are prettily rustic with traditional bamboo ceilings and wood floors (though they also have mod cons including concealed fridge and TV). The owners will also help you arrange canoeing and riding trips nearby.

*Alpenduradas, Zambujeira do Mar* (📞 *00 351 283 961 470; www.monte dopapaleguas.com).* *8 rooms and studios.* **Rates**: *€55–75 including full breakfast and use of bicycles.* **Amenities**: *pool.* **In room**: *fridge, TV.*

## Alvito

**EXPENSIVE**

### Pousada Castelo de Alvito ★★★

This is a grand but child-friendly pousada, housed in a 15th-century castle with turreted battlements and echoing hallways around a paved central courtyard from which you can climb to the ramparts (which for once are reasonably safe for responsible children) for a view over the pretty, dozy little village. In the walled garden there are ponds where frogs croak and goldfish swim, lawns patrolled by a flock of peacocks (including one magical-looking pure albino bird) and a pool that has a shallow end for children. The food is excellent (à la carte dinners but a very good buffet breakfast) and the service is very friendly.

*Castelo do Alvito, Apartado 9 Alvito ( 00 351 284 480 700; www. pousadas.pt). 20 rooms. Rates: €115–150. Amenities: restaurant, bar, pool, gardens. In room: TV, air conditioning, minibar, safe.*

## Évora

EXPENSIVE

### Pousada do Loios ★★★

Every cosy double bedroom in this former 16th-century monastery is different and they are arrayed around cool arcades and public salons and decorated with antique mahogany four posters, gilt-looking glasses and velvet sofas. Not, you might think, ideal for sticky little fingers but the friendly staff treat children with amiable courtesy, the walled courtyard is safe for littler children and away from the street, and there is a small pool. Definitely the best place to stay in Évora, even if the budget and the location mean few families will want to extend that stay for more than a couple of nights.

*Largo do Conde Vila Flor, Évora ( 00 351 266 730 070; www. pousadas.pt). 32 rooms. Rates: €170–200. Amenities: restaurant, bar-terrace, swimming pool. In room: TV, air conditioning, minibar, safe.*

# FAMILY-FRIENDLY DINING

You won't find any imitation English pubs, fish and chip shops, curry restaurants or family menus aimed at British children in the Alentejo, and you will be very lucky indeed to find a restaurant that can produce a high chair on demand (or at all). That said, children are welcome everywhere and all restaurants serve simple, unchallenging dishes as well as less familiar Alentejan offerings such as roast pork with clams (sounds weird but tastes great).

This is one of the richest agricultural areas in Portugal, and is well known for its produce and its food. So we have cherry-picked just a few restaurants in this part of the world that serve a great choice of Alentejan food, in pleasant surroundings, and with a bit of luck should please the entire family. Évora is the happiest hunting ground in the region for foodie families, with a menu of eating places ranging from some of the best in Portugal to simple street cafés. In peaceful little Serpa, you'll find three cheap-and-cheerful pavement cafés next to each other on Praça da República.

## Beja

INEXPENSIVE

**Entre Arcos** ★ This is a cheaper-than-average *petisco* restaurant, much favoured by locals (which is always a good thing) and close to the centre of the old town. To find it, walk down Rua Aresta Branco from the Church of Santa Maria. If you get lost, ask for directions to Pereira's, as the restaurant is commonly known from the name of the family who run it. From the family point of view, it's better for lunch than later in the evening, when it can get quite crowded.

*Rua Jorge Raposo 13, Beja (no tel). Petiscos start at €2.50 – reckon on spending around €10 per person. No credit cards. Reservations not required.*

**Café O Capitel** Certainly the cheapest and one of the nicest places for lunch or a drink in Beja, O Capitel is a favourite with locals who gather beneath the sun-umbrellas overlooking a quiet cobbled square to sip coffee, beer or soft drinks and choose from a menu of *petiscos*, salads and other light meals, cakes and burgers.

*Rua Jacinto Freire de Andrade, Beja (no tel). From around €3. No credit cards. No reservations required.* **Open** *10am–8pm.*

**MODERATE**

**Luis da Rocha** ★ This is a no-frills, regional restaurant and café that serves good Alentejan food in a rather stark upstairs dining room or coffee, snacks and pastries in the café downstairs. It has location going for it, as it's right on the main shopping street, not far from the tourist office. Most of the dishes on the restaurant menu are

recognizable enough (grilled trout, chicken, various grilled meat dishes) and there are plenty of acceptable, child-sized sandwiches and sticky things on the café menu downstairs, which is probably a better bet than the main dining room.

*Rua Capitão João Francisco de Sousa 63 (☎ 00 351 284 323 179). €10–15 for a full meal. Credit cards accepted. No reservation needed.* **Open** *all day until 11pm.*

## Vila Nova de Milfontes

**Restaurante Marisqueira O Pescador** ★★ Senhor and Senhora Moura, who own and run this restaurant, used to be in the fish business themselves and they certainly know their stuff. Most of what appears on your plate was probably swimming around without a care in the world only a few hours (or even minutes) ago – it's that fresh. The locals say the Mouras run the best *marisqueira* (seafood restaurant) for miles around, and some people even drive down from Lisbon at the weekend just to eat here. The big deal is *caldeirada*, a complex, mouth-watering seafood casserole. It's one of these love-it-or-hate-it dishes, and perhaps too challenging for some British children – but if you have picky eaters in tow there are plenty of straightforward grilled fish and prawn dishes to offer them. Not the prettiest restaurant in the world, but it does have air conditioning (which is welcome in summer) and the unpretentious surroundings are quite relaxing

## Petiscos

**Petiscos are the Portuguese version of Spanish *tapas* – tasty bite-sized** snacks, usually but not always served on a slice of crusty bread. Slices of ham, pork, cheese and sausage are mainstays, along with prawns and other seafood, smoked or fresh. They're great for families, because you just order a few at a time as you go along, instead of ordering a full meal and hoping the children will find it acceptable. You can also order a selection to take out – a ready-made, no-hassle picnic.

compared with the heavy furniture and dark décor of some more pretentious upscale Portuguese eating places.

*Largo da Praça 18 (☎ 00 351 282 996 338). €10–15. Credit cards accepted. Reservations recommended. **Open** for lunch and dinner.*

## Évora

**INEXPENSIVE**

### Cafeteria de St Umberto ★

**VALUE** Not to be confused with the similarly named (and much posher) Cozinha de São Humberto nearby, this is a good choice for an open-air snack lunch on a sunny main square. It serves cold drinks including fresh juices, wine and beer and a selection of sandwiches, substantial salads and cakes.

*Praça do Giraldo (no tel). Tuna, ham or chicken toasted sandwich €3.50. Salads from €8. No credit cards. No reservations required.*

**MODERATE**

### Cozinha de São Humberto

★★ In a narrow street off the central Praça do Giraldo, Cozinha de São Humberto is a super place for families to try out local dishes such as simply fried river fish with tomato, filling pork Évora style, and tasty regional cheeses. Children are usually amused by the restaurant's funky style – it's a bit like eating in an eccentric grandparent's home, with old copper pots and kettles hanging from the ceiling, antique muskets and shotguns on the walls and even a grandfather clock, and you sit on padded benches or old-fashioned rush chairs. It's atmospheric and fun.

*Rua do Moeda 39 (☎ 00 351 266 704 251). €12–20. Credit cards accepted. Reservations required. **Open** lunch (midday–4pm) and dinner (7pm–10pm).*

# Appendix:
# Useful Terms & Phrases

**N**o one in the Algarve will expect visitors to have a proficiency in the Portuguese language, but for both politeness and for the opportunity for holiday learning, a knowledge of a few pleasantries goes a long way. Children mixing with Portuguese children on the beach, for example, will also feel more involved and acclimatized if they have a few basic words and phrases. Travelling with children always brings up the possibilities of unforeseen circumstances, whether that's a trip to a pharmacy for minor ailments, decoding a menu for a picky eater, or something more serious, so having a phrase book such as the following is invaluable.

Children also have the advantage that they pick up new languages far more quickly than adults, while in turn' one of the best ways for adults to get to grips with languages in the early stages is to use child-orientated books and televisual aids.

If you want to take this a step further, there are various teaching resources – books, CDs and DVDs – available from sites such as Amazon (*www.amazon.co.uk*) and Multilingual Books (*www.multilingual books.com*). The latter also has a strong focus on teaching children, including picture books, games such as vocabulary cards and even, for slightly older children, the *Harry Potter* series translated into Portuguese. Local stationers will also stock children's comics and colouring books that will help assist in simple language instruction.

# GLOSSARY

## General

| English | Portuguese |
| --- | --- |
| Yes | Sim |
| No | Não |
| Good | Bom |
| Bad | Mau |
| I don't know (a fact) | Não se |
| I don't know a person or place | Não conhesco |
| I don't understand | Não percebo |
| To | Para |
| From | De |
| Day | Dia |
| Week | Semana |
| Month | Mês |
| Year | Ano |
| Why? | Por quê? |
| Where? | Onde? |
| When? | Quando? |

## Basic Pronunciation

'á' as in 'car'

'ch' as sh in shall

'lh' as li in William

'nh' as ni in onion

'ai' as i in ice

'ei' as in 'day'

'au' as in pound

'eu' as the 'e' in set and then 'w'

'ou' as o in note

'ae' as in they but with a more nasal ending

'oe' as oy in boy

'c' before e or i, like s in some, otherwise like 'k'

'g' before e or is, like s in measure, otherwise as English

'h' always silent

'm' generally as in English but if at the end of the word then m is silent and makes preceding letter nasal

's' (the worst letter in the Portuguese language): if between two vowels, like 'z', if at the end, like 'sh', otherwise like English

'u' like oo in boot unless after 'q' when silent

'x' (another horror of Portuguese) generally like 'sh' but (according to all sorts of complicated rules) can sound like z, ss or English x

'ão' as in 'town' but with a more nasal ending

'ay' as in 'ice'

'ç' as the s in 'sit'

'e' as in 'red'

'i' as in machine

'í' as the ee in 'feed'

'j' as the s in 'treasure'

| English | Portuguese |
|---|---|
| How/What did you say? | **Como?** |
| Left | **Esquerda** |
| Right | **Direita** |
| Early | **Cedo** |
| Late | **Tarde** |
| Behind | **Atrás** |
| In front of | **Em frente de** |
| Far | **Longe** |
| Close | **Perto** |
| Where is . . . ? | **Onde fica...?** |

## Greetings & Pleasantries

| English | Portuguese |
|---|---|
| Hello | **Olá** |
| Good morning | **Bom dia** |
| Good evening | **Boa tarde** |
| Goodbye | **Adeus** |
| Please | **Por favor** |
| Thank you | **Obrigado/obrigada (male/female)** |
| How are you? | **Como está?** |
| Very well | **Muito bem** |
| You're welcome | **De nada** |
| Please come in | **Entre** |
| Excuse me (to get by someone) | **Com licença** |
| Excuse me (to begin a question) | **Desculpa** |
| Can you help me please? | **Pode atenderme?** |
| Do you speak English? | **Fala Inglès?** |
| I understand | **Eu percebo** |
| I don't understand | **Não percebo** |
| What's your name? | **Como se chama?** |
| My name is... | **O meu nome é...** |

## Numbers

| English | Portuguese |
|---|---|
| 1 | **um** |
| 2 | **dois** |
| 3 | **tres** |
| 4 | **quatro** |
| 5 | **cinco** |
| 6 | **seis** |
| 7 | **sete** |
| 8 | **oito** |
| 9 | **nove** |
| 10 | **dez** |
| 11 | **onze** |
| 12 | **doze** |
| 13 | **treze** |
| 14 | **quatorze** |
| 15 | **quinze** |

| English | Portuguese |
|---|---|
| 16 | **dizeseis** |
| 17 | **dizesete** |
| 18 | **dizoito** |
| 19 | **dizenove** |
| 20 | **vinte** |
| 30 | **trinta** |
| 40 | **quarenta** |
| 50 | **cinquenta** |
| 60 | **sesenta** |
| 70 | **setenta** |
| 80 | **oitenta** |
| 90 | **noventa** |
| 100 | **cem** |
| 200 | **duzentos** |
| 500 | **quinhentos** |
| 1,000 | **mil** |

## Time

| English | Portuguese |
|---|---|
| Today | **Hoje** |
| Tomorrow | **Amanhã** |
| Yesterday | **Ontem** |
| Every day | **Todos os dias** |
| Now | **Agora** |
| Soon | **Em breve** |
| Later | **Logo/mais tarde** |
| Always | **Sempre** |
| What time is it? | **Que horas são?** |

## Days of the Week & Months of the Year

| English | Portuguese |
|---|---|
| Monday | **Segunda-feira** |
| Tuesday | **Terça-feira** |
| Wednesday | **Quarta-feira** |
| Thursday | **Quinta-feira** |
| Friday | **Sexta-feira** |
| Saturday | **Sábado** |

| English | Portuguese |
|---|---|
| Sunday | **Domingo** |
| January | **Janeiro** |
| February | **Fevereiro** |
| March | **Março** |
| April | **Abril** |
| May | **Maio** |
| June | **Junho** |
| July | **Julho** |
| August | **Agosto** |
| September | **Setembro** |
| October | **Outubro** |
| November | **Novembro** |
| December | **Dezembro** |

## Getting Around

| English | Portuguese |
|---|---|
| I am looking for... | **Queiro procurar** (if looking for something to buy or get) **vol encontrar** (if looking for a place or person etc |
| I want to go to... | **Queiro ir a** |
| Is it far? | **E longe?** |
| How many kilometres to...? | **Quantos quilómetros faltam ainda para chegar a...?** |
| Turn back | **Voltar** |
| Go | **Ir** |
| Left | **Esquerda** |
| Right | **Direita** |
| Straight ahead | **Em frente** |
| Street | **Rua** |
| Square | **Praça** |
| Next to | **Perto de** |
| Here/there | **Aqui/Lá** |
| Map | **Mapa** |
| I would like to buy | **Queiro comprar** |
| Ticket | **Bilhete** |
| Beach | **Praia** |
| Bank | **Banco** |
| Church | **Igreja** |

| English | Portuguese |
| --- | --- |
| Pharmacy | Farmácia |
| Market | Mercado |
| Museum | Museu |
| Park | Jardim público |
| Police | Polícia |
| Post office | Agência do correio |
| Tourist office | Posto de turismo |
| Railway station | Estação de comboios |
| Bus station | Estação de camionetas |
| Airport | Aeroporto |
| Taxi stand | Praça de táxis |
| Exchange office | Cámbios |
| Exchange rate | Cámbio |
| Where can I find a...? | Onde pode encontrar...? |
| Dentist | Dentista |
| Doctor | Medico/a |
| Hospital | Hospital |

## Signs

| English | Portuguese |
| --- | --- |
| Entrance | Entrada |
| Exit | Saída |
| Toilets | Banheiro |
| Prohibited | Proibido |
| No smoking | Não fumar |

## Health

| English | Portuguese |
| --- | --- |
| I am sick | Eu soi enfermo |
| I need a doctor | Eu tem necessidade do medico |
| Fever | Febre |
| Headache | Duente da cabeca |
| Stomach ache | Duente do estomago |
| I have a headache | Eu tem duente da cabeca |
| Pill | Comprimido |
| I am on medication for... | Tomo medecina por... |

# Baby Terms

| English | Portuguese |
| --- | --- |
| Baby | Bebé |
| Baby food | Alimento por bebé |
| Baby's bottle | Garrafa por bebé |
| Carry-cot | Cama portatil |
| Chemist | Farmácia |
| Child | Criança |
| Children's portion | Dose para criança |
| Cleansing lotion | Creme de limpeza |
| Constipation | Obstrucão de ventre |
| Cotton wool | Algodão em rama |
| Cough | Tosse |
| Cough medicine | Medecina por tosse |
| Crèche | Asilo diurno para crianças |
| Diarrhoea | Diarreia |
| Disinfectant | Desinfectante |
| First aid kit | Kit de primeiros socollos |
| Highchair | Cadeira elevada |
| Nappy | Fralda |
| Plasters | Emplastros de colagem |
| Pushchair | Carrinho de bebé |
| Sun block | Bloco do sol |
| Suntan lotion | Loção de bronzear |

# Attractions

| English | Portuguese |
| --- | --- |
| Bridge | ponte |
| Cathedral | catedral |
| Island | ilha |
| Old Town | cidade velha |
| Lake | lago |
| Ruins | ruínas |
| Sea | mar |

## Shopping

| English | Portuguese |
|---|---|
| How much is it? | **Quanto custo?** |
| A little | **Um poco** |
| A lot | **Muito** |
| Enough | **Bastante** |
| This One | **Este** |
| That One | **Esse** |
| Expensive | **Caro** |

## Food & Drink

### Specialities

Not surprisingly, the Algarve's big culinary strength is seafood – from tiddlers such as sardines (a reliable child-pleaser) and anchovies to monster tuna and shark. *Bacalhau* (dried cod) appears in rissoles and stews, and shellfish, clams, prawns and lobster go into the *cataplana*, a seafood stew cooked in a wok-like copper vessel that serves a family of four. Clams also pop up in the cooking of the Alentejo, where they are a key ingredient, along with pork, in another signature dish, *porco Alentejano.* There are several easy-to-eat chicken dishes, and the Alentejo's huge flocks of sheep supply the whole region with lamb and mutton, while Serpa, in the Guadiana valley, is famous for its cheese. Smoked ham and spicy chorizo sausage are popular breakfast buffet servings. Families yearning for the taste of home will also find fish and chips, pizza, pasta, Indian and Chinese food in eat-in and take-away places throughout the Algarve, and locals are fond of *frango assado,* a whole grilled chicken, as a take-away meal.

The region is not noted for its fine wines, though adequate and well-priced red, white and rosé wines are produced locally. The local rocket fuel is *medronho*, a clear spirit distilled from the berries of the arbutus bushes that cloak the Serra de Monchique. Portugal also produces its own good brandies for an after dinner drink. Local lagers (Sagres and Super Bock) are available in bottle or on draught, and most British beers are also sold in the main resorts.

## General

| English | Portuguese |
|---|---|
| Breakfast | **Pequeno almoço** |
| Lunch | **Almoço** |
| Dinner | **Jantar** |
| Knife | **Faca** |

| English | Portuguese |
|---|---|
| Fork | **Garfo** |
| Spoon | **Colher** |
| Glass | **Copo** |
| Plate | **Prato** |
| Menu | **Menú** |
| Bill | **Conta** |
| Cheers! | **Bão saude!** |
| Supermarket | **Supermercado** |
| Open air market | **Mercado** |
| Bakery | **Padaria** |
| Bread | **Pão** |
| Butter | **Manteiga** |
| Pasta | **Massa** |
| Vegetables | **Legumes** |
| Cheese | **Queijo** |
| Ham | **Fiambre** |
| Eggs | **Ovos** |
| Rice | **Arroz** |
| Salt | **Sal** |
| Pepper | **Pimenta** |
| Sugar | **Açúcar** |
| Coffee | **Café** |
| Tea | **Chá** |
| Juice | **Sumo** |
| Water | **Água** |
| Mineral water | **Água mineral** |
| Milk | **Leite** |
| Fish | **Peixe** |
| Meat | **Carne** |
| Potato | **Batata** |

## Meat & Fish

| English | Portuguese |
|---|---|
| Anchovies | **Anchova** |
| Cod | **Bacalhau** (pronounced bakalyow) |
| Mullet | **Mugem** (pronounced mooshem) (sh as in treasure) |
| Sea-bass | **Perca** |

| English | Portuguese |
| --- | --- |
| Mussels | **Mexilhao** (pronounced mesheelyow) |
| John Dory | **Peixe de Sao Pedro** |
| Sole | **Linguado** |
| Octopus | **Polvo** |
| Prawns | **Gambas** |
| Trout | **Truta** |
| Tuna | **Atum** |
| Crab | **Caranguejo** (pronounced carangueshoo) (sh as in treasure) |
| Mackerel | **Cavala** |
| Beef | **Boi** |
| Chicken | **Frango** |
| Lamb | **Borrego** |
| Bacon | **Bacon** |
| Pork | **Porco** |
| Veal | **Vitela** |

## Cooking

| English | Portuguese |
| --- | --- |
| Grilled | **Grelhado** |
| Baked | **Ao forno** |
| Fried | **Fritada** |
| Boiled | **Cozido** |

## Desserts

| English | Portuguese |
| --- | --- |
| Cake | **Bolo** |
| Ice cream | **Gelado** |

## Other Useful Terms

| English | Portuguese |
| --- | --- |
| Restaurant | **Restaurante** |
| White wine | **Vinho branco** |
| Red wine | **Vinho tinto** |
| Beer | **Cerveja** |
| Sandwiches | **Sandes** |
| Waiter | **Empregado/a** |

## Getting a Room

| English | Portuguese |
|---|---|
| Room | **Quarto** |
| Excuse me, is there a hotel near here? | **Desculpe, ha un hotel aqui?** |
| Do you have a room? | **Tem um quarto livre?** |
| Double room | **Quarto de casal** |
| Twin room | **Quarto com duas camas** |
| I would like a room with a... | **Queria um quarto com...** |
| Shower | **Duche** |
| Bathtub | **Casa de banho** |
| Balcony | **Varanda** |
| Air-conditioning | **Ar condicionado** |
| Telephone | **Telefone** |
| How much is the room per night? | **Quanto e um quarto por uma noite?** |
| Per person | **Por persoa** |
| Per week | **Por semana** |
| I'd like to make a reservation | **Queiro fazer reservacão** |
| I will stay for 2 nights | **Eu parare dua noites** |

# FAMILY TRAVEL

There are few things kids find more exciting than the prospect of going on holiday, but as parents it pays to keep a check on the excitement and do a bit of forward planning so that everything goes smoothly. Fortunately the Internet has grasped the concept of family travel full on, and there are plenty of sites that offer advice and information about travelling round the world as a family.

**www.babygoes2.com:** a fantastic site offering all kinds of advice for parents, as well as special offers and details of child-friendly places to stay in a variety of destinations, including the Algarve.

**www.deabirkett.com:** a range of invaluable pieces of information here, compiled by *Guardian* journalist and mother Dea Birkett, but the most useful might be the Travelling with Kids forum where you can share and glean information from other parents about destinations and issues.

**www.babycentre.co.uk:** very much geared towards parents of babies and toddlers, entering 'travel' in the search facility brings up a variety of useful articles, from tips about travel sickness, to the essential accessories.

**www.travellingwithkids.co.uk:** what to pack, forms of transport, health and safety and plenty of other features that will set your mind at ease.

*www.familytravelforum.co.uk:* a vast range of destinations and ideas for holidays with the kids, from fun to culture.

*www.travelwithyourkids.com:* as the intro says, 'written by parents, for parents'. Take a look even if it's only to breathe a sigh of relief that some of these problems haven't happened to you!

*www.family-travel.co.uk:* you need to pay a monthly subscription of £1.20 for the information on this site, which, given the amount of free info on the above sites, seems a little unnecessary. Nevertheless, the information's there if you pay for it.

## RESPONSIBLE TOURISM

In these days when global warming is on the news and political agenda almost every day, it's the responsibility of everyone to consider the environment and in particular to get kids to appreciate the importance of the subject. Tourism, of course, is a tricky issue all round, given the carbon emissions of aircraft and high-rise hotels ruining the landscape. However, there are a number of organizations that offer advice on how to reduce and/or avoid the problems caused by tourism. The Travel Foundation (*www.thetravel foundation.org.uk*) is particularly good for families as it includes a children's guide as well as puzzles, which is a great way to engage young minds on the relevance of the subject.

Other sites offering information include:

*www.responsibletravel.com*
*www.tourismconcern.org.uk*
*www.climatecare.org.uk*

## USEFUL WEBSITES & TELEPHONE NUMBERS

There are a number of organizations and companies that can offer advice and information for all aspects of a family trip to the Algarve.

### Airlines

**British Airways** *www.british airways.com*

**Aer Lingus** *www.flyaerlingus.com*

**Ryanair** *www.ryanair.com*

**Easyjet** *www.easyjet.com*

**British Midland** *www.bmibaby.com*

**Flybe** *www.flybe.com*

**Monarch** *www.flymonarch.com*

### Tourist Boards

**ICEP, Portuguese Embassy**, 11 Belgrave Sq, SW1X 8PP (📞 *0845 355 1212*).

www.visitportugal.com

www.portugaloffice.org.uk

www.algarve.org

## Hotels

www.algarve-web.com

## Pousadas

www.pousadas.pt

## Tour Operators & Specialists

**Destination Portugal** www.destination-portugal.co.uk

**Eurocamp** www.eurocamp.co.uk

**First Choice** www.firstchoice.co.uk

**Sunvil** www.sunvil.co.uk

**EHS Travel** www.ehstravel.co.uk

**Cosmos** www.cosmos.co.uk

**Thomson Holidays** www.thomson.co.uk

## Villas, Apartments & Special Interest

Search the Internet for holidays in the Algarve and there will be a seemingly endless list of companies offering accommodation and activities. These below are some of the more recommended, as well as the tour operators above.

**Premier Villas** www.premiervillas.net

**Classic Collection** www.classic-collection.co.uk

**Villa Retreats** www.villaretreats.com

**Algarve Agency** www.algarveagency.com

**Horse riding** www.ehstravel.co.uk

## Ferries

**Brittany Ferries** www.brittany-ferries.co.uk

## Car Hire

**Avis** www.avis.co.uk

**easyCar** www.easycar.com

**Europcar** www.europcar.com

**Faro Car** www.farocar.com

**Hertz** www.hertz.co.uk

## Rail Travel

**Portugal National Railways** www.cp.pt

**European Rail Guide** www.europeanrailguide.com

**Seat 61** www.seat61.com

## Safety Abroad

www.fco.gov.uk/travel is the website of the British Foreign Office and offers a range of information about safety and health.

# Index

See also Accommodation and Restaurant indexes, below.

## General

### A

Abracadabra (Albufeira), 107
Accommodation, 37–39, 240. *See also*
Accommodation Index
  Albufeira and environs, 108–114
  the Alentejo, 220–224
  Almancil, 70–71
  best, 10–13
  Carrapateira, 141–142
  Faro and environs, 67–72
  Lagos, 142–143
  Portimão, 111–113
  Quarteira, 69–70
  Spain, 199–202
  Tavira and environs, 165–169
  Vilamoura, 71–72
  western Algarve, 140–143
Activity holidays, 32
Adega do Cantor (Albufeira), 107
A Doca (Tavira), 164
A Farrobinha (Tavira), 164
Air tours, Portimão, 105
Air travel, 30–31, 36, 239
  tips for flying with children, 32–33
Albufeira and environs, 77–118
  accommodation, 108–114
    villas, 109
  getting around, 80
  orientation, 79
  restaurants, 114–118
  shopping, 106–108
  sights and activities, 80–106
    for active families, 99–104
    beaches and resorts, 91–96
    castles and historic buildings,
      105–106
    events and entertainment, 81–83
    'living statues,' 86
    miniature road train, 90
    top 10 attractions for children,
      80–81
    towns and villages, 83–91
    water parks and theme parks,
      96–99
  sightseeing in Albufeira itself, 85–86
  travelling to, 79
  visitor information, 79–80
Albufeira Carnival, 24
The Alentejo, 207–226
  accommodation, 220–224
  getting to and around, 210
  orientation, 210
  restaurants, 224–226
  shopping, 220
  sights and activities, 210–220
    animal parks and farms, 218
    beaches and resorts, 215–216

lakes and rivers, 217
    top family attractions, 210
    towns and villages, 210–215
Algar Seco, 104, 105
Aljezur, 128–129
  restaurants, 144
Almancil
  accommodation, 70–71
  restaurants, 75–76
Almancil Karting (Vilamoura), 64–65
Almond blossoms, 58
Alqueva, Lake, 219
Alte, 90–91
Alvito, 212–213, 223–224
Alvor, 96
Animal parks and aquariums, best, 7–8
Apartment purchases in the Algarve, 82
Apumanke (Attractivebn), 107
Aquabus (Lagos), 123
Aqualand (Alcantarilha), 7, 97
Aqualand Bahía de Cádiz, 192
Aquashow (near Quarteira), 63–64
Armação de Pêra, 93–94, 113
Atlantic Park (near Quarteira), 63
ATMs (cashpoint machines), 23
Atrium Faro, 66
Ayuntamiento (Governor's Palace;
  Cádiz), 188

### B

Babysitters, 42
Baelo Claudia Roman Ruins, 197
Banana Boat Arade River Cruises
  (Portimão), 104
Baronigg Ostrich Farm (Alqueva), 218
Barragem de Alqueva, 215, 217
Barragem de Bravura, 16
Barragem de Santa Clara, 217
Barragem do Arade, 16, 104–105
Barrio Santa Cruz (Seville), 181
Beaches, 6. *See also entries starting
  with Praia*
  Albufeira and environs, 91–96
  Faro, 50, 55–56
  guide to, 20
  Lagos, 130, 131
  restaurants on, 14
  safety, 27
  western Algarve, 129–131
The Beach Factory, 130
Beach flags, 92
Bead shop (Tavira), 164
Beja, 210–211, 218
  accommodation, 220–221
  restaurants, 224–225
Belixe, 130
Bella Vista Leisure Park (Albufeira), 99
Belmondo (Faro), 66

241

## Accommodation

## Restaurants